cybercorp
the new business revolution

james martin
www.jamesmartin.com

American Management Association

New York • Atlanta • Boston • Chicago • Kansas City • San Francisco • Washington, D.C.
Brussels • Mexico City • Tokyo • Toronto

This book is available at a special
discount when ordered in bulk quantities.
For information, contact Special Sales Department,
AMACOM, a division of American Management Association,
135 West 50th Street, New York, NY 10020.

This publication is designed to provide accurate and authoritative information in regard to the subject matter covered. It is sold with the understanding that the publisher is not engaged in rendering legal, accounting, or other professional service. If legal advice or other expert assistance is required, the services of a competent professional person should be sought.

Library of Congress Cataloging-in-Publication Data

Martin, James, 1938–
    Cybercorp : the new business revolution / James Martin.
      p.   cm.
    Includes bibliographical references and index.
    ISBN 0-08144-0351-4
    1. Virtual reality in management. 2. Industrial management.
3. Organizational change. 4. International business enterprises—
Computer networks—Management. 5. Corporations—Computer networks—
Management. 6. Internet (Computer network)   I. Title.
HD30.2122.M37   1996
658′ .00285′467—dc20   96 33074
                                                  CIP

Printing number

10 9 8 7 6 5 4 3 2 1

Contents

PART I. Introduction

The planetwide change that is brought by cyberspace is bringing a
revolution in the nature of the corporation. New types of relationships
dramatically change corporate mechanisms and behavior. Every
businessperson needs to "think cybercorp."

The Internet and intranets provide the means for total redesign of
corporate communication channels and structure, and for new forms of
intercorporate relationships.

PART II. Characteristics of the Cybercorp

Modern electronics is changing the nature of marketing and inverts
much of its conventional wisdom.

A key to designing the most effective cybercorp operations is to think of
corporate activities in terms of value streams, whose benefits are clear
and measurable.

5. The Predator Value Stream: Creating Competitive Strength

Successful cybercorps focus intensely on their most critical value stream. How can you design strategic capabilities that are world beaters, and how are these changed by cyberspace?

6. Virtualness

Managers should think in terms of virtual operations, virtual office space, and corporations that use a web of virtual relationships.

7. Networks for Agility

Cybercorp webs link core competences in different companies so that virtual organizations can be assembled and disassembled dynamically to seize new business opportunities.

8. Ecosystems in the Cybercorp Economy

In the cybercorp economy, collections of corporations become linked into cross-industry ecosystems, sometimes with highly complex relationships. Success and survival depends on understanding the ecosystems and managing the relationships.

9. The David Syndrome

Small newcomers are beating the corporate Goliaths, in some cases with astonishing growth rates. The best strategy for aging corporations is to spin off new cybercorps.

10. Agents and Intelligent Documents

Software agents are needed to carry out actions for us in cyberspace. When the documents of business become digital they can have built-in intelligence. Intelligent documents behave in a fundamentally different way from paper documents.

11. Computerized Choreography

Complex operations and interactions with business partners require that responses to events be choreographed with networks, sometimes with complex computing to optimize the results.

12. Counterintuitive Behavior

New control mechanisms can exhibit behavior that defies managers' intuition. How do you take advantage of, rather than be caught by surprise by, cybercorp interactions?

13. Beyond Darwin   212

The successful cybercorp should be designed for very fast evolution, far more advanced than Darwinian evolution.

14. Experiment!   226

Research and experimentation should not be confined to the laboratory. Parts of the cybercorp need to be designed as learning laboratories.

PART III. People and Management

15. An Exciting Place to Work   239

Almost every aspect of traditional employment needs rethinking. How do you make the cybercorp an exciting place to work and maximize employee creativity?

16. The Steepest Possible Learning Curves   256

The cybercorp is constantly learning. How do you design it to learn as rapidly and profitably as possible and modify its behavior accordingly?

17. The Outrageous Cost of Obsolete Thinking   273

We are surrounded everywhere by obsolete thinking. Few executives calculate its cost. In reality, its cost can be enormous.

18. How to Drive a Corporation Nuts   285

In revolutions people get hurt. Ham-fisted corporate reengineering is a disaster. What is the right way to make the cybercorp transition?

19. Power and Propellerheads   297

The cybercorp world has to meld the alien cultures of techies and businesspeople, which are growing farther apart. How can it do this?

Index   313

to korinthia

http://128.197.190.184/stupro/martin

Preface

Most of today's corporations are structured for an age that is gone. But attempts at "business reengineering" have met with failure far more often than success. Executives around the world are asking, "What comes next?" The next giant step in the evolution of the corporate world is the building of corporations that take full advantage of the cyberspace revolution—agile, virtual, global, cybernetic corporations: *cybercorps* for short—fluid and fast-learning so that they do not need to be periodically reengineered. The age of traumatic business reengineering will be replaced by an age of corporations designed to constantly evolve.

This book describes what corporations designed for cyberspace should look like. It is not about building Web pages or establishing a presence on the Internet. It is about the deep structural changes that are necessary for the age of network-centric computing and the new business opportunities that they bring. Many examples exist of executives who have invented such changes and pragmatically improved them, discovering what works well and what does not. In this age of massive change, as we piece together the aspects of the transition that work best a picture emerges of what future corporations must be like. This future bears little resemblance to the 1980s.

Some of the topics are complex, and the book points to where the reader so inclined can explore them in depth in the author's book *The Great Transition.*

This book emphasizes that all businesspeople must "think cybercorp"—in other words, think of business opportunities and operations in terms of cyberspace, radically changed marketing, value streams reinvented for real-time interaction, virtual corporations, agile intercorporate relationships, and new employee teams. Corporate executives reading early versions of the book have put programs into place for adopting cybercorp operations or for transforming their organizations into cybercorps.

Today's seedlings of change will become momentous. The dramatic changes we describe are inevitable because they enrich the customer and enhance competitive capability. There is no question about *whether* they will occur, and little question about *when* they will occur; the important questions relate to which corporations will succeed with them first and which will be knocked out of business—which corporations will take the tide at its flood and which will be swept away by it.

The revolution in the nature of corporations foretells economic changes with wrenching political implications. By 2005 hundreds of billions of dollars a day of electronic cash from consumers will be racing across national frontiers and there will be a growing separation of economy and state. The cybercorp economy will be worldwide. There will be a total reinvention of employment, and the changed nature of work requires new patterns of management, new organizational structures, and a new human-technology partnership. Society is hurtling into the Cybercorp Revolution at warp speed. By the time it has run its course the changes wrought will be far greater even than those of the Industrial Revolution.

Part I
Introduction

1

The Bloodless Revolution?

Early movies often looked like stage plays that had been filmed. It took decades to invent the rapid editing, special effects, and visual storytelling of today's movies. Similarly, early television was like radio shows on a screen. The first "horseless carriages" looked as though they were designed to be pulled by a horse; the radio pioneers thought of radio as "wireless telegraphy" and never dreamed of broadcasting; the "paperless office" looked like the same old office with less paper.

It is by now clear that corporations that take full advantage of information highways and microelectronics bear no resemblance to traditional corporations. Most of today's corporations are structured for an age that is gone. Many employees and managers are cogs in an obsolete machine.

When broadcasting was first proposed, a man who was later to become one of its most distinguished leaders announced that it was difficult to see uses for public broadcasting; about the only regular use he could think of was the broadcasting of Sunday sermons because that was the only occasion when one man addressed a mass public each week. Most executives today are equally unaware of how cyberspace and software will change the world of business. Successful corporations exploit the technology of their era. When technology changes profoundly, some corporations take advantage of the change and some are victims of it. If we rank organizations in terms of how well they put technology to business use, the difference between the best and worst is much greater than it was ten years ago. The standard deviation is increasing. The reason is that some organizations keep up with the changes and others do not. The faster the rate of change, the greater the gap between corporations that learn efficiently and those that do not.

Today mankind has the accelerator pedal of technology pressed hard to the floor. Technology is changing at an unprecedented rate, becoming obsolete before people learn how to use it well. It is increasing in power not linearly but geometrically. This breathless rate of change is likely to continue to increase because there is positive feedback in research and development. Good ideas feed on themselves, and the Internet makes the feedback worldwide. Research results produce better research, and computers make research more effective. Moreover, scientists in so many fields say that the market has barely scratched the potential of their technology yet.

Electronic Organisms

In the year that the Kinsey Report on sexual behavior was first published another book rivaled its success. It went through four printings in its first six months. It was about organisms not orgasms. Most of the public could barely comprehend the book, but its title *Cybernetics* caught on in the popular press.[1] It compared behavior in creatures with behavior in machines. Norbert Weiner, an MIT professor, showed, with much mathematics, how electronic or mechanical devices could have control mechanisms the way creatures do. During World War II, Weiner worked on servomechanisms that could steer ships and weapons. After the war he steadily extended his work to more complex situations, using the flexibility of electronic circuits and then computers. Weiner had an assistant who was a neurologist, and together they applied the theories of servomechanisms to experiments with animals. They found they could predict the behavior of muscles under different loads. Weiner's ideas caught the attention of the mass media when he generalized them to a universal principle: Lifelike self-control could be achieved with electronic circuits.

Weiner defined *cybernetics* as "the science of control and communication in the animal and the machine." We should extend the definition to "control and communication in the corporation." The modern enterprise can be thought of as an organism, rather like a biological organism, except that it consists of people and electronics, organized to achieve certain goals. It has a nervous system that extends to every employee's desk. A corporation, like an animal, is exceedingly complex and cannot be described with simple equations. The mechanisms for corporate control and communications are changing greatly as we race into the era of information highways and complex software. New forms of corporations have been referred to as "virtual corporations," "adaptive corporations," or "learning enterprises," but such terms describe only one aspect of the cybernetic corporation. We need a word that encompasses all of them. Corporations now emerging have a vast web of electronic links to other corporations. They have virtual operations worldwide, are designed to adapt rapidly and continually to changing environments, and learn and evolve constantly at all levels. We refer to this human-electronic organism as a *cybernetic corporation—a cybercorp* for short.

Today's ubiquitous networks are making the cybercorp reality. The word *cybernetics* derives from the Greek word for "steersman," which was also used in ancient Greece to denote a governor of a country. The Latin version of the word *kubernetes* means "governor." The famous physicist Ampère described cybernetics as the science of governance.

The prefix *cyber* became popular when hackers started to discover that roaming the world on computer networks was very different from roaming the world physically. Personal computer users could connect to any site almost instantly and explore complex realms of software. The traditional sense of geographic space was replaced by *cyberspace.*

Cyberspace is the universe behind the computer screen. As tens of millions of computers become interlinked worldwide a form of global collective consciousness is being created. Cyberspace explorers can find themselves in a world in many ways richer and more complex than the physical world. The modern enterprise exists in cyberspace (whether or not it takes advantage of it).

Managers, executives, change agents, and creative people everywhere need to ask, "What should my corporation look like if it takes maximum advantage of cyberspace, cybernetics, and superhighways?" For many in traditional corporations the answers are startling.

It does not usually make much sense to say, "Is such-and-such corporation a cybercorp or not?" Corporations may be thought of as having cybercorp characteristics or mechanisms. Some have extensive cybercorp characteristics; some have just a touch of cybercorp. Almost all corporations would benefit from having more cybercorp characteristics than they have today.

Cybercorp \ˈsī-bər-kȯrp\ *noun*
[from Greek *kybernētēs,* governor, from *kybernan,* to govern]

A corporation designed using the principles of cybernetics. A corporation optimized for the age of cyberspace. A cybernetic corporation with senses constantly alert, capable of reacting in real time to changes in its environment, competition, and customer needs, with virtual operations or agile linkages of competencies in different organizations when necessary. A corporation designed for fast change, which can learn, evolve, and transform itself rapidly.

Society's massive institutions are manifestations of the technology of their age. Cyberspace brings new ways of thinking about business that affect managers everywhere (whether they know it or not). The corporation that can compete best in the age of cyberspace has an architecture quite different from the corporations of the 1980s. The ordered hierarchies of the 1980s are doomed; new organizational structures are taking their place. A designer in London interacts with a designer in Tokyo as though they were in the same room. New teams with new technology deliver new results. Jobs are being reinvented so that all employees are challenged to improve corporate know-how. Agile networks of cybercorps can share competencies so that they can seize new opportunities fast.

While mass production is being replaced by agile networks of producers, mass marketing is giving way to individualized marketing and the ability to deliver customized solutions. Standardized long-lived products and services are giving way to constantly changeable products and services. The entire nature of enterprises and employment is at the start of a massive historical transformation. The Internet enables chain reactions of technology feeding technology and people stimulating people worldwide. In aggregate it spells a momentous change that will affect the whole planet. The cybercorp world is characterized by intense competition bypassing national frontiers and unions. It is spanned by dynamic computerized relationships among corporations using worldwide networks, with electronic reaction times, virtual operations, and massive automation. The Cybercorp Revolution will be bloodless (one hopes) and by its end will have brought deeper changes worldwide than most violent revolutions.

In such an environment we all need to concentrate on how we delight our customers. How can we understand customer needs better? How do we eliminate defects? How do we cut costs? How do we improve quality? How do we make exciting products? How can we climb learning curves more rapidly even though complexity is higher?

Jungle Creatures

A creature in the jungle stalking its prey is constantly alert. It may itself be stalked. It monitors its environment in real time and can make immediate adjustments. It has a clearly defined goal, but its tactic for achieving that goal may switch instantly. Its entire behavior is sharply focused on the goal. It can suddenly move at great speed when it needs to. This paragraph will increasingly describe the survivor in the corporate jungle—the cybercorp.

Today's electronics enables a corporation to react to events at great speed. The more corporations use software, computer networks, and sensors that are constantly alert, the more they acquire characteristics that are in some ways similar to those of nature's creatures. New models of business management are appearing that are concerned with a real-time business environment in which response times are as fast as they need to be.

The cybercorp, however, is not confined in one small skin; it can be worldwide. Public networks, such as the Internet and Integrated Services

Digital Network (ISDN; a switched service of higher capacity than telephone service), and in-house computer networks take it into every nook and cranny of the planet. Computers in New Zealand or Stockholm can decide to make a financial trade in Chicago and move the money in a fracion of a second. Bad weather can close airports, and computers can reschedule the operations of flights, crews, and maintenance worldwide to minimize disruption in service and maximize airlines' profits. Customers of shops in Cape Town change their buying patterns, and a distributor's computer in Paris takes action. The culture of Netscape is summed up by one of its founders, Jim Clark, as recognizing "how quickly the predator can become the prey."

Electronic Reaction Times

One of the key characteristics of the cybercorp is that *things happen fast.* When separate organizational locations are linked by a computer network, an event in one location is immediately felt in a different location. As separate corporations become linked electronically, one can nudge the other into action at electronic speed.

The windows of opportunity in business are of shorter duration when corporations are linked electronically. Price advantages have to be used quickly. Computers in many corporations scan the prices of possible vendors electronically and may transmit electronic purchase orders. To minimize inventory-holding costs with "just-in-time" inventory control, suppliers have to deliver exactly when computers tell them to. Computers help generate sales proposals while the salesman is with the customer. Networks connecting manufacturers to suppliers facilitate quality control on the supplier's premises and just-in-time delivery. We have "just-in-time" manufacturing, "just-in-time" education, "just-in-time" everything. Not long ago, customers wanting a mortgage, insurance, credit, financial quotations, or other such information had to wait for weeks; now it can be provided in minutes. We have rapid food delivery, eyeglasses made while we wait, news whenever we switch on the TV, e-mail not snail mail, instant travel bookings, instant cameras, instant gratification of most things that can be gratified.

Worldwide events affect computerized stock markets immediately. An event anywhere causes reactions to ripple instantly through worldwide computer networks. Because of computers, corporations can design new products and bring them to market quickly with automated production lines. The time between a customer's ordering a product and the product's being delivered is reduced to the minimum. Some products are delivered within hours of being ordered. Funds move between banks on opposite sides of the earth in seconds. Switched video links reduce executive travel and expand the ability to help customers.

Constant Monitoring and Reaction

Networks and software make possible the constant monitoring of events in a corporation.

> **The cybercorp, like the jungle creature, should be constantly alert, electronically monitoring what is important to it, and constantly able to make adjustments.**

Airlines continuously monitor bookings and adjust the allocation of seats to different prices, offerings, or deals. Supermarkets continuously monitor the sales of items and take action to increase the sales of slow-moving items and replenish fast-moving ones. Goods that are moving slowly are featured in sales and special advertising. Some supermarkets have experimented with shopping carts outfitted with small televisions. Electronics sense the position of the cart, and the television may advertise goods that are on the shelves the shopper is next to. Other stores have tried electronic price displays on some shelves so that prices can be changed, several times a day if necessary, by a computer that is trying to maximize profits. The information about what is selling is used to adjust the restocking of the stores, the bulk purchasing of goods, and the warehousing and distribution of inventory.

Nu-Skin, a Utah-based company making personal care and health products, uses 300,000 independent dealers who work on an intricate commission scheme. It monitors sales and pays commissions immediately by electronic funds transfer. Nu-Skin's dealers are in eight countries. With the Internet, it will be common for companies like Nu-Skin to have dealers worldwide, linked with computers.

Nature's creatures have conditioned reflexes. The cybercorp also needs conditioned reflexes. Some decision making can be automated using sets of rules built into software. Exceptions needing human attention are automatically routed to the right person. Automated decision making leads to much faster reaction times.

Sensors

Like a creature, a cybercorp needs senses. Humans provide some of the senses, but also a diversity of automatic sensors are used. Bar codes read at supermarket checkout counters can provide immediate information about sales to computerized systems that plan purchasing, restocking, distribution, pricing, and advertising. Containers shipped around the world can have transponders so that their whereabouts are known. Satellite transmitters on trucks are inexpensive. Global Positioning Satellite (GPS) electronics enable computers to be aware of the position of cars, trucks, containers, and so forth, accurate to 100 feet or less. Computers can track the location of people who use portable phones.

When Federal Express picks up a package, the courier uses a handheld menu-driven computer called a Supertracker to scan the smart bar code on the package. He keys in information such as the type of service and the desti-nation zip code. The Supertracker knows the time and date, which route it is on, its own zip code, and who the courier is. When the courier returns to his van he places the Supertracker in a port in the van computer that radios details to the dispatch center. FedEx knows the whereabouts of the package at all times as it moves through the FedEx system and ensures that no pack-ages are delayed. Many different industries could use handheld computers with sensors and radio transmission, for example, for inventory checking.

The cybercorp needs sensors that tell it immediately when public buying habits shift. When credit cards are used, customer information can be linked to sales information. Smart cards can be used for a diversity of purposes. A mass of information can be collected from the Internet.

It is inexpensive to make chips that send radio signals, like car keys that unlock your car door with a radio signal. Vending machines, for example, should send radio signals to their supplier whenever items are bought. This gives the supplier immediate information about what is selling. Soft drink machines can transmit real-time data about the changing mix of drinks sold in a summer heat wave, and this information should feed directly into pro-duction scheduling. Devices like cars and computers can send a radio signal when they are stolen. Chips can be designed so that their memory can be interrogated or updated by radio. Some clothing manufacturers have put chips in clothes that can indicate where and when the item was made, when it arrived in which store, when it was sold, who purchased it, and for how much. Many goods should have a "memory" to provide information that helps management. It is intriguing to reflect what personal information might be exchanged in the future between radio chips that people wear.

Controlling Wealth-Generating Processes in Real Time

Benetton's customers are fickle. They constantly change their minds about what they would like to buy or about what is fashionable. Customers in different countries have different tastes and experience different fashion shifts. Benetton continuously monitors what the customers ask for, what col-ors they want, what stock is in the pipeline, and so on. To do this, each store has a personal computer connected to Benetton's worldwide nervous system. Central computers near Rome enable Benetton to constantly adjust its manufacturing and distribution to adapt to customer desires. It often ships white clothes to a warehouse near the customer and, when the customer places an order, uses a computerized dye works to create clothes of the color the customer requests.

Benetton is a human-electronic organism monitoring its wealth generation continuously and adapting itself to the changing wishes of its customers.

The cybercorp should monitor its wealth-generating processes in real time and continuously make adjustments.

In all industries, technology is rapidly changing what is possible. The clothing industry now has machines that can do a three-dimensional body scan, generate color separations to print a chosen pattern on a chosen fabric, and design and cut the fabric. The customer may be shipped clothes that are a perfect fit by overnight courier. Body-scan measurements may be stored on a customer card or may be stored by the vendor. When a body scan is not used the customer may be instructed about how to measure herself and the measurements transmitted over the Internet. What will this technology do to future Benettons? Or to Britain's overpriced Savile Row?

The business change that results from electronic networks is accelerating at a rate that will increasingly leave unprepared companies struggling to survive. The models and methods that have served business well for many decades are being replaced with models that are appropriate for real time junglelike interaction.

Corporations need to learn from nature and apply the science of cybernetics to business. Top management should be concerned with three things. First, is its corporation *designed* to be a cybercorp? If we think of a cybercorp as being like a racehorse, management should ask, "Do we have a racehorse or is it more like a camel?" Does it have the right internal systems, teams, software, and sensors? It is difficult to reengineer a camel and turn it into a racehorse. Second, does it know where to race? Is the *strategic vision* well thought out? Third, is it *trained to win?* Are the key players ready for their roles? Are all the employees alert and excited? Do they clearly understand the vision?

Minimum Concept-to-Cash Time

The ubiquitous spread of computer networks is causing everything in business to speed up. Networks make it *possible* to react faster and at the same time make it *necessary* because of competition. Speed is the deciding factor in many competitive situations:

- Identifying new product needs
- Getting products to market
- Implementing new services
- Making product improvements
- Responding to fashion trends
- Satisfying new customer demands
- Controlling inventories and distribution

Particularly important is the need to minimize the time from having the concept of a new product or service to having cash flowing from its sale. The car industry, for example, used to take six or seven years to go from the concept of a new car to the first customer delivery; it battled to drive that figure down to five years by the end of the 1980s, to three years by the mid-1990s, and now in some cases to less than three years. The *concept to-cash time* is much lower with products less complex than cars.

> **An important characteristic of cybercorp design is the minimization of** *concept-to-cash time.*

Fast Evolution

The more we learn about nature's creatures the more we are impressed by the way they are designed. They have evolved over hundreds of millions of years. As corporations compete, we are witnessing a process of evolution happening at immense speed compared with nature's evolution. However, there is another difference: in nature it is *species* that evolve; in the corporate jungle *individual* creatures evolve. Corporations are often replaced by more efficient corporations and die.

To handle the rate of change the cybercorp needs to be designed to change constantly. Most older corporations were not designed for change. They do change, but it is a painful process like renovating an ancient building. To change at a rapid rate the cybercorp needs an infrastructure *designed* to facilitate change and a culture that regards change as a constant process, not a problem. Many corporations have computer systems that make change extremely difficult; cybercorp computing needs to be built with techniques that support the maximum rate of change.

Three types of change are necessary. First, the cybercorp needs to react to events twisting rapidly in new directions. Second, it needs to constantly improve products and invent new products. Third, it should be designed to evolve its processes, both with continuous improvement and with quantum-leap changes.

> **The cybercorp should be designed to *thrive* on change and uncertainty and use it to gain competitive advantage over corporations that find change a problem. Change and uncertainty are continuous sources of competitive opportunity.**

Luciana Benetton constantly reinvents how the clothing business should operate. He has revenues of over $2 billion with only 2,100 employees (almost a million dollars per employee, because much of the work is outsourced). He comments, "The world is changing and we're changing with it. I like it. I go looking for it!"[2]

Strategic Speed

When the world changes with cybercorp speed, *strategic* decisions need to be made fast and implemented fast.

Rupert Murdoch has repeatedly beaten other tycoons in the news and entertainment business because he moves faster. Murdoch's president of telecom and television, Preston Padden, says, "We have no five-year plan. We have no strategic planning group. It's really a sort of personal business being executed on a scale you don't normally see."[3] Murdoch doesn't need to call a committee, or do battle with a contentious board as at Time Warner. He makes sure he is in control so that he can act on good ideas fast. If a jungle animal sensing a new predator had to convene a committee before it could act, it wouldn't survive long.

Electronic Confrontation

Do you remember the days when there were movies like *Doctor Strangelove* and *Fail-Safe?* In those days nuclear bombers took twelve hours to reach the USSR, or vice versa. The United States built the SAGE defense system to warn President Kennedy if Soviet bombers were on their way.

Ten years later ICBMs could make the trip in twenty-five minutes, and so NATO built the BMEWS system, which had radars in multiple places, designed to detect Soviet ICBMs and funnel this information to a science-fiction-like computer center deep in the rock of Cheyenne Mountain in Colorado. It would take half of the twenty-five minutes to confirm that the Soviets had really launched an attack (and that it was not a computer error) and then a frenzied few minutes in which nuclear bombers took off, ICBMs were activated, and President Nixon could decide to launch a counterattack.

Then we got submarines like *Red October.* That class of Soviet "boomer" carried twenty missiles each with ten independently targeted warheads, so it could vaporize 200 cities with a much shorter flight time than ICBMs making the long journey around the planet. There would barely be time to wake up President Reagan.

In the 1980s the game speeded up even more. Cruise missiles were built, like those that slid under the radar defenses into Baghdad. Such missiles were designed to carry a nuclear warhead immensely more powerful than the Hiroshima bomb. They could be hidden, undetectable, for example, in a cargo ship approaching the coast near Washington, D.C. There was massive publicity for Star Wars, but no publicity at all for nuclear command-and-control systems designed so that they could be set to "Launch On Warning"—meaning that at the very highest level of alert, if the United States or Soviet Union were attacked, nuclear retaliation would be automatic, with preprogrammed missiles because there was no time for the head of state to press "the button."

The two sides had built a computerized nuclear creature. It was chained up with superb security. It had many safety catches that could be successively released as a crisis grew (DEFCON 5, DEFCON 4, DEFCON 3, etc.). Fortunately, no crisis reached the alert level of the Cuban missile crisis (DEFCON 2) before the Soviet Union collapsed and the superpowers were able to back away from their confrontation and rethink.

What happened in this scary period of history illustrates the inexorable logic of the computer age. Computers become steadily more powerful and become linked to an electronic nervous system. The system has senses that are constantly alert. Corporations confront one another with computerized systems. It is inevitable in war and competition that electronic complexity increases and reaction times decrease as computerized systems become more advanced. The leisurely pace of *Doctor Strangelove* changes to automated Launch On Warning.

The ultimate consequence of computerized competition is that the battle between the competing cybercorps becomes fast-moving, automated, agile, worldwide, and cybercorps are electronically linked to numerous partners.

Many enterprises are becoming cybercorps, organisms like jungle creatures, constantly alert, with worldwide nervous systems and value streams designed to be as fast and efficient as possible. Isolated cybercorps would change the world, society, employment, and the way we live. However, the revolution now in progress is about something much more powerful than isolated cybercorps: *cybercorps linked electronically.*

Intercorporate Computing

An order placed in Spain with an order-entry computer in France triggers manufacturing planning software in New York to place items into a manufacturing schedule in Dallas, which requires chips from Japan to be built into circuit boards in Singapore, with final assembly in the robotic factory in Dallas and computer-controlled shipment from a warehouse in Milan.

It does not make sense for a computer in one enterprise to print purchase orders and send them to another corporation to be entered (with errors) into another computer. Orders should be transmitted electronically from computer to computer. This electronic data interchange saves money for both the sending and receiving parties. However, the true advantage does not lie in cost savings (although these are substantial) but in interlinking businesses so they can help each other better. A manufacturer can know exactly what is sold by retail stores and hence is alerted immediately to changes in sales patterns. A supplier can supply parts or materials at just the right time. A computer-aided design (CAD) department can link to a subcontractor's design department, so that they cooperate intimately in developing a new product. An enterprise no longer battles its suppliers; it joins forces with them to bring products to market faster, or to achieve other mutual advantages. As relationships between enterprises are reinvented, there are major changes in philosophy and attitude.

Some interactions between computers in separate corporations become elaborate. A computer in a firm that drills and cuts steel girders to shape interacts with a building company whose schedules change frequently, and the steel company constantly adjusts the times of its manufacture and delivery. Boeing's design of its 777 jetliner was done with many corporations around the world creating components with the same CAD software; the components were fitted together, tested, explored with vitual reality, and modified many times in the software before physical assembly began.

While some intercorporate computing connects two corporations for a specific purpose, most intercorporate computing connects vast numbers of corporations. Travel agents' computers worldwide interact with airlines' computers; electronic orders come from thousands of corporations; tax returns are computed and transmitted automatically to government computers; a potential purchaser explores electronically the catalogs of multiple suppliers.

Intercorporate networks and intercorporate computing are fundamentally changing worldwide patterns of commerce.

Intercorporate Monitoring

Toyota cars have several thousand parts that come from several hundred suppliers. Suppliers deliver parts not only just in time but on pallets *in the right sequence for production,* even though the production mix changes constantly with thousands of variations. That coordination requires the supplier computers to have up-to-the-minute knowledge of Toyota's production planning.

When parts are used, the Toyota computers signal the supplier computers to deliver the next batch and indicate the sequence of items in the batch.

As electronic links are built between corporations, the process of monitoring and continuous adjustment becomes an intercorporate process. The computers in one corporation monitor a situation and signal the computers in another corporation to take action. As goods are consumed in a factory and the factory changes its production schedule, a supplier corporation monitors this and ships goods in the correct sequence for the changing production schedule. Chosen suppliers are allocated certain shelf space in supermarkets. As goods are sold, the store computers inform the supplier computers so that they resupply the store. The store may pay its supplier only when the goods are sold. This gives the store a zero inventory-holding cost for these goods.

When cybercorps are linked and each monitors its wealth-generating processes, each makes constant adjustments to those processes and so affects its trading partners.

Virtualness

In the cybercorp world, corporations are increasingly intertwined in electronic interdependencies with other corporations. The term *virtual corporation* is used to describe a situation where people or facilities that are *not* part of a corporation are linked to it as though they were. Resources from different companies may be assembled so that they work together, through electronic links, to achieve some well-defined corporate goal. During its high-growth period Benetton opened over 8,000 shops in over 100 countries, but it did not own the shops. Separate owners were computer-linked into the Benetton system.

The term *virtual* means that something appears to exist when in actuality it does not. The dictionary defines the use of the term in computing, for example, to mean "not physically existing as such but made by software to do so."[4] A corporation may appear to own the facilities of a traditional corporation, but in reality does not own them. Much of a cybercorp can be virtual. People can be linked together with computer networks, work-group facilities, design tools, and software in general so that they cooperate closely even though they are in different locations and different organizations. A corporation does not need to officially employ much of the talent it puts to work or own much of the plant and equipment it uses. It can choose to outsource any part of its activities. You can dial a local number for local service, but in reality the phone rings in Singapore. In an extreme case, a corporation could be a shell that outsources its product design, its manufacturing, its production of marketing brochures, its selling, its order fulfillment, and its accounting. It might do this because it has a great idea in a very fast-changing market. Its management might sense that a certain market will have sudden massive growth or that a new type of product will have explosive worldwide sales. If the corporation had to build its own design, manufacturing, marketing, and sales capability, it would miss the boat. The only way to be a player is to make use of facilities that already exist.

Most corporations of the future will not be purely virtual or nonvirtual; they will have elements of virtualness. Almost no corporation will be purely virtual, so it usually makes more sense to talk about *virtual operations* than a *virtual corporation.* A virtual operation can have a cohesive structure, tightly knit with computer networks, but be scattered to the winds geographically and organizationally.

> **The possibility of virtualness is an important consideration in the design of processes everywhere. Cybercorp managers need to ask, "What should be done in-house, and what should be farmed out?"**

The corporation of the future may decide that the only work that should be done in-house is that for which the corporation has exceptional knowledge or capability, or which is strategically essential. It may use service organizations to run the cafeteria and perform operations such as making components, packaging, order fulfillment, and distribution. If the work depends on strategic ideas, inventiveness, unique skills, or world-class capability in general, it may be done in-house.

> **A corporation should be building capabilities that make it *uniquely* competitive in certain ways. Many great corporate success stories relate to using technology to build processes that the competition cannot copy.**

Agile Webs

Virtualness may be relatively static—for example, two partners agree to co-operate and steadily build a way of working together. However we are now seeing a much more dynamic form of virtualness. Corporations are forming networks of partners, rather like clubs, where different club members can rapidly associate in order to bid on a new contract. Groupings of prequalified partners can be assembled and disassembled rapidly. This ever-shifting dynamic association of partners is referred to as *agile* operation.

> ***Agility* is concerned with the dynamic assembly of core competences from different corporations to react to a fast-changing marketplace that demands excellence and very flexible capabilities.**

When corporations share competences (as opposed to buying parts from one another), it becomes possible to tackle jobs that no single corporation could tackle alone; the agile grouping is greater than the sum of its parts. In the best cases the assembly of core competences from different companies enables corporations to build an all-star team, selecting players from different organizations who have the highest-level capabilities.

When traditional corporations provide complex products or services they are often excellent at some of the activities needed but less than competent at others. This is not good enough. By forming partnerships the corporation can replace its less-than-competent areas. This is increasingly essential for world-class competition. Today's networks, video conferencing, and computerized tools make possible agile but tightly coupled linkages between corporations. Agile webs of corporations are starting to become a vital part of the cybercorp world and will fundamentally change future commerce. There is much to learn about how to make agile manufacturing and agile services work as well as possible, and some organizations are spreading that know-how—for example, the Iacocca Institute in Bethlehem, Pennsylvania.[5]

Agility is about shifting patterns of virtual relationships. Business on a planet laced by electronic highways is becoming turbulent, fast-changing, unpredictable, and highly competitive. Agility is needed to respond to the turbulence and make money out of it.

The cybercorp will increasingly be a cluster of common activities in the midst of a vast fabric of relationships. It may be a nerve center linking many resources where none of the resources are wholly owned. The activities may change rapidly in response to customer demands or changing capabilities.

Global Reach

Many corporations have reorganized themselves to be global in scope. In 1994, Ford announced that it was merging all its activities, distributed among 30 countries, into a single global operation. It electronically merged its seven automotive design centers on four continents. Ford developed its "world car" and split vehicle development by vehicle type, not geographic market. At about the same time IBM reorganized itself by industry type, instead of geography. AT&T implemented its Global Information Systems Architecture (GISA) to standardize its manufacturing systems worldwide and split into three separate businesses. Britain's giant conglomerate Hanson split into four separate companies each with a worldwide focus.

Large companies are shifting from being geographically specific and product diversified to being product specific and geographically diversified.

An Internet call across town costs the same as an Internet call across the planet. Corporations everywhere have set up Web sites that are accessed worldwide; the culture of the Net is global. Many corporations use private networks that also encircle the earth. Distance disappears. Corporations use worldwide networks today that are not "superhighways," but meanwhile superhighways are being built. Fiber optics are spreading at a furious rate and will change the speed and nature of both machine and human interaction. Many corporations are *leasing* fiber-optic circuits. The cybercorp does not need to wait for public superhighways. It can be electronically linked to its suppliers, agents, customers, and trading partners so that computers in one corporation can interact almost instantly with computers in other corporations worldwide.

VISA created a cybercorp vision of a computer system for the entire planet that would capture and refine the knowledge that it collects from credit card processing worldwide. This knowledge, encapsulated in tens of thousands of computerized rules, would be used to help VISA grow faster than its competition. Every transaction from many millions of retailers around the world is funneled through *nine million miles* of fiber-optic cable to one of two large computer centers, one in England and the other in the United States. Every transaction from every retailer in the world has a unique identifying number that stays with the transaction for its life.

The unique number for each transaction enables the computer system to know a great deal about the card user. Gold cardholders can be spotted immediately and given a different level of service. Computerized categorization of the cardholders enables powerful marketing techniques. When the card is used the system can know what activities the cardholder is allowed, such as use of cash dispensers, debit transactions, very large transactions, telephone charges, frequent-flier services, automatic travel insurance, parking fees, and so on. In addition, VISA introduced smart cards that give customers the electronic equivalent of purses of money. With electronic cash the cost of processing a transaction is very low.

It is estimated that with VISA's new system the volume of card transactions could grow from $458 billion in 1993 to $1.1 trillion in 1998 and that VISA's growth in transactions will be more than $220 billion larger by 1998 than it would have been without the system.[6]

We often see images on television of the trading floors of stock markets or commodities markets with a mass of agitated traders frantically gesticulating at one another. This is not necessarily an efficient way to make trades. Much of what happens on such trading floors is being replaced by computerized systems in which some customers enter sell orders, others enter buy orders, and a computer matches them. When the computer establishes a potential trade the buyer and seller are notified of the price and quantity. Verification of the trade is sent to a clearing center and buyer's and seller's accounts are adjusted. *When the trading process is automated it need not be confined to one room full of people hand-waving; it can be worldwide.* Buyers and sellers anywhere in cyberspace can interact.

When trading happens in cyberspace it can bypass the Securities and Exchange Commission regulations and any national regulations. Funds are transferred around the globe at the speed of light, in and out of tax havens, and sometimes into banks such as those in the Cayman Islands that guarantee bank secrecy.

Cyberspace is changing the world's patterns of commerce.

New laws are needed for commerce in cyberspace, but whereas cyberspace mechanisms change at warp speed, the law changes very slowly. Some corporations take advantage of this gap.

Brutal New Competition

Worldwide networks will make certain types of competition brutally intense.

Simple operations that have been profitable in the past may generate little profit in the future because of the new forms of electronics-aided competition. Computers are being used to find the lowest price of goods and services on the Internet, so when corporations each say, "We will not be undersold," vicious price wars will ensue. Price wars will be fought, not between a handful of local gas stations, but between corporations worldwide. Electronics can link to cheap-labor countries where workers who earn a tenth of the wages paid in the West are trained to do high-quality work. Low-salary designers, programmers, and knowledge workers in distant countries will be increasingly used, linked by the Internet. The more the economy shifts to knowledge work, the more "virtual aliens" will be employed to underprice competitors.

Managers everywhere need to understand under what circumstances the cybercorp economy drives down profits, and what new business approaches lead to sustainable high margins.

In the traditional economy, corporations knew who their competition was. In the cybercorp economy totally unexpected competition can come from anywhere because it depends on knowledge that can be transmitted anywhere. In 1995 Microsoft tried to buy the financial software company Intuit. The acquisition was blocked by the Justice Department because the financial industry was worried. *Fortune* commented, "Microsoft would become, in effect, a nationwide consumer bank."[7] Microsoft wanted its customers to pay bills, buy stocks, manage investments, and carry out other banking functions from their personal computer (PC) screens. The Intuit deal was blocked, but it is inevitable that other newcomers will provide Internet banking. Other Internet-based companies will attack the customer bases of travel agents, insurance brokers, and almost all service organizations. Newcomers with networks can skim the cream of service companies, and unless these companies design their strategies ingeniously, cream skimming will wipe out their profits.

Profits will come from doing more complex work that is difficult to emulate. High profits will come from unique skills. Many service or middleman organizations will have to move higher up the food chain in order to survive.

Knowledge Is Money

Francis Bacon said, "Knowledge is power"; the modern executive should say, "Knowledge is money." Knowledge creates money in many different ways. It translates into good marketing, good design, satisfied customers, better production methods, just-in-time inventory control, more profitable decisions. As knowledge flows over networks it enables events to happen efficiently, beautifully choreographed; it makes possible more automated operations.

Knowledge, constantly renewed and enhanced, is the primary source of competitive advantage. Because of this the cybercorp must be designed to expand the knowledge of all employees. The more we enhance the way employees use knowledge, the more they contribute to corporate profits. Corporations succeed because they have greater expertise than their competition in such fields as design, service, and marketing. Human expertise can be amplified with computing, especially network-centric computing. The modern corporation should enhance the knowledge of all workers and support them with software that encapsulates knowledge.

> The cybercorp needs a *knowledge infrastructure* to capture and create knowledge, store it, improve it, clarify it, disseminate it to all employees, and put it to use.

Corporations in the knowledge era must constantly *learn*. The most successful corporations will be the ones that learn in every way possible and put what is learned to the best use. Most knowledge can be copied. Only a tiny fraction of knowledge can be protected with copyright or patent laws. Corporations rapidly learn to do what their competition has done. Almost no process improvements can be protected with intellectual property laws. Because of this the only way to stay ahead is to learn faster and better than one's competition. A corporation must encourage constant experimentation at all levels.

> **The cybercorp should be *designed* to climb the fastest learning curves that are practical.**

The Cybercorp Economy

Peter Drucker points out that a new form of capitalist society has evolved, which he calls "postcapitalist."[8] The classical resources of capitalism described by economists are capital, equipment, labor, land, and natural resources. Today the most important resource is none of these. It is *knowledge.* Value is created by applying knowledge to work.

> **An era in which the key economic resource is knowledge is startlingly different from an era in which the key resources were capital, raw materials, land, and labor.**

Most knowledge, unlike traditional economic resources, is endlessly replicable. It can reside in computers and on disks; it may reside in exceedingly complex software. It can be transmitted worldwide in a fraction of a second. Customs officials have no idea that the most valuable economic resource has just flitted past them.

A corporation should employ all the knowledge it can muster. If this knowledge is not shared with other corporations it provides a unique advantage. We might say, "Unshared knowledge is money." However, it must be fully shared *within* the corporation. Intellectual property rights can protect little corporate knowledge (with a few striking exceptions) because most knowledge leaks to other corporations. Therefore, learning that creates new knowledge provides the primary competitive advantage.

The total worldwide investment in information and communication technologies is now more than a trillion dollars per year. An ongoing investment of this magnitude on technologies so potent is bound to change the world economy. We are heading toward a totally different type of economy. The term *information economy* is repeatedly used, but it does not fully describe what is happening. What is evolving is a *cybercorp economy,* with corporations designed for worldwide real-time interaction over information superhighways and an interlaced mesh of virtual operations. Such corporations will increasingly be "nonnational," with capital, management, talent, and resources coming from around the planet. In various ways there will be a *separation of state and economy.*[9]

> **The cybercorp economy is not simply a speeding up of the old economic environment but a fundamentally new kind of economic environment.**

Cybercorp Ecosystems

Most managers think about competing products within one industry. The cybercorp economy is more complex than that. Increasingly, corporations are interleaved in complex cross-industry relationships. As in nature, complex ecosystems form and companies battle for dominance within these ecosystems, as described in Chapter 8. As commerce becomes globally computerized, product-to-product competition will be brutally intense and the key to sustaining profits will be deep understanding of the ecosystems in which you play, and how to carve out key roles in those ecosystems.

This reshuffling of the cybercorp economy has been likened to the early days of the universe after the big bang, before the galaxies started to congeal. New corporations will congeal into *cybercorp ecosystems* linking diverse players that cut across traditional industries.

> **Management everywhere will need much vision and understanding of how to dominate cybercorp ecosystems if they are to be among the winners.**

Many corporations will go under because of the brutal intensity of electronics-aided competition, but others will use the new mechanisms to achieve dominance of global ecosystems. The fastest growth rates will be much faster than in previous corporate history.

Breakdown in Accounting

> **Where knowledge is a primary source of value in a corporation, traditional accounting practices are misleading and can lead to wrong business decisions.**

This breakdown in accounting is discussed in the book *Relevance Lost,* by two foremost authorities Johnson and Kaplan.[10] No fully satisfactory form of accounting for knowledge has evolved yet, especially because so much valuable knowledge resides in the heads of individuals.

Johnson describes how accounting led to wrong decisions in the microchip industry.[11] Around 1980, U.S. manufacturers made both low-density and high-density chips. High-density chips required far more skill and knowledge overhead. Low-density chips sold for less but appeared to have similar costs to high-density chips because accountants allocated costs on the basis of direct labor. The accountants' computations made low-density chips appear unprofitable when in fact they were not. Various U.S. chip manufacturers surrendered what appeared to be unprofitable lines to foreign competitors who generated major growth and profits with them. This mistake, and others like it, led to a loss of U.S. industrial capacity.[12]

The cybercorp revolution is even more knowledge dependent than microchip production, and irrelevant traditional accounting would argue against many critically important new directions. Various institutes have studied alternative accounting practices that might be useful.[13]

Learning-Intensive Work

The great rate of change means that cybercorp work must be *learning intensive.* If employees have spent ten years doing routine work they have probably lost the ability to do learning-intensive work. The corporation with its eye on the future keeps its employees constantly learning. All employees should be encouraged to think creatively about how their procedures can be improved.

The most successful corporations spend more than one percent of gross revenue on training and education. IBM in its great days spent almost 2 percent on internal education and customer education. Motorola requires many of its employees to spend a total of one month per year of their time on training. At Chaparral Steel, at any given time 85 percent of its personnel are in part-time training courses, and all personnel take an educational sabbatical during which they visit customers' plants, other steel companies, or universities. This is the price that must be paid to succeed with high levels of technology.

> **We must grow human potential as fast as we grow technological potential.**

As computerized tools, robot machinery, and automated processes become ever more powerful, people tend to move into jobs requiring higher skills. Humans no longer need to act like robots on a relentlessly moving production line; robotlike jobs are done by robots. Bookkeepers no longer add up columns of figures. Staffs of many types, working with spreadsheet and decision-support tools, are expected to make better and larger-scale decisions. Designers have tools of great power that enable them to be more creative. In many jobs, computers should do the drudgery and people should do the work that is uniquely human. The annual revenue generated per person is often several times higher in highly automated corporations than in corporations with little automation. The computer can be an intellect amplifier. Automated corporations demand greater skill for greater pay.

> **The cybercorp is the culmination of the twentieth-century journey from treating employees like dumb slaves who must be made to obey orders to challenging every employee to use his or her wits in devising new ways to add value.**

The century started with Kafkaesque bureaucracy and contempt for employees, with Frederick Taylor timing every motion of workers with a stopwatch. It ends with the challenge of regarding the entire corporation as a cybercorp that must climb the steepest learning curve, where everybody is challenged to strive for their full potential. In the past what was good for the corporation was often bad for the individual. We created soul-destroying jobs. The best corporations today are creating work environments where difficult challenges energize and excite people and everybody cares about them. They are reinventing work so that what is good for the corporation is good for the individual. They aim for the highest of Maslow's hierarchy of human needs so that everybody tries to achieve full potential. Most boring jobs can be abolished (but not quite all). The dehumanizing methods of early mass production are gone. The intense competition and emphasis on quality means that we can buy far more interesting goods and services. Unlike in Adam Smith's revolution, the wealth of nations is maximized by maximizing the value added by everybody.

Reinventing Automation

> **Many corporations with a high level of automation have automated *existing* operations. The challenge of the cybercorp era is to use automation to invent *new* types of operations.**

Software, for example, has been widely used to create and process purchase orders, but a more interesting challenge is to create *intelligent* purchase orders. An intelligent purchase order order behaves in a fundamentally different way from a traditional purchase order. An intelligent purchase order can monitor the inventory and spring into action when the inventory drops to a predetermined level. It decides what quantity should be ordered and what supplier to order from. It may monitor the requirements of many different departments so that bulk discounts can be obtained. Purchase orders for some goods may search the Internet to find the lowest prices. Some purchase orders may be allowed to travel to the supplier on their own initiative; others may not. In the latter case the purchase order goes to the screen of a person who can give authorization. If the person does not respond within a predetermined time, the purchase order sends a message to someone else indicating that attention is needed. When it receives authorization the intelligent purchase order travels to the supplier's computer. It checks that the supplier is responding quickly enough. Most traditional business documents can become similarly intelligent.

> **Instead of dumb paper documents a cybercorp will use objects with built-in intelligence that can move worldwide in seconds.**

As technology evolves, machines become more impressive, dwarfing humans in their capabilities but ultimately needing the human. A giant excavator is formidable compared with the frail biological creature who drives it. The excavator can be highly automated, but it needs a driver. Bond traders have worldwide networks of computers that can detect and take advantage of fleeting investment opportunities. A jumbo jet pilot has little to do as more and more functions are performed more reliably by computers than by the pilot, but jumbo jets are not likely to fly without human pilots. By contrast, the flight attendant's job has little automation. The more the basic mechanisms become automated, the greater the need for people to concentrate on *uniquely human* roles such as inventing new ways to delight the customers.

The cybercorp has much in common with the bond trader network and jumbo jet. Its operation is highly automated. Many functions are performed better by machines than by people. Information flashes between locations automatically to keep the jet safe in the sky, but both the human pilot and the human traffic controllers are vital. The competiveness and survival of advanced corporations depend on how effectively they use automation, but as automation improves, greater skills are demanded of people. Human services need intensely caring people.

The Strategic Importance of Software

Much of a corporation's expertise and procedures are represented in its software. Corporate software is rapidly growing in complexity, encapsulating an ever-growing body of human know-how. Software that can be purchased is growing more comprehensive and sophisticated. Designers of corporate operations need to ask what should be done purely by software, what purely by humans, and what by a human-software combination. The optimal mix is steadily changing.

> **Software should not merely replicate existing operations; it should facilitate entirely different types of operations.**

In the airline business, for example, software fundamentally changed the booking process worldwide and made it possible to have many prices for the same seat so that revenue from the flight could be maximized. When American Airlines was highly profitable, its CEO, Robert Crandell, was asked if he would sell the airline. He replied that given the choice of selling the airline or selling its software, SABRE (which links the airline to booking agencies worldwide), he would rather sell the airline; the software was more valuable. European airlines struggled to combat the effects of SABRE's moving into Europe. Two airline consortia built competing systems of great complexity for their time, AMADEUS and GALILEO. The airline business, like other businesses, became a battlefield of competing software.

Many enterprises have been badly hurt by failures to acquire the software they needed and put it to work effectively. The London Stock Exchange was so badly damaged by its failure to build its TAURUS system for electronic share registration that the *London Sunday Times* described the fiasco as "the beginning of the end for the London Stock Exchange."[14]

Most software, like most machine tools, should not be built in-house, but some software needs to be custom built because it gives the corporation a unique competitive advantage. Some software has become a valuable strategic resource that cannot be replicated quickly by competing organizations. Software that makes a competitive difference, which cannot be bought off-the-shelf, must be built, either in-house or by a contractor, and usually it needs to be built *quickly*. If your competition can build a competitive system in three months and it takes you three years, you will be in trouble. Fast change is essential for survival.

In many corporations programmers have laboriously coded software line by line, rather like monks in their cells copying manuscripts before Gutenberg. This is much too slow for the pace of cybercorp evolution. As software becomes more complex and strategic, it is necessary either to buy it or to automate its construction. Complex corporate software cannot sensibly be built without rigorous engineering with automated tools. Corporations cannot design and maintain the complex integration of systems that is needed unless computers themselves are used for that task. The *automation of automation* is essential.

Business rules can be built into software. Rule-based systems make it easy to change the rules the computer uses. By contrast, when rules are buried in hand-coded programs it is extremely difficult to change the programs when the rules need to change.

> **A key reason for stating business rules explicitly and expressing them in software is that certain rules may change, rapidly. When they change it is desirable to be able to make a corresponding change to software, *almost immediately*.**

The "artificial intelligence" systems that evolved in the 1980s represented knowledge in the form of rules. Large numbers of rules were stored, and a computer could deal with certain types of problems by searching for rules and logically chaining them together in order to do inferential reasoning. Computers are able to reason better than humans about certain problems such as scheduling, diagnosis, reconfiguring, simulation, and optimization. The most advanced systems for automated reasoning far exceed human capability. But for most situations human insight needs to be combined with automated reasoning. The combination makes it possible to build more complex products and design more complex operations. Products can be designed knowing that computers will diagnose their problems. Factory networks can be designed knowing that there will be automated scheduling and automated purchasing. Worldwide logistics can be intricately choreographed for computerized management.

Data Mining

A deluge of data is produced by cybercorp sensors, information collected on the Internet, and other information sources. *Data-warehousing* tools are designed to capture and stove overwhelming quantities of data in such a way that they can be searched and understood. Decision makers can then use *data-analysis* tools to explore complex data in useful ways and *data-visualization* tools to chart data so that they help provide insight.

Often data are too amorphous and complex for humans to recognize the patterns they contain that could be used to understand situations and manage them better. *Data-mining* software uses various techniques including neural networks (based on brain mechanisms) to "mine" an ocean of data, searching for patterns that might lead to better decision making. When a pattern is discovered the decision maker needs to find out whether it could *really* lead to better decisions. She uses it with historical data to see whether it would have provided better results. It might indicate, for example, that customers with certain characteristics are more likely to buy specific goods. Those customers should be targeted in the marketing.

Data mining can reveal what segmentation produces the best results with a large mailing list, or where spare parts should be stored in a worldwide airline operation. It is used in sophisticated ways in the financial community to design derivatives and to improve investment decisions. The pharmaceutical industry uses it to understand factors that correlate with the incidence of disease and to study the effectiveness of drugs. It is used in banks and insurance companies to manage risks better. Wal-Mart did thorough data mining and Kmart did not, and this was a factor in helping Wal-Mart beat Kmart in the marketplace.

To make data mining effective it is necessary to collect the most useful data. Some large stores, for example, ask customers for their zip codes and correlate this with bar-code data collected at the cash register. The ability to collect the most valuable data and mine them is important in every industry.

> **Data analysis, data mining and data visualization will increasingly be part of the cybercorp creature's instinct for survival.**

Designing the Creature

The cybercorp, a creature designed to prosper in the corporate jungle, needs many parts that work together to make it creaturelike, constantly alert, ready to spring into action.

Russell Ackoff describes corporations as complex systems. He describes an important property of such systems: "If each part of a system, considered separately, is made to operate as efficiently as possible, the system as a whole will not operate as effectively as possible."[15] Ackoff comments that if many types of cars were examined by engineers, and engineers identified which components were the best designed and then assembled a car from those best components, that car would not work. The parts would not operate well together. The performance of a system depends more on how its parts interact than on how well they work independent of one another.

In a corporation that consists of many departments, we could try to make each department work as efficiently as possible, using the most advanced computer systems for that department. But this would not make the corporation as a whole efficient. This is especially true in an era of great reinvention such as today. When machines or corporations are reinvented many of the old parts are scrapped.

> **Optimizing the parts of a corporation independently can be highly inefficient compared with optimizing the whole.**

If the designer of a jungle creature perfected the stomach without thinking about the teeth, or optimized the ability to run without thinking about the senses, the creature would not survive long. Unfortunately, most corporations do just that. An enormous amount of money has been spent on localized redesign, personal computers, ISO 9000 applied to existing processes, departmental client-server systems, and so on, without redesigning the end-to-end behavior. When total quality management (TQM) of ISO 9000 is applied within an obsolete organizational structure, it has the effect of optimizing and polishing procedures that ought to be scrapped. It is a waste of money to automate or reengineer departments that ought to be replaced because the overall cybercorp architecture needs to be different. Builders of the cybercorp must be concerned with end-to-end streams of activities.

> If we pull out a piece of a successful cybercorp to examine it, it comes out trailing roots back into a tightly interconnected structure. Only when we have designed the structure well should we be concerned with optimizing the components.

To understand cybercorp interconnectedness we need to see, not snapshots, but a dynamic picture of how the parts of the system interact with one another, constantly changing with time. Like appreciating a football game we must understand the holistic interplay of activities, but unlike a football game the activities may be far apart in time and space.

Forces of Disintegration

While the key to cybercorp operation is connectivity and intergration, the forces of *dis*integration are great. Left to their own devices, individual departments tend to design their own data and select their own software. A mess of incompatibility spreads so that future change requires conversion efforts that are slow, painful, and expensive. Flexible connectivity requires common data and objects rather than the same data and objects having different representations in different systems. This needs architected planning rather than each department doing its own thing.

It is appalling how many authorities on "business process reengineering" advocate modeling and modifying an existing business process when the right thing to do is to scrap the process and take an integrated approach to building cybercorp mechanisms. This cybercorp view has the largest payoff and raises vital questions about the enterprise's overall architecture and information technology (IT). It raises questions about where "business reengineering" is a good idea; it is usually easier to build new cybercorp units. Answering these questions effectively should result in the planning of a corporate journey, with a pragmatic timetable for the changes that are needed.

> Most managers in most corporations think about their own areas and what they do. The cybercorp should be conceived in terms of end-to-end activities that often span multiple departments, multiple divisions, and sometimes multiple corporations.

Employees need to be encouraged to understand a broad viewpoint; otherwise they cast into concrete obsolete procedures rather than helping to create cybercorp procedures. The spread of PCs and local area networks (LANs) led to an era of downsizing in IT. There are clear advantages when business units build and perfect their own systems. However, if those systems are built with no cybercorp viewpoint they are the wrong systems, expensive because of hidden costs, and often difficult to change. The many localized "client-server" systems being built today will become the mother of all legacy problems. You cannot build a cybercorp out of incompatible fragments.

Top management needs to understand the business payoff from architected planning. When a city is well planned, has good roads, services, and telecommunications, the flexibility of activities that can take place in the city is enhanced. The cybercorp needs a nervous system, but it is only likely to work well when it conforms to a well-designed architecture.

The cybercorp needs the right mix of top-down design of infrastructure and bottom-up design of activities.

Small Cybercorps

The cybercorp need not be a large corporation. We will see how cybercorp characteristics are enabling start-up corporations to achieve results and grow faster than would have been possible ten years ago. Traditional advertising favors the large corporation; the cybermarketing techniques discussed in Chapter 3 favor the small corporation. Some new corporations are growing at lightning speed, taking advantage of power tools and the Internet. Virtual operations have enabled some new operations to grow at astonishing rates. A small corporation can outsource its bread-and-butter activities so that it can focus on the services or products that make it unique. It can have partnerships with other corporations using networks and computer-to-computer interaction.

The cybercorp world is full of David-and-Goliath battles that David can win.

Reengineer or Build New Units?

It is difficult to reengineer a corporation with a deeply established culture. Roughly 70 percent of attempts at business reengineering are abandoned before completion,[16] and of those completed the CSC Index *State of Reengineering Report* stated that "67% were judged as producing mediocre, marginal, or failed results."[17] Similarly, many attempts at introducing TQM have failed. A vital question for all top executives is, "Should we attempt the traumatic reengineering of an old organization, or should we build new units with cybercorp principles?" Building fundamentally new units is usually easier, more exciting, and more successful. Many say, "Let's swing the old corporation around slowly and cautiously, and steady as you go," but new-paradigm newcomers are racing fast to take business away from cautious competitors. This is an age in which small corporations can easily outmaneuver old ones.

Top executives of traditional corporations must ask, "Can we convert today's corporation to the new world, or is its embedded culture too difficult to convert?" Particularly important, "Can we convert *fast enough*?" If reengineering a business takes years and has a high probability of failure, it is much more prudent to start new subsidiaries or affiliates that can move fast. They should be cybercorps that avoid old-world inflexible structures. We are entering an age when many executives realize that instead of attempting to reengineer arthritic corporations, it is far better to create cybercorp start-ups. New corporations with cybercorp thinking are streaking ahead of old corporations that are struggling to reengineer old structures.

Every chief executive must ask, "Should we reengineer, or should we create new cybercorp units?" Creating new units is usually more successful.

The new corporations or subsidiaries should be designed so that they will not need quantum-leap reengineering themselves in the future because they are *designed to evolve continuously*.

"Think Cybercorp"

Given the dramatic changes that are happening it is vital that business leaders, managers, entrepreneurs, and IT professionals everywhere understand the potentials of the cybercorp world and "think cybercorp." They should think about business in terms of cybercorp mechanisms, opportunities, and competitive threats. Many businesses contain the seeds of their own destruction. Unless their executives think in a cybercorp way, those seeds will sprout. Relentless missionary work is needed to help executives think in terms of cybercorp capabilities. While many are skeptical, bewildered, and uneducated about the possibilities, others are racing to seize the new opportunities.

The capability to think cybercorp is essential for entrepreneurs. Many small corporations are growing in very different ways from the past. A newcomer can latch onto an exploding market segment and operate as a virtual corporation from the start. In large corporations, cybercorp thinking should pervade all aspects of the business. However, older corporations are buried in noncybercorp structures, and many executives are anxious to protect obsolete turf.

The Sound Barrier

Given the breathless reckless rate of change, what do managers have to do? In this revolution who are the survivors? Davids of the new world are attacking

Goliaths of the old. As we plunge into cyberspace, what are the guidelines? The cybercorp outdates most management textbooks; what will the textbooks of the future say?

The cybercorp does not change the fundamental wisdom of management expressed in classic books such as James Collins and Jerry Porras's *Built to Last*, Peter Drucker's *Managing for Results*, James Heskett's *Corporate Culture and Performance*, Gary Hamel and C. K. Prahalad's *Competing for the Future*, and Masaaki Imai's *Kaizen*.[18] Great corporations need core values, strong cultures, clearly articulated vision, audacious goals, continuous process improvement, and management who pay careful attention to detail. They need consistent alignment of their multifold activities with their goals and vision. The cybercorp, however, needs different clockwork, different architecture, changed marketing; it should use virtual operations, be as fluid as mercury, and be able to dynamically link competences from agile webs of associates. It must be designed for very fast evolution. It needs new thinking. Few executives calculate the cost of obsolete thinking, but as discussed in Chapter 17 this cost can be appallingly high. This book does not repeat or replace the wisdom of the classic management books. It assumes that such wisdom should be in place in a corporate world that may have otherwise changed beyond recognition.

Corporations have to pass through a great transition,[19] from the world of the 1980s to the world of cyberspace. When planes of the 1950s first approached the sound barrier a most violent juddering set in. Then engineers learned how to penetrate the sound barrier so that the plane streaks into the blue skies, the great speed becoming unnoticeable. In the great corporate transition the juddering is just beginning.

References

1. Norbert Weiner, *Cybernetics* (New York: Wiley, 1948).
2. Curtis Bill Pepper, "Fast Forward," *Business Month*, February 1989.
3. Michael Hirsh, "Setting Course," Special report on Rupert Murdoch, *Time*, February 12, 1996.
4. *Concise Oxford Dictionary*, s.v. "Virtual."
5. S. L. Goldman, ed., *Agility Initial Survey*, Working Paper no. 94-03 (Agility Forum, Iacocca Institute at Lehigh University, Bethlehem, PA, 1994).
6. "Visa International, Digital Credit," *Economist*, September 25, 1993.
7. Terrence P. Paré, "Why the Banks Lined Up against Bill Gates," *Fortune*, May 19, 1995.
8. Peter Drucker, *Post-Capitalist Society* (New York: Harper Business, 1993).
9. Kelley Holland and Amy Cortese, "The Future of Money," *Business Week*, June 12, 1995.

10. T. H. Johnson and R. L. Kaplan, *Relevance Lost* (Boston: Harvard Business School Press, 1987).
11. T. H. Johnson, *Relevance Regained* (New York: Free Press, 1992).
12. Ibid.
13. E.g., Iacocca Institute, Lehigh University, Bethlehem, PA, fax: (610) 758-6550.
14. "Taurus: Bank Takes Bull by the Horns," *Sunday Times*, Business section, March 14, 1993.
15. Russell L. Ackoff, *Creating the Corporate Future* (New York: Wiley, 1981).
16. Statistic quoted by Mike Hammer in his lectures, 1995.
17. *Fast Company* 1, no. 1 (1995): 71.
18. James C. Collins and Jerry I. Porras, *Built to Last* (New York: Random House, 1994); Peter Drucker, *Managing for Results* (New York: Harper Business, 1964); James Heskett, *Corporate Culture and Performance* (New York: Macmillan, 1992); Gary Hamel and C. K. Prahalad, *Competing for the Future* (Boston: Harvard Business School Press, 1994); Masaaki Imai, *Kaizen: The Key to Japan's Competitive Success* (New York: McGraw-Hill, 1986).
19. James Martin, *The Great Transition* (New York: AMACOM, 1995).

2

The Nervous System

To be creaturelike, the cybercorp needs a *nervous system.* A reason why cybercorp mechanisms began to evolve fast in the mid-1990s was the spread of the Internet. After the World Wide Web made it easy to navigate the Internet, the Internet became high fashion; news media everywhere talked about it. Corporations started to use it for commerce.

Throughout history, when changes in communication patterns have occurred they have caused changes in society and its institutions. The World Wide Web, implemented as both private networks and the public Internet, brings a sudden change from highly restricted computer communication channels to worldwide, any-to-any communication. The effects of this transition, when mature, will be a total reinvention of the structure of computerized enterprises. The crude communication paths of an earlier era led to restrictive forms of organization structure.

Many corporations have used the Internet only in simplistic ways. They set up Web pages for marketing but failed to realize that the ubiquitous nervous system breaks down the walls within corporations and hence can fundamentally change the organizational structure.

> **The deep structural changes are much more important than the use of conventional Web sites.**

The 1990s is a decade of explosive growth in worldwide networks. As well as the Internet, the world is laced with private networks like those of McDonald's and American Express and multicorporate networks like those handling funds transfer, travel bookings, stock market trading, goods distribution, and so on.

Intranets

A cybercorp should have two nervous systems: an *internal* one that is private and secure and the *external* public one linking it to customers, suppliers, and the public at large.

When the Internet became high fashion it became clear that the easiest way to build an *internal* corporate network was to use the same technology and software. Corporations around the world began to build their own private versions of the Internet, called *intranets*. It steadily became understood that all manner of valuable information should be made usable on the corporate intranet. Before long, far more money was being spent on intranets than on the public Internet.

The corporate intranet has closed borders. It uses "firewall" software to keep unwanted visitors out. Computer users inside the corporation can access both the public Internet and the private intranet, but security measures keep the internal network private.

Not all corporate networking needs can be met with Internet-like facilities. A corporation may have a separate network for high-volume transaction processing and for video interaction. Collectively, these networks make up the cybercorp nervous system.

New Communication Patterns

The Internet has one very important characteristic: computers of all types can use it. Prior to the Internet, different computers had often been incompatible and could not "talk" to one another. Suddenly, there was a way for all the world's computers to intercommunicate. The World Wide Web, its bulletin boards, and software for easily browsing its contents with a mouse-clicking dialog made it easy for people to interact with computers anywhere. Suddenly, an astonishing worldwide nervous system was in place and the stage was set for the rapid evolution of corporate behavior.

Information technology *frees information from the constraints of geography and time.* Information in electronic form can be made available at any place at any time, whereas information on paper is tied to a physical location. Paper information has to be searched for in a filing cabinet; it is mailed and photocopied and accumulates in disorganized piles. A nurse in a typical hospital walks about eight miles a day. If the hospital computer systems make information available where he is (for example, in or near the patient's room), he need walk only two miles a day. He should spend his time doing what he wants to do—nursing.

Software tools can make communication detailed and precise. Chrysler, for example, decrees that its suppliers employ uniform CAD tools, linked over networks. Tools for the automation of software development enable developers in different countries to communicate with computerized precision. Different locations can exchange business "objects" with encoded behavior. The new Hollywood studio DreamWorks, started by Steven Spielberg and his friends, has an intranet used to track animation objects and coordination scenes shot in different locations.

The Informality of Cyberspace

Cyberspace not only frees communication from the constraints of geography and time; it also frees it from some human constraints. People say different things to one another in cyberspace than they would face to face. E-mail messages are usually short and go straight to the point. People tend to be direct and frank when addressing each other with a keyboard. There is no body language, no facial expression, no vocal inflection. Cyberspace is a sensory deprivation tank. It is sometimes thought that the keyboard character set is too restricted for intimate human dialog, but it has a different sort of intimacy because it conveys raw ideas without the constraining courtesies of facial interaction.

There is an easygoing informality to cyberspace that means that people are often more willing to say what they think. This candor can oil the channels of communication and achieve knowledge transfer that may have been blocked in other media. Employees who would never dream of telephoning a top executive do send e-mail to her. E-mail can help to overcome language barriers. Many people who would not talk on the telephone in a foreign language are willing to send e-mail with computerized spell-checking.

The Global City

Marshal McLuhan popularized the term "global village." The Internet is not a global village because in a village everybody knows what everybody else does; the Internet is a *global city.* It has vast numbers of separate communities with separate interests. Its population is many times larger than London's or New York's. Soon it will be larger than the United States'. No one in the global city can know what most other people do. Different communities in the global city have radically different cultures, but they coexist, sharing the same streets, often stimulating one another, sometimes antagonistic to one another. Like a great city, the Net puts many cultures into close proximity so that they learn from each other. It is a worldwide melting pot, a vast information resource, a nervous system for the explosion of electronics around the planet. It grows the way society grows but at a lightning pace.

There is an immense diversity of information sources, shopping malls, playthings, bulletin boards, libraries, and discussion groups whose members do not meet physically but have a close rapport electronically. One can "surf" the Net endlessly and not exhaust its possibilities. People meet and make friends in cyberspace and are often generous in helping one another. There is crime and craziness in the global city, but businesses and ordinary citizens learn to protect themselves from it. Some learn how to find their way around the labyrinthine city; some have just one or two sites they visit; others are bewildered by the city and become net-phobic.

In many ways the Net is primitive today, but because it does more with less on a dramatic scale, it is a juggernaut. The Internet will change incredibly in the next ten years. It will change the entire electronics industry. Some aspects of its use are fads and will fade away like the hula hoop, but it has a massively important role to play in the planet's commercial and social infrastructure.

The Internet is building a worldwide nervous system over mankind's culture. Nothing like this has ever happened before. The long-term effects will be immense. Corporations everywhere need to constantly reassess the new opportunities and threats.

While intranets provide an internal nervous system within the corporation, the Internet provides an external nervous system linking to customers, agents, and affiliate corporations worldwide. Some groups of corporations build a shared intranet for their collective use, for example, a network linking insurance brokers, or a network to aid in sharing competences in agile manufacturing.

Bulletin Boards

An Internet *bulletin board* might be likened to a corkboard in an office on which anybody can pin notices; however, the notices can be posted or read worldwide. Basically, anybody with a computer can start a board. Boards can be cheap, and they can be contacted at no cost to the person running the board—the caller pays the phone bill.

The Internet has hundreds of thousands of *bulletin board systems* that provide information or act as the focus of discussion groups. Corporate intranets employ similar boards to communicate among employees or provide databases for all manner of corporate functions. They are proliferating at a rapid rate. Some contain vast quantities of information. Hewlett-Packard (HP), for example, operates an internal board called a "software vending machine," so that software developers can check what's in it before writing code. Not long after establishing its intranet, Silicon Graphics had 144,000 Web pages of valuable information accessible to its 7,200 employees.

Some boards are designed for discussion groups; some are read-only, and the audience does not contribute. Such a board may be a shopping "mall," a collection of information about corporate products, a timetable, the world airline guide, an art gallery, a listing of film or theater reviews, and so on.

The person or organization who sets up an Internet site and operates it is referred to as the *sysop*. Sysops vary enormously in the amount of effort they put into running their boards, validating users, adding to (or purging) contents, or generally controlling them.

There are many different types of boards:

Open boards. Anyone can connect to the board and say anything about its subject matter. The sysop makes little or no attempt to supervise the board's contents. The board may be a source of lively discussion or may degenerate into anarchy or silence.

Controlled discussion boards. The sysop runs a tidy board, issues announcements, controls the subject matter, calms brawls, and tries to rid the board of troublemakers or clowns.

Electronic publications. The board is run rather like a magazine with editorial control but is much more flexible than a paper magazine. Users around the planet may contribute.

Boards with refereed or heavily supervised contents. The sysop sternly urges responsible or academic behavior, may referee the content or grade its quality, and removes offensive or irrelevant content.

Information databases. The board makes available a vast amount of information, some of which may be updated by board users.

Ease of Implementation

Bulletin boards provide a relatively easy way to get valuable information to employees on intranets, or to customers on the Internet. In many corporations bulletin boards make information immediately available where previously employees had to submit requests to experts specially trained to extract the information from databases—a process that could take several days. At HBO it took just seven days to put the Human Resource department's 150-page database on-line.[1]

Federal Express set up a Web site that customers could interrogate to find the status and location of items in shipment. This tracking capability proved extremely popular with customers and was a reason to choose FedEx over its competition. UPS quickly followed suit, but customers could find out about a package only after it had been delivered.

Some entrepreneurs set up bulletin boards to serve an industry; for example, Polygon Internet serves corporations in the gem trade.[2] By accessing its home page and entering a password, companies can see diamonds and other gems offered for sale, declare their own trading interests, check with labs on stone quality, or read details of thefts. They can download color images of stones and search a database of diamonds for sale.

Some years ago, Hilton, Marriott, and Budget Rent-A-Car made a catastrophic attempt to establish a joint booking system. After years of effort and $165 million spent on software development, the project was written off, with mass firings of those responsible. Then World Wide Web software became available and a new enterprise called TravelWeb quickly set up a system that enabled the public to search for accommodation at 7,000 hotels in 30 chains, and make reservations on-line.

Java and the World Wide Web

In 1994 the Internet took a great step forward because the World Wide Web (WWW) came into general use. Like multimedia software, the Web allows users to mouse-click on highlighted words or icons to select new pages or files of information. The data selected in this way can be anywhere on the Net. You can click on YAHOO! on a Web page in Ireland and be linked to a computer in California that provides you with menus; you click on a shopping "mall" and are connected to a computer in New York; you click on a clothing "store" and are connected to its Web site in Italy; you choose woolen sweaters from its catalog and are linked to a collection of colorful designs in Australia; you choose one and are connected to an electronic bank in Bermuda for payment. As you surf the Web, exploring subject matter, you skip from computer to computer not necessarily knowing which country your responses are coming from. Travel in the global city happens at magical speed.

In 1996 another innovation represented a quantum leap in Web capability—the downloading of not just messages and data from the Net but also chunks of program that could be executed in one's computer. The program chunks called *applets* (little applications) are written in a language called Java. All different types of computers can have an interpreter that enables them to run Java applets. The information obtained from the Net can then be brought to life. There can be animated Web pages, cartoonlike helpers, applications for placing orders or calculating expense reports, chunks of artificial intelligence, details of a product's options packaged with programs to compute its total cost, all-singing-all-dancing advertisements, and all the diversity that programming can bring.

There are vast numbers of potential applications for software downloaded from the Net that nobody has thought of yet.

Most computer programs run on certain types of computers but not others. A Macintosh program won't run on a Sun machine, for example. Java is designed to run efficiently on *all* computers because they can all have Hot Java software that converts the applets to their machine code. Java thus provides a new "openness" in computing.

The World Wide Web has been likened to a "global brain" linking vast numbers of computers and people around the entire planet. It is growing into something awesome. National governments may fight it, but it skips across frontiers; there are no immigration laws in cyberspace. It is larger than any government and will eventually change the nature of global democracy. It will also fundamentally change the capability of corporations, and how corporations interact.

New Highways

Much of this book was written in a twelfth-century castle in Ireland but the local telephone company had no difficulty connecting an ISDN circuit to the castle for a $1,000 fee. The heating did not work well, but video conferencing, virtual board meetings, and intercontinental computerized editing worked wonderfully. Digital television can be squeezed into a number of bits small enough to send over ISDN circuits. When this is done there is a loss of picture quality. Talking heads and still landscapes look fine, but Sylvester Stallone smashing up thugs looks terrible.

A corporation can use multiple different types of highways in addition to the normal telephone system:

1. *The Internet.* The Internet will eventually be as ubiquitous as the telephone network. Because most customers can access it, it is one of the most important corporate highways. The Net became relatively easy to use with the availability of the World Wide Web and mouse-pointing software.

2. *An intranet.* An intranet is a private internal version of the Internet using similar software.

3. *Corporate networks.* Many corporations have in-house networks that are not like the Internet. These may be designed for fast response times and good video. Some corporations, for example, VISA International, have a pri-

vate network with optical fibers for handling extremely high transaction volumes.

4. *Private circuits of all types.* Private circuits can be leased between locations with heavy traffic or video. Some medical clinics, for example, have leased circuits to a major hospital so that doctors can do remote examinations.

5. *Multicorporate private networks.* Some private networks serve multiple related corporations—for example, networks handling reservations for the airlines around the world and networks handling electronic funds transfer for banks. The U.S. National Science Foundation (NSF) operates a superhighway (not linked to the Internet, which the NSF once funded) for connecting supercomputers at universities and research establishments at extremely high speed.

6. *ISDN circuits.* ISDN circuits can be installed that give access to the world's switched ISDN network. ISDN operates at higher speeds than regular telephone service (64,000 or 128,000 bits per second and sometimes higher, whereas telephone circuits are commonly used at 14,400 or 28,800 bits per second). ISDN circuits allow us to interact with graphic images with a faster response time and to transmit music with high quality and video with poor quality (often small video windows are used).

7. *Frame relay networks.* Frame relay is switched service used to link corporate locations at megabit speeds. It is used for video interaction or high-capacity data transmission.

8. *The Internet linked to cable TV.* Cable TV linked to the Internet is a potentially powerful combination. Internet dialogs can have responses with segments of television as well as other images, music, and applets of program code.

Firehose to the Home

Some countries plan to build fiber-optic cables to homes in order to deliver high-quality television and a deluge of interactive services. Such rewiring will cost many billions of dollars and take years to complete. Meanwhile, many homes are already fed by an information "firehose"—the cable TV circuit. While not originally designed to carry computer data, cable TV can be linked to the Internet by using a cable TV modem. This combination will become a dramatic medium for home Internet use and for marketing that combines the pizzazz of television advertising with the ubiquitous capabilities of the Net. It is estimated that cable TV modems will drop in cost to about $150.

Many TV cables are one way. To use the Net with them requires a (low-capacity) telephone link *from* the home as well as the cable TV link *to* the

Exhibit 2-1. Types of connection possible to the Internet

Type of circuit	Speed (thousands of bits per second)	Time to Download a Megabyte	Availability (in USA)
Telephone voice line	14.4	9.3 min	Everywhere
	28.8	4.6 min	
ISDN	128	1 min	High percentage of phone customers
DirecPC (satellite downlink)	128	1 min	Everywhere
T1	1,440	5.5 sec	Everywhere, at a price
Cable TV modem	4,000	2 sec	Fraction of cable TV customers
Advanced cable TV modem	40,000	0.2 sec	In development
Optical fiber	80,000+	0.1 sec	Some office locations

home. This can work well because most interactions do not send video from the home.

Exhibit 2-1 shows different methods of connecting to the Internet and the time they take to download one megabyte. The amount of video that can be encoded in a megabyte varies greatly with the picture quality. A megabyte can range from carrying about five seconds of television with a good-quality image to about sixty seconds with a highly compressed image. The highly compressed image may be acceptable for a talking head or a picture with little movement. It is often used for computer video windows the size of a postage stamp. The same megabyte chunk could carry 500 pages of text, an interesting slice of software, one minute of good-quality music, or five minutes of speech. Any of the above could be sent to the subscriber after a delay of about two seconds with cable TV, whereas with a telephone circuit the delay would be several minutes. With cable TV circuits, exciting interaction with high-quality video images becomes possible.

Because home Internet links with good video have such great potential for entertainment and marketing, much money is being spent on the marriage of cable TV and the Internet. People who use this combination comment that going back to telephone modems feels like visiting the Stone Age.

Research

The first major use of the Internet in corporations was for research. Scientists and engineers could submit jobs to remote supercomputers. They joined virtual communities of researchers with like interests from different enterprises and different countries and could often get questions answered, acquire useful knowledge, or solicit help with problems. Vast libraries of papers and databases of research information could be searched. Researchers or designers could gain access to specialized expertise. By the mid-1990s, *millions* of researchers were connected to the Internet, and it transformed the nature of much of their work.[3]

Science has increasingly become a collaborative activity that requires the interchange of ideas across a broad community and the pooling of data. Good ideas are more likely to emerge when knowledge and debate is interchanged among diverse communities. Isolated monolithic laboratories are giving way to partnerships, foundations, and consortia. The expense and risk of research can be lessened by working in collaboration with other organizations. The Internet evolved as a vehicle for such interchange, much encouraged by the NSF, which operated the backbone of the Net in the 1980s.

It is common to hear researchers who use the Internet say that when they start to explore new issues they begin by finding Usenet groups on the Internet and asking for suggestions, information, and references. They commonly say that they are never disappointed. Douglas Adams, author of *The Hitchhiker's Guide to the Galaxy,* describes using the Internet as the intellectual equivalent of casual sex.[4] He comments: "I wonder how I could have done any of my work beforehand. It left me with this sensation of being handed around the world by supportive, friendly people." Researchers often send requests to special-interest groups on the Net and find that they receive a flood of information from people they will meet only in cyberspace. Some of the responses give the researcher vital leads in making research progress.

Information that should remain internal to a corporation needs to be classified and secure.

> **A corporation needs to protect its competitive information assets while at the same time optimizing its information exchange.**

All Corporate Staff

The need to interchange knowledge, to search diverse sources of information, and to collaborate with other organizations applies not only to the research community but to all parts of corporations. Researchers need to communicate with product designers; product designers need to communicate with manufacturing engineers; marketing staff members need to communicate with designers and manufacturers so that the right products can be built with features that customers want; designers need to communicate with maintenance staff so that repairs can be done quickly and easily. Everybody needs to communicate with customers; customers need to communicate with one another to discuss product usage. This constant interchange of knowledge and dialog is what the Internet and intranets are ideal for.

Dealers around the world can feed forecasts for sales to a central production planning process. Customers can obtain better support from vendors. The Internet provides everybody with a richer diversity of information sources.

However, there is something much more fundamental. Communications slice across the traditional hierarchies and organizational structures. The Net allows instant interaction with business partners and service providers and opens up questions about what work should be done inside the corporation and what should be outsourced. Work can be done in countries where salaries are low. Swissair, for example, does its accounting in India. Particularly important, competences from differences places can be interlinked. This possibility makes more ambitious goals practical. Virtual teams can be designed to serve customers better.

Internet tools make it relatively easy to make corporate information available. A Mitre consulting vice president comments, "We want every employee to know everything the company knows."[5] The biggest change brought about by well-planned intranets will be sociological, not technical.

The Internet and intranets provide valuable new opportunities *in every area of business,* so it is critical that corporations be structured with a coherent strategy and architecture rather than having sporadic uncoordinated use of the Internet.

Cybercorp strategy needs to identify the uses of external and internal networks. It should be concerned with the overall implementation of the corporate nervous system, with its security, and with the missionary work and training needed to make users everywhere comfortable with the Net.

The future corporation will bear no resemblance to traditional corporations, so the transition to a cybercorp is a strategic issue not a tactical one.

Impact on All Employees

Exhibit 2-2 lists business uses of the Internet and how they affect almost every part of the organization.

Exhibit 2-2. Business uses of the Internet

Selling

- Electronic shops and "shopping malls," worldwide
- Customer access to on-line catalogs, with changing prices, features, and details; information constantly updated, worldwide
- On-line order taking
- Inexpensive communication with new potential customers, worldwide
- Electronic distribution of software, publications, and music
- Guidance to potential purchasers
- Open communication channels
- Avoidance of purchase orders for continuously supplied goods
- Contact with more customers; enhanced telesales capability

Product Design

- Better knowledge of available components and of vendors' information, worldwide
- Knowledge of low-cost facilities in distant countries
- Links to suppliers for joint design
- Links to design consultants
- Research
- Access to remote knowledge sources
- Ability to search for information, worldwide
- Literature searches; vast amounts of literature accessible on-line
- Knowledge interchange with communities of common interest
- Collaboration with universities and other research establishments
- Constant awareness of global technology trends
- Access to remote supercomputers

Marketing

- A different form of advertising, interactive, when the potential customer wants it, customized, on-demand
- "Micromarketing" linked to individual requirements, tastes, and profiles
- Fast user community feedback: product reviews, information about problems, suggestions, and concerns, worldwide
- Data for market research; knowledge of related products
- Knowledge of customer wishes, e.g., colors or features
- Continuous forecast of sales from dealers; worldwide facilities; better production planning; less inventory stockpiles

Support to Customers

- On-line guidance to users
- Faster problem resolution

(*continued*)

Exhibit 2-2. (*continued*)

- Fast access to expertise
- Customer newsletters, on-line
- User community interchange of product knowledge and guidance on product use
- On-line answers to frequently asked questions
- Customer tracking of orders and delivery

Manufacturing

- Better selection of suppliers; identification of low-cost components, worldwide
- Direct communications with suppliers
- On-line forecasts and tracking to lower inventory
- User-group discussions of problems and solutions

Expertise

- Membership of special-interest communities
- Communication of specialist knowledge; spreading of knowledge
- Exchange of experience
- Ability to search for relevant experience, literature, data, or technology

Human Resources

- Electronic résumés
- Access to many education resources; self-education
- Knowledge of job opportunities within the corporation
- Empowerment of employees; making employees more self-sufficient
- Use of remote contract employees
- Teams based on experience, not location; location-independent work

Executive Information

- Access by top management to critical external knowledge
- Early warning of breaking trends
- Access to industry knowledge, market research, and economic trends
- Participation in communities with external viewpoint
- Participation in customer groups concerned with the products

General Administration

- Corporatewide e-mail
- Savings in telecommunications cost for some operations (shared lines, fast message relay, fewer phone calls, worldwide e-mail the same cost as local e-mail)
- Flexible work arrangements, virtual offices, telecommuting, and location-independent work

(*continued*)

Exhibit 2-2. (*continued*)

- Connectivity of diverse hardware, software, and networks
- Electronic money transfer (using "digicash" or similar high-security interaction)
- Closer, fast-response, links to business partners; greater diversity of business partners, worldwide
- Service functions in countries with low salaries
- Use of education facilities on the Internet (including CD-ROMs with Internet access)

Value Streams in General

- Small, empowered teams with access to the resources they need; teams that are smaller, self-sufficient, less dependent on other departments
- Virtual operations (virtual corporation) in which external resources are used as though they were internal
- Value-stream teams that are scattered geographically
- Access to specialized expertise, bulletin boards, and remote computers
- Direct contact with value-stream customers
- Instant response to value-stream customers or users

Webmasters

One problem with the Internet is that it can suck up so much time. Inexperienced users waste endless time surfing the Net without achieving much. The Internet is a vast ocean of trivia with isolated islands of great value. Employees should not have to wade through that ocean or struggle to find what they need; they should be able to go directly to what they need when they need it by clicking on bookmarks in their PCs. Specialists are required who can help users find the resources they need and set up these bookmarks. Without help at the beginning, potential users often become net-phobic.

The term *webmaster* is used for a corporate expert on the Web. Employees discuss their needs with the webmaster, who acts as a cyberspace guide and librarian. He can help users find information they need, set up bookmarks in their PCs, and help them put the Net to use in diverse ways. He becomes familiar with the most useful Web sites, news-filtering services, business-related Usenet groups, and so forth. The webmaster may be able to design Web home pages and bulletin boards and generally put the Web to use. He may be an expert on advertising on the Net.

The webmaster should be skilled at using a corporation's private intranet along with its links to the public Net. He should set up internal sources of information, bulletin boards for specific value streams, and possibly an e-mail magazine with a "what's new" section or "webmaster's picks" of favorite Web sites.

Sometimes groups of companies form a multicorporate intranet—for example, a network for insurance brokers. When this is done they must decide whether they need a private network or whether their needs can be met using secure bulletin boards on the public Internet. High traffic volumes or performance demands have led some groups to build private shared intranets. Some intranets use circuits of much higher capacity than those commonly used on the public Internet.

Crackpots and Criminals

Many IT executives have opposed the use of the Internet on the grounds that it is a leper colony of crackpots who spread viruses and worms, hack their way into corporate computer systems, delete files, steal passwords, and leave time bombs. The last thing a corporation needs are Trojan horses in every stable.

New network technology has often been treated with alarm and derision by security experts. However, as the technology evolves, ways are found to make it acceptably secure. When the electric telegraph first came into use the French government fought it bitterly. France at that time had a nation-wide semaphore system with stone towers on hilltops that relayed messages with huge semaphore arms. A government semaphore expert Dr. Barbay expressed the nineteenth-century equivalent of the security expert's argument:

> The electric telegraph is not a sound invention. It will always be at the mercy of the slightest disruption, wild youths, drunkards, bums, etc. . . . The electric telegraph meets those destructive elements with only a few meters of wire over which supervision is impossible. A single man could, without being seen, cut the wires leading to Paris, and in twenty-four hours cut in ten different places the wires of the same line, without being arrested. The visual telegraph, on the contrary, has its towers, its high walls, its gates well-guarded from inside by strong armed men. Yes, I declare, substitution of the electric telegraph for the visual one is a dreadful measure, *a truly idiotic act.*[6]

Dr. Barbay would have been astonished by today's whiz kids and hairy-eyed cyberpunk anarchists.

The Cyberspace Underworld

After the movie *War Games* hundreds of thousands of teenagers asked their parents for modems and stayed up hacking into the early hours, totally addicted to the world behind the screen.

One sixteen-year-old in Indiana called himself "Fry Guy" because he succeeded in breaking into a McDonald's mainframe and changing the records to give his hamburger-flipping friends spectacular pay raises. Fry Guy learned how to tamper with telephone switching computers. He gleefully arranged that all callers to the Probation Department of Palm Beach County, Florida, found themselves in conversation with a pornographic phone-sex worker called "Tina" in New York State. He graduated from what his friends thought were hilarious practical jokes to raiding credit card agencies and telephone billing computers. He stored vast numbers of credit card details and telephone long-distance access codes. Fry Guy learned how to pretend to be a cardholder on the telephone and persuade Western Union to send him cash advances. Western Union would call the customer back to verify the transaction, and Fry Guy would switch the call-back to a local pay phone where he answered with the number that Western Union expected. He and a friend stole $6,000. Fry Guy might have gotten away with such antics for some time, but he called representatives of Indiana Bell security and told them that he and associates in the Legion of Doom hacker club were going to crash the national telephone network on July the Fourth. His unsuspecting parents were scared witless when the Secret Service showed up in force, armed to the teeth like in a Schwarzenegger movie, raided the house, and seized all electronic equipment.

In 1988, Robert Morris, a Cornell University undergraduate and the son of the CIA security chief, introduced a "worm" to explore the Internet, and due to bad programming it quickly crashed 6,000 computers. Eight years later when the Net had grown large the same worm might have crashed a million computers.

Firewalls

Some systems are highly secure, for example, in banks and the military. However, in many organizations computer security measures are feeble, and this weakness invites misuse. A corporate network should be designed to have tight security and should not be connected to the Internet without protection. There should be airlocks between public networks and private internal networks.

The term *firewall* describes a small computer through which traffic has to pass to travel from an insecure network to a secure network. It may be used to authenticate messages from the Internet before passing them to the corporate intranet. Messages are taken into a filter and subjected to various tests before they are put on the internal corporate network. Some systems automatically translate internal network addresses, so that the internal systems are shielded, and allow only certain types of packets to reach certain machines. Sometimes multiple firewalls are used within an organization to isolate separate security domains. The software and hardware facilities designed to provide protection are constantly being improved.

As in real cities, security in the global city is never likely to be perfect, but the dangers can be reduced to an acceptable level. The value of the Internet far outweighs the risks. The simplest form of protection is to ensure that PCs connected to the Internet are *not* connected to the internal corporate network. This is often done when the Internet is used only by one department or team. To make full use of the Internet, however, it is desirable for machines on the corporate network to be able to use the Net without inconvenience to the user.

Cryptography

An essential technique in achieving good security is *cryptography.* Cryptography is used to encode traffic so that messages cannot be read by unauthorized eyes and phony messages cannot masquerade as genuine. It is also used for trustworthy identification of a machine or credit card.

Stories of breaking enemy codes are among the legends of past warfare. However, code breakers have a difficult time when computer chips are very powerful. In the battle between cryptographers and code breakers, an inexpensive processor chip can scramble a message so formidably that no code breaker is likely to unscramble it. A common misconception is that any cryptography can be broken. There have been much-publicized instances in which Internet security has been broken, and the press has reported, "The Internet is not secure." It should be understood that *if a code is cracked it can be made immensely more secure by doubling the size of the key.* Computers can handle very large keys, and they do not need to be very large to stop code breaking. Some transmissions that have been cracked have used a 40-bit key; the KGB used a 100-bit key that was probably never cracked; computers can easily use a 1,000-bit key or much larger if necessary. Widespread use is made of *public key* encryption. This relies on each party's having a private key, which no one else knows, and a public key, which is made available to chosen recipients of messages. These keys work in tandem. Messages encoded with the private key can be decoded by recipients using the public key of the sender. In effect, the sender "signs" messages with the private key, and recipients can check the signature with the public key.

Powerful cryptography is essential for cyberspace security, but it is not sufficient by itself. It must be used in conjunction with other security techniques.

Security Servers

Cryptography works well if sender and recipient have agreed ahead of time about what key will be used. However, the user may need to communicate securely with a new party whom he or she has never dealt with before. In such a situation cryptography can be used if both parties use a common security service. A server computer on the Net is used to provide security; only this server knows the keys of all parties. The user's machine enciphers the message and sends it to the security server, which knows the user's public key. The security server decodes the user's message and then reenciphers it so that it can be sent securely to the destination computer. This security procedure is inexpensive and transparent so that the user is not aware of it; it all occurs under the covers.

Social Engineering

However good the firewalls, cryptography, and other measures, ingenious hackers have sometimes violated security by human techniques. Hackers use the term "social engineering" to describe ingeniously talking their way into having changes made that enable them to bypass security:

> "Hello, I'm Tony Boyle. Henry told me my password has been compromised and that I must call you immediately to get it fixed. I haven't used it for some time and a hacker may be using it. Henry says we must fix it like pronto."
> "OK. What do you want me to do?"
> "Just change the password for my login on your machine. Make it real secure. Change it to YINOFEAP7260 and make sure it's hashed."
> "Can you give me that again?"

Tight security needs tight administrative procedures. People responsible for security need to understand that they must not be talked into bypassing the correct procedures.

The End of Security Amateurism

In the early years of cyberspace, security was amateurish at best. Fourteen-year-old kids rampaged through networks that were largely unprotected. Break-ins, which sometimes occurred on an astonishing scale, were more comical than criminal.

Then the U.S. Secret Service and law enforcement agencies started to get serious. There was a high-power crackdown on the hackers. Paranoia swept through the hacker underground. Most teenagers got the message: Your number is up; don't get your fingers broken; keep out of corporate systems. The Net grew at a furious pace, and there was an infinity of exciting things for teenagers to do that were legal. Wizened old hackers of twenty-one gave up the game when they graduated, and most of the new kids on the block attacked things in the computer *game* world rather than things in the real world. A hard core of dangerous hackers stayed active, but antisocial computer intrusion did not become a mass epidemic as some had suggested. Meanwhile, a more alarming trend started. Real criminals learned how to manipulate systems; electronic theft and fraud grew by leaps and bounds.

If the teenage hackers were amateurish, most corporate security was far more so. Powerful security measures existed, but few corporations used them or even knew about them. Most software was built without the security features software should have. It is trivial to encipher electronic mail, but most e-mail software lacked this capability. As the game matures, both the good guys and the bad guys evolve from amateur to skilled professional. Virus protection and authentication schemes become used routinely. Firewalls and cryptography become tough, ubiquitous, and unobtrusive. The administration of security needs to be done with skill.

Security should not be a reason for avoiding cyberspace, but any corporation that remains amateurish about security is asking for trouble.

E-Cash

There are many places to buy things in the global city. In order to get the service they want, customers need electronic money.

Just as the Internet has e-mail, it needs e-cash. Before long, e-cash will be a standard feature of society, flowing in enormous volumes over the world's networks. There will eventually be millions of e-cash transactions, some for very small amounts, flooding through the Internet. E-cash needs the tightest electronic security, otherwise it would make no sense. Hackers around the world will be devilishly ingenious in trying to create e-cash forgeries or break the e-cash mint. E-cash requires a powerful cryptography system that ensures that transactions are legitimate while at the same time protecting the privacy of the sender. With today's cryptography techniques, e-cash will be *immensely more secure than today's credit cards*. In the future when cryptography is automatic and unobtrusive we will look back at credit cards, amazed that such insecure instruments could have had such widespread acceptance.

Three Types of E-Cash

There are three main ways to provide e-cash: credit cards, smart cards, and cash transfers from computers. Once confidence in its safety grows, it seems inevitable that e-cash will become very popular, probably in all of these forms:

Credit Cards

For credit cards to be an acceptable means of payment on the Internet the card number must not be transmitted in an unprotected form. Most schemes for using credit cards encipher the card number. VISA teamed up with Microsoft to develop a credit card payment system that they hope will become a standard on the Net. Playing the same game, MasterCard joined forces with Netscape.

Credit cards will be widely used on the Net because customers are familiar with them, but they have some disadvantages. They have a cash limit; they are not anonymous; they are not suitable for the Internet's style of grassroots, person-to-person interaction in which any individual can sell things. Particularly important, their use is likely to be more expensive than the use of pure e-cash.

Smart Cards

A smart card, about the size of a credit card, can contain an electronic "purse" that the user fills with e-cash and then uses for making purchases. Mondex, a subsidiary of the National Westminster Bank, pioneered smart cards, explaining to customers that they should think of Mondex money as being similar to physical money. Smart cards cost more than simple credit cards, but the processing of smart-card transactions is very inexpensive, so they can be used for very small payments. For example, smart cards are in use in parts of Europe to pay for bus fares or school lunches. It is likely that in the future, parking meters and vending machines will operate with smart cards. Some cards can be interrogated by radio and e-cash deducted without the card's having to be fed into a machine slot.

The smart-card user may have a smart-card reader at home connected to a telephone so that he or she can fill the "purse" with money without having to go out to a bank machine. The consumer can then use the gadget to buy things at home, for example, goods advertised on television.

In 1995 the First Bank of Internet™ (FBOI) opened its (virtual) doors, announcing the start of transaction-processing services for commerce on the Net. The service is based on VISA smart cards, which can be filled with cash at over 200,000 VISA/PLUS ATMs in eighty-three countries. The card is protected with a personal identification number (PIN). FBOI is not a lending institution nor is it chartered. In the FBOI scheme, when the consumer places an order with a vendor she sends the vendor an e-mail "check." The vendor sends FBOI an e-mail "invoice." FBOI reconciles the transaction and sends e-mail "receipts" to both vendor and customer. Cash is taken from the customer's ATM account and credited to the vendor for later payment. All these e-mail messages are securely enciphered. The ATM card and PIN provide customer authentication. FBOI transmits no sensitive information over the Net, so the scheme protects customer privacy. FBOI charges the vendor a commission on each transaction. FBOI hopes to benefit from a very large consumer base because the VISA ATM network is worldwide.

While smart cards can provide an extremely convenient form of e-cash, they have certain disadvantages. Perhaps the most serious is that if you lose your smart card you have in effect lost a purse of money. For this reason you might want to use a smart card for small items but not large-cost items.

Computer Transactions

A particularly convenient form of e-cash is the ability to pay for purchases from your computer screen at the click of a mouse.

David Chaum, a Berkeley Ph.D. in cryptography, designed mechanisms for e-cash transfer that are both ultrasecure and private. Digicash, an Amsterdam-based company, was one of the first to use David Chaum's e-cash. It requires "electronic banks," which operate secure unmanned e-cash servers on the Net. Exhibit 2-3 shows how it works.

A purchaser, Alice, finds something in an Internet shopping mall that she wants to buy. The software indicates the price, fourteen dollars, say. Her notebook computer sends a request for payment of fourteen dollars to an Internet bank, enciphering the request with her private key, which acts like a signature. The bank computer has Alice's public key on file. It uses this to decipher the message. It determines that Alice has enough money in her account and creates an enciphered packet of fourteen dollars containing the "signature" of the bank, which it sends to Alice's computer. Alice's computer sends the packet of e-cash to the shop in question. The shop's computer verifies the bank's signature and agrees to have the goods dispatched to Alice. The shop sends the packet of fourteen dollars to *its* bank, using the shop's private key. The shop's bank contacts Alice's bank, which verifies that the e-cash it authorized is used only once. Alice's bank remits the funds electronically to the shop's bank. All of this happens automatically when Alice triggers the process with a mouse-click on her computer screen. The encryption and authorization process is not visible to Alice. The total processing cost is minute.

This payment process is designed so that Alice's privacy is protected.

Alice's bank does not know what Alice is using the packet of cash for, or to what shop it is sent. Similarly, the shop's bank does not know what the e-cash is used for, or that it comes from Alice. Nobody can assemble a detailed dossier of Alice's activities or preferences.

E-cash mechanisms must be designed to be both secure and private.

On the Net anyone with a computer and a telephone line can become a small business. There is no need to lease a real shop front or seek approval as a credit-card-accepting merchant; any willing seller and willing buyer can interchange e-cash. The Net today contains instructions on how to become an e-cash merchant. PC software packages will do the accounting. Such low-cost-of-entry facilities will encourage a massive growth of entrepreneurship *worldwide.*

The combination of PCs and electronic money represents a massive market revolution. Many people will want to buy goods and services at the click of a mouse.

Money Becomes Software

Money is information. But coins and notes are a very crude way of representing information. E-cash is information designed to be processed by software and so can have endless subtle variations that traditional money cannot have. For example, you could give your children smart-card cash with a code indicating that it can only be used for bus fares and school meals, or wire your teenagers money that can be spent on tuition fees and books but nothing else. An office might have electronic petty cash that can be used for office items but not beer. Governments, in the future, might want to have different types of e-cash relating to future taxation schemes or to schemes for preventing money laundering.

Massive Financial Volume

About a trillion dollars per day are transmitted over networks between banks today. E-cash will enable such transactions to occur between pocket devices, smart cards, and notebook computers owned by ordinary people. The convergence of e-cash, PCs, and the Internet will change the mechanisms of commerce. It is a form of downsizing. Instead of large transactions between large mainframes in large banks, e-cash will facilitate small transactions between small computers owned by anybody.

Exhibit 2-3. A purchase automatically paid for with e-cash

Alice

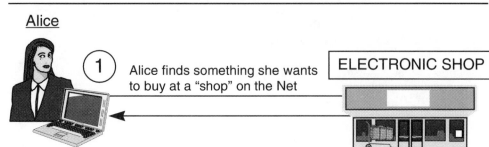

1) Alice finds something she wants to buy at a "shop" on the Net

ELECTRONIC SHOP

2) Alice's computer sends an enciphered request for payment

3) The electronic bank sends back a secure packet of e-cash

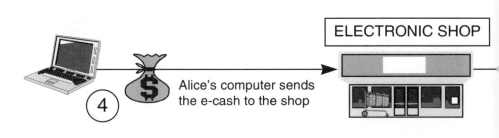

ELECTRONIC SHOP

4) Alice's computer sends the e-cash to the shop

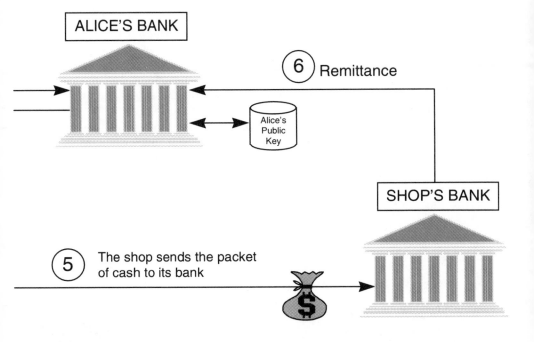

ALICE'S BANK

6 Remittance

Alice's
Public
Key

SHOP'S BANK

5 The shop sends the packet
of cash to its bank

The e-cash "banks" are secure servers on the
net. Alice's privacy is protected; the bank does
not know how Alice uses the packet of e-cash.

Some Internet transactions will involve very small amounts of money. E-cash will be used to pay royalties for the use of Internet documents, music, software, and so forth. Software objects may pay automatically for the use of other objects. There will be billions of tiny transactions constantly interchanged around the world among computers. Other transactions will be very large, as many electronic funds transfers are today.

E-cash will encourage instant settlement of many payments. Small companies today often wait months for big companies to pay their bills. With e-cash, many transactions will be paid for when they occur. E-cash will be worldwide, very inexpensive, and usable at the click of a mouse button. The use of e-cash raises important questions for banks (who will not be able to profit from it much if there is no float) and for national taxation authorities (because it crosses borders in an enciphered, invisible form). Internet users today are interacting across national frontiers all the time, sometimes without even knowing it; the same will be true with Internet cash. E-cash can flow in and out of countries at lightning speed and will sometimes do so in vast quantities to avoid market crises. The Internet encourages stateless cash from stateless corporations.

By the year 2000 the world volume of purchases will be over $10 trillion per year. Before many years a tenth of that volume will involve electronic money, and the proportion will grow rapidly. A study for the U.S. Commerce Department indicates that by 2005 the Internet will probably carry $1.25 trillion of e-cash a year (and that would be less than half of all consumers' electronic money).[7] The battle to be e-cash providers will be intense.

References

1. "The Net Rules," *Information Week,* January 29, 1996.
2. Roger L. Kay, "Diamond Lines," *WebMaster,* March/April 1996.
3. William J. Broad, "Doing Science on the Network: A Long Way from Gutenberg," *New York Times,* May 18, 1993, pp. C1, C10.
4. Douglas Adams, interviewed in Bob Berger, "Surfer's Guide to the Galaxy," *Net Guide,* December 1994.
5. Berger, "Surfer's Guide."
6. Bruce Sterling, *The Hacker Crackdown: Law and Disorder on the Electronic Frontier* (New York: Bantam, 1992; London: Penguin, 1994).
7. Kelley Holland and Amy Cortese, "The Future of Money," *Business Week,* June 12, 1995.

Part II
Characteristics of the Cybercorp

3

Cybermarketing: An Inversion of Tradition

Hong Kong is a place where you can truly shop till you drop: a city filled with shopping malls where bustling crowds exhaust themselves in the search for bargains. I shopped there for camera lenses and other items. Then in relative comfort I searched for the same goods on the Internet, where I found that I could buy them for half the price.

Just as e-mail is so much more convenient that paper mail, electronic shopping is immensely more convenient than physical shopping. My family would laugh me out of the house if I suggested that they give up physical shopping, but a huge amount of shopping and other commerce will be done in cyberspace. My daughter, for example, may find it attractive to explore exotic silk scarf designs on the Net, discover a uniquely beautiful scarf in Thailand, and buy it at the click of a mouse button.

As the capability for selling on the Net spreads and interlinks with television, shopping and advertising may become the aspect of the Internet that the mass public is most familiar with. The Internet dialog may often use a telephone circuit from the home and a cable TV link to the home. Some of the Internet's old-timers are enraged to see their Net being corrupted in this way, but commerce will pay for the high-capacity trunks that make the Net a truly global city.

Almost $100 billion worth of goods are bought through direct marketing channels each year in the United States alone. As it matures, shopping on the Net will become much more interesting than shopping with paper catalogs because there will be such a great diversity of shops and goods; you will be able to explore the world and shop around for low prices. The glossy pictures of paper catalogs are more appealing than the early Net catalogs, but as Internet business develops, new technology will bring video, music, and a level of pizzazz not possible with paper catalogs.

Highly customized goods will be bought over the Net for computerized fabrication and overnight delivery, for example, clothes where the buyer's body-scan measurements are in the computer. In the U.S. clothing industry today, $25 billion worth of clothing remains in stores unsold or sells only after deep discounts, so selling to order is appealing. The same is true with other goods. Only 27 percent of women who purchase jeans are happy with the fit, so a start-up called Custom Clothing Technology formed a deal with Levi Strauss to link stores, Internet users, and jeans manufacturers to produce customized jeans. In the Levi store where the service began, sales of jeans jumped 300 percent in the first year.[1] Many stores will be replaced with Internet shops and FedEx trucks.

It is far from sure how many shoppers will bypass shops in the future, so a safe strategy for stores would be to back all horses: mail order, Net order, and physical shops.

Comp-U-Card (CUC) International operates a range of home shopping services that have more than 30 million subscribers (mostly not on the Internet yet) who pay fees to access the company's database of 250,000 products. The subscribers can compare prices. They place orders with CUC, which has no inventory of its own, and CUC relays the orders to vendors for home delivery at the best discount prices. Services like this can operate on the Net *automatically*. Software called an *agent* scans the Web searching for the lowest prices. On the World Wide Web one can find the lowest price for any music tape or disk, for example.

Internet Malls

The shopping malls of the Net can have interactive advertising and "infomercials." A whole new set of skills is needed in the advertising world to use the Net effectively: Madison Avenue skills, which most hackers do not have, and hacker skills, which most Madison Avenue people do not have.

Interactive selling and marketing is very different from traditional advertising and mail order. It enables potential customers to drill down into highly detailed information sources and interact with them in enticing ways.

The Internet has evolved its own consensual code of good manners called *netiquette*. The Net, like an exclusive club, can make life miserable for serious netiquette violators: "Flaming" has become an art form. You must not use the club's notice boards for posting private e-mail or for blatant selling. You must not send unsolicited junk mail. A marketing person needs to approach the Net with netiquette sensitivity. Vast numbers of people search the Net for items of interest. They want to find out about products and services, look up details, have questions answered, and decide whether to make purchases. They want to find marketing information *when they look for it,* but they do not want it thrust at them like television advertising when they are not looking for it. A rule must be that advertisements are never intrusive. They may be icons the size of a postage stamp that surfers can click on if they want. They should link to a substantial quantity of useful information, data, reports, literature, user reviews, and the like. This is entirely different from the work of traditional advertising agencies.

Kraft, for example, is working on attractive ways for the public to obtain recipes and cooking advice from the Internet. It has been pursuing famous chefs and television personalities who might attract Internet users, world-wide, and as a by-product of their cooking advice let viewers know more about Kraft products.

Internet "shop windows" can lead the viewer to extensive catalogs. Catalogs on the Net can have great advantages over conventional catalogs (see Exhibit 3-1).

Apple Computer used to advertise its e-World as a "clean, well-lighted place with friendly people, with products and services selected for value and quality." As you entered this world you received an image of a town center complete with the sound of bustling street traffic. You could click on a number of centers, for example, a learning center opening with a picture of a library, a mail center, a newsstand, an information booth, a market, and a business and finance center. Each center allowed you to mouse-click down into detailed resources or visit "cafes" for special-interest discussion (including a Horse Laugh Cafe).

Infomercials or catalog items should be immediately convertible into orders and computer-processable transactions, using electronic payment mechanisms. Part of the convenience of shopping on the Net is the ability to pay for goods when you buy them. If payment is easy, merchants will make more goods available to be purchased.

> **A basic rule should be: When an Internet user discovers something he or she might like, the fleeting desire should be converted into an order before it fades.**

Marketing on the Net

On the Net, orders can be placed worldwide; advertisements and catalogs can be seen worldwide. If the goods can be represented digitally—for example, reports, information, games, pictures, software, or music—they can be shipped over the Net, immediately. Theater bookings, airline reservations, hotel bookings, car rental bookings, and so on, can be made on the Net.

Holiday Inn was one of the first hotels to establish a Web site, and it

Exhibit 3-1. Catalogs on the Net

Internet product catalogs have the following advantages over paper catalogs:

- Electronic catalogs can be enormous, enabling customers or prospects to explore vast amounts of product variations or details. For example, a bookshop catalog may be linked to the text of some chapters of the book, possibly viewable for a limited time. Paper catalogs are limited in the amount of information they can contain.
- Paper catalogs are expensive to change; electronic catalogs are not.
- The product sets of many large corporations change daily. Internet catalogs can reflect changes, whereas paper catalogs may be shipped out once a year.
- Mass distribution of large paper catalogs is expensive.
- Large paper catalogs are usually boring and do not contain the glossy appeal of advertising brochures. Advertising brochures communicate information in valuable ways that catalogs do not. Internet catalogs can link a jazzy sales pitch, glossy pictures, music, the advertiser's product discussion, and massive product detail.
- CD-ROMs may be linked to the Net, where the Net has the information that needs rapid updating.
- Internet catalogs may link to education facilities, user advice, discussion groups, and so forth.
- Electronic catalogs can have customized variants for specific customers and locations.
- Catalogs on the Net permit micromarketing to the numerous special-interest groups on the Net.
- Internet catalogs can have music, animation, and possibly video.
- Internet catalogs can have built-in segments of program.
- Last and often the most important, catalogs on the Net have worldwide availability. They can be designed to be seen by many people whom salesmen do not reach. A global audience can enter sales@ibm.com or a similar address.

quickly attracted 700 Internet bookings per week. When a customer books directly or through a travel agent it costs the hotel six to eighteen dollars per reservation; the cost of an Internet booking is almost zero once the Web site is established. Holiday Inn's vice president of marketing, Martin Gray, predicts that in five years time 60 percent of bookings will be made electronically.[2] Some hotels have their own Web site for booking; some share a Web site called TravelWeb. A danger is that another company—Microsoft, for example—could get into the reservation business. Gray says, "We don't ever want to cede that to another company."[3] In many industries there will be new battles for control of the distribution channels.

Virtual Vineyards is direct marketer of wines and gourmet foods. Customers place orders directly on the Web. The president comments, "Since we started marketing wine on the Web our revenues have been increasing 30 percent each month."[4] The orders come from all over the world.

The U.S. Internet commerce research company ActivMedia states, "Many companies have tripled their exports by going on-line."[5]

> **The Net promises the buyer *worldwide* marketplaces and the ability to find the best prices.**
> **The Net promises the seller *worldwide* access at low costs to highly specialized or prequalified customers.**

The Net has global reach, and it can give access to far more detailed information than can be offered in paper catalogs. Marketing staff can obtain feedback from their user community. They can receive and give information about how to deal with problems, or how to make better use of the product. Increasingly, the key to business success is to listen sensitively to customers, react to what they say, and help them to succeed. The Internet is a powerful medium for such interaction.

The Internet enables marketers to collect knowledge about customers' wishes for product features, such as different color, new functionality, less confusing human factoring, better instruction manuals, new variations on the product, add-on markets, and so on. Dealers can tell the manufacturer what customers are asking for and what is attracting them to competing products.

The Internet, especially when linked to cable TV, has dramatic potential for providing new marketing channels into the home. Eighty percent of companies sell not to the home but to companies that themselves have customers. These companies should use multiple electronic facilities, not only the Internet, to change how they do marketing. Marketing on the Net is worldwide.

At the end of 1994 the Rolling Stones had a spectacular rock concert with new music. They were the first rock band to send out a live concert on the Internet. A New York multimedia company multicast the first five songs of the concert over the World Wide Web. Customers could hear and record these songs free and were encouraged to buy the others, which could be delivered over the Net. This was the start of a new era: The world began to use the Internet for global marketing. The customer wants to buy things from around the planet; the marketer wants to market to the whole planet.

Web Pages

Many corporations have a "home page" on the World Wide Web that may link to a mass of marketing information. At the time of writing, new sites on the Web are appearing at the rate of *about one per minute.* We are seeing the explosive growth of an entirely new marketing economy with fundamentally different characteristics from traditional marketing and advertising.

> **The mere existence of a home page does not guarantee that people will visit it, or that if they do the corporation will make money. Many corporations have not.**

The address of the page needs to be quoted on corporate literature, business cards, product packaging, and other forms of advertising. Some corporations "bait" the home page with interesting information, jokes, cartoons, free offers, agents that shop for minimum-price goods, and so forth. For example, a life insurance company might entice Web visitors with actuarial computations that allow them to estimate their life expectancy and how they could live longer if they change their lifestyle.

A visit to a home page does not necessarily result in business. Many Web sites are a waste of money, and some have been abandoned. Much thought is needed about how to turn visitors into qualified prospects or actual customers.

Net-Order Firms

Net-order firms are the Internet equivalent of mail-order firms. They can be much more convenient because one can access them worldwide and drill down into much more product detail than in a mail-order catalog or magazine page. Many new opportunities exist for Net-order selling. Unlike a mail-order firm, the Net-order firm doesn't need an army of keypunchers; the details are entered by the customer on the Web screen. As with today's mail-order (or telephone order) firms the prices from Net-order firms may be much lower than in shops. The Net user may employ a software agent to shop the world looking for the best price.

As commented earlier, a principle of Net-order firms, and of cybermarketing in general, is that when the Net user discovers something she would like she should be able to buy it there and then, placing the order with the click of a mouse before she changes her mind, and paying electronically if possible.

Paradigm Shift

When a paradigm shift occurs, managers and professionals have to unlearn deeply held habits of the past. Some old dogs cling to the old views. Cybermarketing is the most severe paradigm shift to have occurred in marketing for a long time. It offers ways for small corporations to outmaneuver large corporations that are set in their ways.

Cybermarketing enables corporations to do the following at low cost:

- Establish new sales channels to PC users
- Make contact with new prospects
- Provide new channels of in-depth advertising
- Provide one-to-one marketing rather than mass marketing
- Make large amounts of (changeable) information available on request
- Collect large amounts of information about customers so that marketing to them can be targeted and specific
- Set up effective channels for solving problems and answer many customer questions automatically
- Provide substantial help to salespeople
- Set up channels between customers so that they can help one another
- Obtain sensitive feedback from customers with which to improve products, services, and selling
- Set up fan clubs

From Mass to Individualized Marketing

In the 1950s, mass marketing began to change society with television advertising, shopping malls, supermarkets, large mass-production factories, and a society geared to mass consumption. Large companies spent enormous sums on mass consumer advertising. By capturing market share they grew large, generated profits, and made it difficult for new entrants to penetrate their territory. It was the era of General Motors, General Foods, Disney, IBM, and the big television networks.

As the twentieth century nears its end the world is becoming laced with computer networks spreading at a phenomenal rate. Homes are acquiring computers and Internet access. Teenagers are talking to the world from their PCs. Electronics has brought an era of miniaturization, downsizing, diversification, and rapidly growing complexity. Massive cheap-labor countries compete with the affluent countries. Instead of national markets with a low level of consumer choice, there are global markets with immense consumer choice. Computerized manufacturing allows a rich diversity of options in products to meet the specific needs of specific customers.

> **We are changing from standard catalog items mass-produced with little variation, to individualized, short-lived, information-rich goods and services that have endless variations.**

We have come from Henry Ford's "You can have whatever color you want so long as it's black" to products with so many features that it takes a week to read the manual. The customer wants neither of these but instead an easy-to-use product designed *for that customer.* Manufacturers need dialog with customers to understand their specific wishes.

From Megabrand to Diversity

The key phrase for salespeople in IBM's great days was "account control." The sales teams were trained to understand and control customer corporations so that they bought only from IBM. IBM would go to the corporation's top management if lower-level management showed the deviant inclination to buy from non-IBM sources. Today, the customer does not want to be controlled, but rather to be free to buy the "best of breed."

If we ask who owns the largest share of the market for computers or software it is not IBM; it is a mass of small companies. If you test binoculars in a Singapore shop so that you can buy the best, you will probably buy binoculars made by a company whose name you do not know. Trying out the beers in London pubs, you may find that the beer with the nicest taste is one you've never seen advertisements for. Regis McKenna comments that the largest share of the cookie market is not Nabisco; it's "other." This is the way the world is changing.

"Other" brands are growing fast because modern technology allows them to be made cheaper. Cybermarketing allows them to be marketed worldwide at low cost. In the days of mass marketing small companies could not compete with the big-budget advertising of large companies, but in the era of cyberspace very small companies can reach special-interest groups.

Technology has allowed the old power structure to be eroded by nimble newcomers. The giant telephone companies were challenged by new kids on the block brimming with new ideas. Doug Terman, the thriller writer, operates a basement full of electronics in his Vermont cottage that allows foreign subscribers to make cheap international calls.

Today's customers are more educated and because of the diverse choices available tend to be fickle. They know that all soaps are similar and that the camera lenses that give them the best results are no longer Nikon. They are less likely to believe in the glossy market images of traditional advertising.

The trend from mass markets to fragmented markets would have happened without the Internet, but the Internet greatly amplifies the trend. The Internet consists of vast numbers of special-interest communities. If your interest is single-malt scotch you can find more about single-malt scotch on the Internet than you can in any library. There are special-interest communities on organically grown coffee, California mountain biking, Mendelian inheritance in men, Japanese dairy cattle improvement, Lewis Carroll, U.S. Southern gospel music, German nobility, ancient Middle Eastern trans-desert trade routes, hydroponics—you name it!

A large magazine stand sells hundreds of magazines, each carrying much specialist advertising; narrowcasting has the ability to deliver to affinity groups. Imagine this fragmenting continuing to the point of infinity, and you will understand the business potential of the Net.

One of the effects of the Net is rapid growth of certain low-volume products targeted to narrowly focused consumer groups worldwide.

From Monolog to Dialog

In the past marketing has been a monolog. Television and newspapers bombard us with one-way messages. Advertisers design campaigns to tell customers what to think and ask themselves, "How many impressions did we make today?" But increasingly, television viewers do not want to be captive; they change the channel as soon as the ad starts.

Marketing is a complex two-way learning process. The customer wants to learn about goods or services that are of interest to her: she would like to explore details of the product or service and ask questions before buying it. The marketer wants to learn about the potential customer. He wants to understand customers so that he can target the marketing. He wants to learn about the customer's needs and wishes so that he can customize and constantly improve the product or create new products that satisfy the customer's wishes better. Conventional television is useless in this regard. Its brief and very expensive commercials do little more than create a market image. Magazines can give some detail but not the detail that the potential buyer needs.

Most traditional media provide one-to-many communication; computer networks provide one-to-one communication. With the help of computers the prospect or customer can be engaged in a dialog.

Dialog is the essence of cybermarketing.

Traditional advertising companies are wedded to traditional advertising and want their customers to have large budgets for it. Such advertising creates awareness and market image, which is important. Today, however, much more is needed. In 1983 Texas Instruments (TI) was the largest advertiser in personal computers; shortly afterward, they ditched their PC operation because it was suffering intolerable losses. In 1992 IBM and Digital Equipment Corporation were the largest advertisers in the computer industry; both were heading for disaster. TI, IBM, and Digital had great market images; what led customers elsewhere was not market image but detailed knowledge of products.

To acquire the detailed knowledge needed for a purchasing decision the customer must be able to investigate information about the product. If marketing is to succeed it should make it easy for the customer to do this. As choices increase and products become more complex, customers are more in need of detailed help. The learning process needs a dialog.

Evan I. Schwartz pictures the process of prospecting for customers as a giant funnel.[6] Traditional mass marketing on TV is at the wide mouth of the funnel and seeks mass exposure. The Web is at the deep spout of the funnel and seeks to deliver highly qualified leads or sales.

The traditional Nielsen-like measurements that form the basis for advertising charges are irrelevant to the Net because Net use is concerned with the *quality* of the contacts it attracts, not just exposure. Web site visitors who return frequently are much more valuable than TV watchers who ignore most commercials.

Marketers are on the Web for results, not exposure.

Rich Everett, manager of interactive communications for the Chrysler Corporation, says that Web use should link interested buyers into a virtual showroom and give them enough detail so that they can decide whether they are actually going to purchase a car.

Bidirectional Uncontrolled Media

The advertising industry has always claimed that it does not influence the content of television programs or press articles; publishers and editors claim that they are not influenced by advertisers or sponsors. Yet companies often tell editors that they will pull their ads if views critical of the company are published. Silvio Berlusconi when prime minister of Italy owned three television networks that vigorously attacked his political opposition, but Berlusconi protested that there was no conflict of interest. A variety of research studies have demonstrated that media are far from unbiased by the organizations that finance them.

The Internet is different. Its anarchical nature allows anyone to advertise anything (with appropriate netiquette) and anyone to air his or her views about the products advertised. Advertisers do not have the one-way control that they do with traditional media because the specialist groups that the advertisers want to reach have their own forums. The Net would not be a good place to advertise that cigarettes are unharmful. If the ads are nonintrusive and informative or amusing, though, the Internet community is likely to respond to them well. The vast number of special-interest groups offer unparalleled opportunities for effective ads.

Web Servers

A Web server can make a vast amount of information available. It often lists topics such as product catalog, new announcements, optional features, price lists, help with problems, frequently asked questions (FAQs), user comments, suggestions, and so forth. Users who contact the Web site can select a topic, explore its contents, and post messages. They can download files or exchange information with other users. They may post questions that a specialist will answer. The site may contain operating manuals, maintenance manuals, troubleshooting guidelines, software, photographs, lectures, or presentations. Changes can be posted constantly and are thus immediately available to all users. This is far faster and cheaper than distributing amendments to large paper documents. Information becomes fluid because it is easy to change.

Some information on a bulletin board may be open for everybody to read; other information—for example, that sent by salespeople to management—may be electronically locked so that only authorized people can read it. Some data may be made available only if users pay for it.

Web servers can allow customers to communicate with one another. One customer may post a question or ask for help, and other customers answer. There may be a suggestions forum, a fan club, a list of solutions to common problems, or phone numbers of other companies that provide services. Some companies are nervous about having an open forum in which customers can discuss problems because the problems are made known. However, if the company does not know about the problems, it could be in trouble. Most problems can be fixed once the company knows about them. The customer interactions are available to marketing, manufacturing, and engineering and may initiate many improvements in products, literature, or services.

Database Marketing

Database marketing aims to segment the market in detail and use information to do rifle-shot marketing rather than mass marketing.

Highly targeted marketing is essential today because of the growing diversity of products and customer needs. The age when the same thing could be sold to every customer is gone.

It is generally more profitable to expand business done with an existing customer than to sign up new customers. The consultant Bain & Co. has a customer loyalty/retention practice. Fred Reichheld, founder of this practice, estimates that in regional banks, a fourteen-year customer is worth 85 percent more in profits than a ten-year customer because over time their balances grow and they take out new house and car loans.[7] American Airlines estimates that persuading new customers to choose American is five times as expensive as persuading old ones. Other companies have quoted similar ratios ranging from 3:1 to 10:1. A Bain study showed that a 5 percent increase in customer loyalty can translate into a 60 percent increase in profits.[8] Boosting customer retention 2 percent can have the same effect on profits as cutting costs 10 percent.

Just as statistical quality control allowed the quality movement to take off in manufacturing, so statistics about customer retention and growth are important measures in marketing. *Zero defects* is an important goal in manufacturing; *zero defections* should be an important goal in customer service. There are various early warning signs of possible defections. If they are detected, special skills should be used to persuade the customer to stay.

Feedback

Marketers use the Internet to collect valuable information about potential customers. To be induced to disclose information about themselves, people need to be rewarded in some way. They may be offered a discount when making a purchase, or free options of some type. They may be promised customized services, or information about new product offerings—"Send us details and we will give you advance booking information on the new Lloyd Webber musical before the box office opens to the public."

Some Web sites provide entertaining activities in exchange for information. The Stolichnaya Vodka Web site has a fully stocked virtual bar. You can submit recipes for favorite drinks using ingredients from screen menus. Your name then appears along with the name of the recipe you created. Customers are invited to vote for their favorite recipe. For a time a concoction called "I'll Have What the Guy on the Floor Is Having" was the winner. This site encourages customers to try out Stoli's different flavors and gives Stoli feedback about customer preferences.

Silicon Graphics announced an on-line competition offering prizes to those who described how to use the company's tools to improve the Internet. Within five weeks there were 5,000 entries from around the world. This gave Silicon Graphics priceless information about potential customers.[9]

More serious sites engage customers in ongoing dialogs about how to improve products and services.

Selling Advertising

A few months after *Playboy* opened its Web site on the Internet, the site was logging over three million visitors per day. Such a site can sell advertising and charge a substantial amount. Visitors to the site may be invited to click on colorful advertising buttons the size of postage stamps that will link them to the advertiser's Web site on some other computer. The most popular Web sites, such as *Playboy, HotWired,* ESPNET *SportsZone,* and Time Warner's *Pathfinder,* charge $30,000 to $100,000 for a three-month placement of such an advertising button. When IBM's computer Deep Blue challenged the chess grand master Zakarov, 5 million people per day visited the match's Internet site—a highly specialized marketing target.

Charges can be more directly related to user behavior than is the case with magazine advertising. Nobody knows how many readers read a magazine ad, but on the Net is it possible to know exactly how many users click on an ad button and download the Web page. Prospects are much more likely to click on a Web button than to return a card in a magazine. *USA Today* charges twenty dollars for every 1,000 customers who click on an ad button over a two-month period. It is charging advertisers, not for the number of visitors to the *USA Today* site, but for the number of visitors it lures to the advertiser's Web site.

This turns the economics of traditional advertising upside down. It makes it logical to have *no charge* for an ad placement, but only a charge *for results.* This appeals to advertisers because the ad can be specifically targeted and there is no charge unless it delivers qualified leads. The ad is like a sales representative working only on commission. Results can be measured in terms of the number of prospects routed to the advertiser's site—or even with more precision, in terms of the number of response panels filled in. Companies that call themselves *cybermetricians* sell or use software for measuring and validating such results.

There is such a deluge of free information on the Net that that most Internet users are remarkably reluctant to pay for information. A Forrester Research analyst comments, "They treat information charges as damage and route around them." [10] Because of this, many magazines and other organizations have found it impractical to charge a subscription fee. They can charge for advertising but not for information. There are exceptions, for example, Individual Inc., of Burlington, Massachusetts, scans stories from 600 daily and weekly publications and provides an Internet service called NewsPage. Subscribers pay to receive only those news stories they are interested in, chosen from a menu of 850 business topics. Individual Inc. then knows the specific interests of its subscribers so it can enable advertisers to target the customers they want. Various advertisers have sponsored news sections on specific topics; for example, 3Com Corporation, which sells network products, sponsored the section on LANs.

Cyberspace makes possible news media and related marketing tailored to the interests of individuals.

Data Deluge

In the cybercorp world, enormous amounts of data can be collected at little cost. These data can be used to make a change from mass marketing to focused marketing. Data-warehousing technology with sophisticated on-line data analysis is essential for taking advantage of the data deluge.

We commented that when Visa redesigned its card-processing system it introduced a transaction number that indicated the customer, the merchant, the bank, and the card. It could also include the type of product purchased. Such information can be used for marketing to the customer more directly.

As manufacturing changes from mass production to customization, marketing should change from mass marketing to individualization.

The supermarket checkout assistant uses a laser wand to read Universal Product Codes (UPCs) on goods. This technology helps make the checkout process fast and accurate and provides itemized bills for the customer. Information collected at the checkout counter is used to help replenish the shelves efficiently. It can also be used to help communicate with the customers better. If the customer uses a credit or debit card, the customer's identity can be recorded along with details of the purchase. Managers everywhere should ask how they can collect information about customers. Some stores ask for the customer's zip code, for example. Many businesses should employ a frequent-customer program similar to airlines' frequent-flier programs.

When individualized products are manufactured for a customer much more information is needed than for traditional catalog products.

The cybercorp should use electronics to record information about customers that can be used to help the customers. It should adapt its marketing accordingly.

Pizzazz

Marketing needs pizzazz.

Many consumers today are addicted to video games and CD-ROMs, and now images and sound are common on the Internet and cyberspace services. It is becoming almost mandatory in some companies that presentations be done with a computer and flashy graphics.

CD-ROMs are used for dramatic presentations. As well as being used by salespeople, they can be given to customers, mass-mailed, packaged with magazines, or handled like literature. More than just sales presentations, CD-ROMs can link a graphic presentation to a warehouse of useful information so that their recipient keeps them for future reference. They can be reproduced in quantity for less than a dollar. Coca-Cola distributes CD-ROMs to organizations, telling them all about operating soft-drink vending machines. Some companies doing product announcements give CD-ROMs to salespeople, dealers, and agents around the world, often to back up live presentations with masses of detail.

The CD-ROM can be even more useful when it is automatically linked to the Internet. Video, graphics, and unchangeable information can be on the CD-ROM and changeable information on the Net, automatically accessed when needed. The package can be well indexed, easy to navigate, and focused on customer needs. A CD-ROM can enable an Internet dialog to link to better pictures, music, and video.

There is much to be gained from integrating CD-ROMs or the Internet with other marketing channels. A chain of video stores or bookshops, for example, might provide its customers with a catalog containing details, snippets, and reviews.

It is sometimes said that the Internet will replace CD-ROMs because it gives access to a world of information that is constantly updated. However, in order to compete with the pizzazz of the CD-ROM, Internet circuits will have to be able to handle interactive video with fast response times. Today, waiting for a still picture on the Net can be frustrating, and video is not really usable over voice-grade lines. The CD-ROM is being replaced with the digital video disk, which is designed for high-quality television at low cost. To compete with this advance, the slow lanes of the Internet need to evolve into fast highways.

Information superhighways, as they mature, will have a major effect on marketing. Digital television and multimedia presentations will be relayed directly to customers. One-to-one communication will be common over video circuits. It is often thought that this is in the distant future when fiber-optic circuits are wired to all customer locations, but in fact much can be done today.

When corporations use the World Wide Web for luring new customers, the opening Web page needs to be attractive and enticing. The art and skill that goes into building catalogs and advertising now needs to go into Web pages, but design options are constrained by the limited bandwidth. Customer do not want to be bored by having to sit through time-consuming sound-and-graphics sequences that they have seen before.

New talents exist in service companies for creating Web dialogs. These talents span the skills of the advertising world and the skills of the hacker. Good Internet marketing designers have more often learned their trade in film and advertising than in programming or computer science.

> **The design of interactive marketing needs to look different when targeted at the home with a telephone-grade Internet connection than when aimed at corporations with higher-capacity circuits.**

Ways to Use Cybermarketing

Exhibit 3-2 summarizes some of the ways to use cybermarketing.

Exhibit 3-2. Ways to use cybermarketing

Selling

- Offer goods for sale on World Wide Web shops and malls.
- Facilitate impulse buying: allow customers to order goods as soon as they find them on the Web.
- Convert advertising and infomercials directly into orders and transactions wherever possible, using credit cards, smart cards, or e-cash.

New Prospects

- Put appropriate information on Internet special-interest bulletin boards.
- Establish a Web page on the Internet.
- Bait the Web site: put something exciting, amusing, or valuable at the Web site to attract potential customers to it. (Most Web sites are boring!)
- Use a service firm with good skills in designing World Wide Web facilities with color pictures and sound.
- Display the Web page address on all print advertisements.

Narrowly Focused Marketing

- Do "micromarketing" linked to individual requirements, tastes, and profiles.
- Do highly focused marketing targeted at narrow communities with specific interests.
- Use on-demand infomercials, tailored to customer needs, that potential customers can explore when they want, rather than traditional advertising.

Advertising

- Examine the possibility of advertising your Web site on frequently accessed Web sites (such as *HotWired, Playboy,* or specialist sites).
- Use advertisements in which customers can drill down into great detail when they want.
- Distribute multimedia presentations to customers, possibly with automatic links to the Net.

(continued)

Exhibit 3-2. (*continued*)

Changing Prices

- Post changing prices on the Net.
- Change prices in real time, based on computations about how to maximize earnings (as some airlines do).

Help With Ordering

- Encourage customers to do electronic order entry rather than having order-entry clerks decipher customer requests.

New Information to Customers

- Announce new products or features by sending e-mail to existing customers. Enable these customers to explore details about the products on bulletin boards.
- Send customers information about discounts and lower prices.
- Provide free upgrades (e.g., software companies can distribute version changes over the Net).
- Create a news bulletin board containing stories about the product.
- In paper catalogs and literature, describe how new information can be found on the Net.

Bulletin Boards for Customers

- Enable customers to access bulletin boards of product details.
- Where products have many pricing options, make these accessible on a bulletin board.
- Enable customers to access bulletin boards of service information, diagnostic information, and technical manuals.

Information to Salespeople

- Use e-mail to tell an entire sales force about product or price changes, or about breaking news.
- Put the sales manual on-line (with appropriate privacy locks).
- Enable salespeople or agents to access bulletin boards with the very latest information or news.
- Give salespeople on-line access to product details that change.
- Put pricing options that change frequently on-line.
- Use a computer system that does complex pricing calculations for salespeople (especially when items of pricing change).
- Store proposal pages on bulletin boards so that salespeople can download them into their computers.
- Use an expert system to help salespeople understand sales arguments and generate proposals.

(*continued*)

Exhibit 3-2. (*continued*)

- Use a computer system that helps salespeople establish complex deals or configurations.

Press Relations

- Distribute news releases to the press by e-mail rather than regular mail. Most journalists would prefer news releases to go directly into their computer.
- Set up a bulletin board for the press.

News Dissemination

- Back up information in the company magazine with more detailed or variable information on the Net.
- Provide information on product-related seminars or conferences, possibly making the proceedings or papers available on-line.
- Offer contests or sweepstakes on-line. As well as creating news, this can be a way to troll for new e-mail addresses.

Product Support

- Use person-to-person video communications via ISDN to provide better support to customers.
- Offer technical support via e-mail.
- Offer advice by e-mail (e.g., a food company can offer recipes, or a flower seller can offer pictures of flower arrangements).
- Offer e-mail services for customers to find out about add-on products or other models.
- List answers to FAQs about the products or services.
- Send customers stories about the company, its service philosophy, its new directions.
- Try to make customers feel like part of the family.
- Send reminders to regular customers (e.g., send suggestions before a spouse's birthday).

Feedback From Web Site Visitors

- Collect information for qualified leads.
- Reward Web site visitors for providing information that can be used in marketing (with discounts, free offers, promises of information, etc.).

Feedback From Customers

- Obtain user feedback: product comments, information about problems, suggestions, concerns—worldwide.
- Obtain data for market research; learn about related products.

(*continued*)

Exhibit 3-2. (*continued*)

- Solicit knowledge of customer wishes (e.g., color or features).
- Create an electronic suggestion box. Invite all customers to send comments and suggestions.
- Provide survey forms to customers for electronic response. For mass-market products a large amount of feedback can be obtained cheaply.
- Prompt customers for comments on specific items ("We've just added a new option on . . . Is it useful to you?").
- Print your e-mail address prominently with every product shipped, and ask for comments.

Feedback From Salespeople

- Prompt salespeople for comments on specific items ("How are customers reacting to the new feature? How would they change it?").
- Use e-mail to solicit constant feedback from the field.
- Encourage salespeople to provide information to management or engineering that would help to close sales or keep customers happy.
- Set up conferences or bulletin boards shared between marketing or sales and engineering or manufacturing to facilitate communication.
- Encourage salespeople to provide information about competitive products.

User Groups

- Start newsgroups where customers can exchange information and help one another.

Fan Clubs

- Create an electronic fan club where fans can trade information and tell other fans what they like.
- Provide fans with interesting trivia, and ask for comments about future directions.
- Ask fans for testimonials.
- In a company that sells information, books, music, or anything that can be transmitted, allow fans to download snippets.
- Offer product users a chance to have their names on the bulletin board by inviting them to say what they like about the product.

Help in Using the Product

- Use person-to-person video communications via ISDN to provide help.
- Set up bulletin boards with hints about how to use the product well (e.g., how to improve filming and editing with a camcorder).
- Enable customers to exchange tips on bulletin boards about how to use the product well, or how to solve problems.
- Set up an electronic magazine about the product or services.

References

1. Don Tapscott, *The Digital Economy* (New York: McGraw-Hill, 1996).
2. "Rooms with a View," *WebMaster,* March/April 1996.
3. Ibid.
4. Robert Olson, president of Virtual Vineyards, at www.virtualvin.com.
5. Jeanne Dietsch, vice president of ActivMedia, quoted in Fred Hapgood, "Foreign Entanglements," *WebMaster,* January/February 1996.
6. Evan I. Schwartz, "Advertising Webonomics 101," *Wired,* February 1996.
7. *A Business Week Guide: The Quality Imperative* (New York: McGraw-Hill, 1994).
8. Seth Godin, *eMarketing* (New York: Perigee, 1995).
9. "Lessons of the Valley," *WebMaster,* March/April 1996.
10. Josh Bernoff of Forrester Research, Inc., Boston.

4

Value Streams: Creatures Within a Creature

Cyberspace drastically changes the communication patterns in corporations. Fundamentally new types of operation become possible that can achieve better results. At the same time cyberspace increases the potential complexity of business because it greatly increases the number of options to choose from. In the phrase of cyberneticians, it increases the *variety*.[1] It is essential to have organizational structures that make this complexity manageable.

However, corporations are so complex that it can be difficult to comprehend what structures would be optimal, or how today's fast-moving technologies can be put to the best use. The accelerating changes in technology would be difficult enough to cope with, but in addition there are radically new views about how to organize people better. Many corporations that require fundamental redesign today are paying lip service to reengineering but in reality are missing the boat. They are not carrying through or even understanding the reinvention that the cybercorp world demands.

A necessary way to cut through this confusion is to think of an enterprise in terms of *value streams*.[2] When we map a corporation as a *collection of value streams* we can then for each value stream ask: How can it be optimized? How should it use cyberspace? Should it be totally reinvented? What value streams are strategically important? (Chapter 5). And particularly interesting: What value streams should be *virtual?* (Chapter 6).

What Are Value Streams?

A *value stream* is an end-to-end collection of activities that has a clear reason
for its existence—to deliver a result to a customer or end user. This may be
the *external* customer of the corporation, or it may be a user of the value
stream *within the corporation.* The customer or user has certain desires, and
the value stream consists of activities dedicated to satisfying those desires.
How well it does this can be measured.

The value streams in a company correspond to natural business behavior. If the cybercorp is thought of as a jungle creature, constantly alert, the
value stream is a creature within the creature, designed to be as responsive
as possible to its customers (internal or external) and to meet their needs as
effectively as possible.

A cybercorp is a collection of value streams. Some of them are critical
for competitive success; some are not. Understanding value streams is essential for thinking about cybercorp design.

Managers should map and comprehend the corporation in terms of its value
streams and understand that most value streams need *radical* reinventing.

Value streams and their customers cannot be separated. The value
stream integrates the end-to-end work activities that are dedicated to serving,
or delighting, that customer (Exhibit 4-1). This is true whether the customer
is the ultimate external customer or a "customer" within the enterprise. An
example of a value stream that supplies a customer within the corporation is
the materials acquisition value stream that supplies materials to a company's
manufacturing operations—the customer is the manufacturing function.

In most corporations the value streams have been unnamed and largely
unmanaged because the corporation has been structured around vertical
functions that evolve their own power structures.

Value streams in traditional corporations fragment work activities
across traditional departments or functional areas and hence are slow and
clumsy in operation. Today's technology allows us to synthesize work rather
than fragment it. Small teams of employees can often be established to tackle
the entire end-to-end value stream in an integrated, alert, creaturelike fashion. The team can move fast and delight the customer.

There are numerous examples of value-stream teams achieving tenfold
improvements over traditional hierarchical structures. For example, some
telephone companies have reduced the time to respond to customer requests
for circuits from months to one or two days. Some manufacturers have dramatically shrunk the time it takes to design a new product and get it to mar-

Exhibit 4-1. Value stream: An end-to-end set of activities that collectively create value for a customer or end user

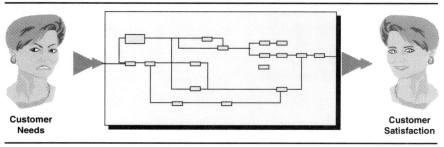

Customer
Needs

Customer
Satisfaction

ket. Harley-Davidson reduced the time for manufacturing motorbike frames from seventy-two days to two. Iomega reduced the time it took to make disk drives from twenty-eight days to one and a half. More important, some corporations have rebuilt a strategic capability so that they do it far better than their competition. Wal-Mart reinvented its distribution and logistics capacity so that it could get goods on its supermarket shelves at lower cost than other stores.

Many corporations have old mainframe systems, often called "stovepipe systems," because of their narrow vertical set of functions. The crude technology of an earlier era led to crude forms of organizational structure. The cybercorp needs value streams with instant responsiveness and information systems designed to make the value stream as effective as possible. As we set out to invent cybercorp mechanisms we need to understand which value streams are important, how we should measure them, and how we can drastically improve the measurements by using today's technology well.

> **It is essential for executives to understand value streams and how they are being reinvented. This book only summarizes the subject; the reader who wants more detail should read Part II, "Value-Stream Reinvention," of my book *The Great Transition*.**[3]

In the cyberspace world, fundamentally new types of value streams can be invented.

"Value stream" is a much simpler concept than Michael Porter's "value chain."[4] Porter's value chain refers to the entire enterprise. "Value stream" refers to a stream of activities within that enterprise that achieve a particular re-

sult. Understanding value streams, and how to give them creaturelike responsiveness, is essential for thinking about cybercorp design.

Porter's value-chain perspective is driven by a functional business view evaluating costs and margins as a basis for competitive comparisons. The value-stream perspective is based on the fact that within every enterprise there are streams of work activities that deliver a particular result for a particular type of customer or end user. The streams often straggle across multiple departments and functional areas and are clumsy and slow; they can be made straight and fast.

The Term "Process"

A value stream is sometimes referred to as a "process." The term "process," although it has a precise definition, is vague because it is used to refer to everything from adding a comma to a sentence to responding to a nuclear attack. The word is used in many different ways by different professionals. Systems analysts call "accounts receivable" a process, for example. "Accounts receivable" is not a value stream—an end-to-end stream of activities designed to satisfy a customer. The term "value stream," rather than "process," should be used to define the end-to-end stream of activities. Sometimes the term "cross-functional process" is used; sometimes "core process." A value stream is a more precisely defined concept—the end-to-end set of activities that deliver particular results for a given customer (external or internal).

Clumsy Value Streams

As shown in Exhibit 4-2, the value streams in traditional enterprises often straggle across several functional areas. Multiple handovers occur as work progresses from one area to another. This causes delays and errors. Each department has a queue of jobs waiting to be done, so the overall cycle time is much longer than it need be. It is difficult to trace things that have "fallen through the cracks." Exceptions are time-consuming. There is no manager in charge of the value stream as a whole. The sequence of work handover in Exhibit 4-2 causes many problems.

In the cybercorp, value-stream structures like that in Exhibit 4-2 should be anathema. The clunky, slow, throw-it-over-the-wall-it's-his-problem set of activities needs to be replaced with a tightly coupled *team* that can finish the job, *empowered* to find the best way to please the customer. There needs to be a new work flow that is as fast, simple, and automated as possible, per-

Exhibit 4-2. Value streams in traditional corporations are slow and error-prone because they straggle across multiple functional areas.

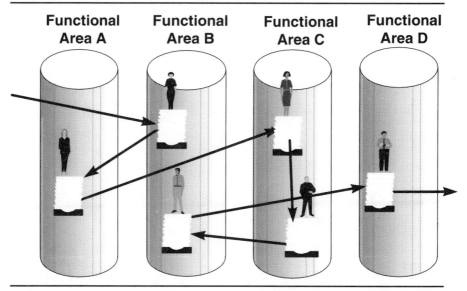

In the cybercorp, value-stream structures like this are avoided. Computer networks can take the work to an empowered team with access to all the information they need. The work should be done as simply and directly as possible, with the team focusing intensely on the needs of the value-stream customer.

formed by a team sharply focused on the customer like a jungle creature stalking its prey.

The main reason why value streams are being reinvented is that the technology that makes the cybercorp possible provides fundamentally better ways to operate end-to-end streams of activities.

Fast Reaction

In some nonphysical value streams such as processing an insurance claim, obtaining finance, or obtaining a price estimate, the customer has to wait weeks or months because there are so many handovers. With the right use of information systems, the activity could be done in an hour or so. Sometimes work that could be dealt with in one telephone call takes weeks because it waits in multiple in-baskets.

When a credit card user find errors in her statement she may write a letter, and the bank writes back. Often the problem takes weeks to resolve. Citibank reinvented this process so that the customer can telephone and be switched to a person at a computer screen that displays an image of the credit slip in question. Usually, the error can be corrected *while the customer is on the telephone,* and the customer's next bill is adjusted accordingly.

Similarly, CitiCorp cut its time to respond to requests for mortgages from thirty to sixty days down to fifteen minutes for most cases. Building a system for Chubb Insurance in London, we redesigned and automated the underwriting process so that the policy production that used to take thirty days is now done in thirty minutes.

> **Redesigning the value stream can sometimes bring the total response time down from weeks or days to hours or minutes. This is essential to the fast-reacting nature of the cybercorp.**

Integration of Work

Value-stream teams combine what were previously multiple jobs. The team must have the ability to execute the entire value stream. There are no queues as work passes to different functional areas. The value-stream team must be empowered to make decisions and should not have to say, "I must pass this up the management chain for approval." The team rule is "Just do it!" Employees must be trained to do the collection of tasks that meet the customer's needs.

At some General Motors plants there were as many as 183 job classifications. GM built a totally new car factory in California, the New United Motor Manufacturing Inc. (NUMMI) plant, which had only 4 job classifications because teams of workers learned to do many types of work. Decision making is not separated from work; it is now part of the work because only the people who do the work have detailed knowledge about it. Having a team with all the knowledge and information systems to finish the job greatly reduces overhead costs and enables the organization to be much more responsive to customers. It helps eliminate nasty surprises and "things falling through the cracks." It avoids jobs' being sent back for rework or reconciliation, which is so time consuming and expensive.

The cybercorp value stream should minimize the need for checking and reconciling different pieces of paper. Checking should be done as events happen, where possible, because then mistakes are easy to correct. A wrong shipment should be detected on the shipping dock and sent back. Computers should be used to catch design errors as they are made, if possible. The value team should do its own checking and reconciliation; these should not be done by some other department at some other time.

Value-stream design identifies the end-to-end work that has to be done and designs efficient teams to do it in the cleanest and simplest way possible, with no handovers, no boundaries, no politics, and the most powerful use of technology.

Some value streams involve work that is geographically scattered. Maintenance of aircraft requires worldwide logistics. Supplying a supermarket chain requires continentwide control. Even a simple task, such as installing a home telephone, requires work in multiple places. Today's electronics allow team members to work well together when distance intervenes. Magazine editors in different countries can debate the layout of color pages, which they can manipulate together on their computer screens. Doctors can interact with a distant specialist. At Digital the designers who created the complex mechanisms of Digital's network software were on both sides of the Atlantic, working together in the most intricate way with powerful workstations.

Typical Value Streams

Most large companies can be broken down into one or two dozen value streams. IBM identified eighteen major value streams, Ameritech fifteen, Dow Chemical nine, and Xerox fourteen in its document-processing business.[5] A major insurance company envisions itself as fourteen value streams. Exhibit 4-3 lists a typical collection of value streams in a corporation. The list of value streams differs somewhat from one type of enterprise to another. An insurance company may have a separate value stream for claims processing. An airline needs a value stream for maintenance of aircraft, worldwide.

In the top three value streams in Exhibit 4-3, the corporate customer is the value-stream customer. In the other value streams the "customer" is internal. However, each value stream has clear customers, and its goal should be to satisfy those customers in the simplest, most direct way. Although a value stream has many work steps, these should be tightly coordinated and compressed into the minimum time in order to maximize responsiveness to the customer. Work steps should be done in parallel where this is practical, to increase speed. Unnecessary work should be eliminated. Handovers from one

Exhibit 4-3. A typical collection of value streams in a corporation

1. *Customer engagement*—Acquiring customers, determining their needs, selling, ensuring that they are pleased
2. *Order fulfillment*—Receiving orders, fulfilling the orders, collecting payment
3. *Customer services*—Providing customers with services such as help in using the product, planning, consulting
4. *Manufacturing*—Production of goods, maintenance of inventory, interaction with suppliers
5. *Procurement services*—Assistance in supplier selection, contracting, and management
6. *Product design engineering*—Designing of products and the facilities for manufacturing them
7. *Research*—Exploration of potentially valuable science and technology
8. *Marketing*—Determining what customers need, what products to build, what features are needed; advertising
9. *Market information capture*—Capture of information about sales; intelligence about competition
10. *Product maintenance*—Repair of products and preventive maintenance on customer sites
11. *IT application development*—Developing and modifying systems and software
12. *IT infrastructure*—Building the corporation-wide network, database, and cyberspace infrastructure
13. *Human resources*—Assistance in recruiting, training, management compensation, career planning
14. *Financial management*—Accounting, negotiation with banks, cash management

---

group to another, which tend to cause errors or to allow things to "slip through the cracks," should be avoided where possible.

In identifying value streams that are candidates for reinvention, it is important to identify clearly where they start and where they end. This clarifies what the value stream is. Exhibit 4-4 shows the start and finish of typical value streams.

Silos and Stovepipes

Traditional enterprises are organized by function with an executive heading each functional area with a title like "vice president of marketing" or "vice

Exhibit 4-4. To clarify what the value stream is, its start and finish activities can be named

Value stream	*Start*	*Finish*
Order acquisition	Prospect, lead	Order
Order fulfillment	Customer order	Delivery
Procurement	Requirements determination	Payment
Mortgage request	Inquiry	Resolution
Manufacturing	Procurement	Shipment
Product design	Concept	Prototype
Software application	Concept	Cutover
Strategy development	Market requirements	Business strategy
Customer communications	Customer inquiries	Customer interest in products
Claims processing	Accident report	Claim payment

Exhibit 4-5. Functional silos in traditional corporate structure

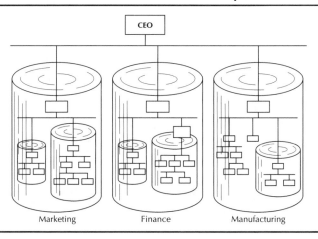

president of finance." Often the functional areas are largely autonomous, and there is limited communication among functions. An employee in manufacturing does not normally pick up the phone and make joint decisions with an employee in marketing. Sometimes enterprises are described as being organized into functional "silos" (Exhibit 4-5).

Computer systems in traditional corporations have usually been de-

Exhibit 4-6. The cybercorp value stream needs computer systems quite different from the old stovepipe systems.

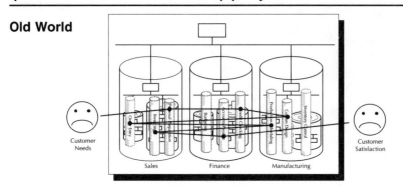

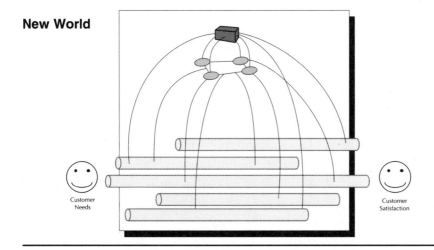

signed to support functional silos rather than cross-functional value streams. Often systems have been created with a database to support one function or department rather than with data designed to be shared across the value stream. The cybercorp value stream requires information systems completely different from those of the past.

The computer applications within each function have often been built independently by separate noncommunicating development teams. They are sometimes referred to as stovepipe systems (Exhibit 4-6). The stovepipe systems often use incompatible data. This prevents or makes difficult communication between the systems (even if they are "open" systems).

Primary vs. Support Value Streams

Some value streams are *primary* activities of the corporation, such as product design, customer engagement, distribution logistics, manufacturing, and marketing. Other value streams are needed for basic *support* of the business; they enable the business to operate. Support value streams include purchasing, operational finance, human resources, facilities management, and IT services. Most of the primary value streams have customers external to the enterprise. The support value streams have customers inside the enterprise.

One, or maybe more than one, of the primary value streams may be regarded as a *strategic* capability that top management wants to perform with world-beating excellence. Part of the strategic vision is to make the corporation so excellent in one aspect of the business that it is uniquely differentiated from its competition. Building such a capability may only be achievable by means of complex and unique computer systems.

One-Person Value Streams

A useful way to think about most value streams is to ask, "If a single person operated the entire value stream, with the goal of delighting the value-stream customer, what would that person do?" Sometimes it is more sensible to think about a small tightly knit team than about one person. With very complex operations, such as constructing a skyscraper or designing a jet fighter, the one-person question is not helpful, but for processing an insurance claim, responding to a customer order, purchasing materials, obtaining mortgage approval, and most of the ordinary processes of business, the question makes good sense. The one person might need much help from specialists or new computer systems. It should be assumed that the one person or team has the information systems needed (often systems not yet in place) and that the work is automated where possible.

A one-person value stream is very different from a value stream that passes work around multiple departments: Work is designed to meet the goals of the customer rather than goals of function managers who don't think about the customer. Because the person spends her entire time thinking about her customers she can grow to understand their needs very well and invent ways of pleasing them. She can think about how to eliminate work and meet customer needs as fast as possible.

Value-Stream Teams

Value-stream teams assume a diversity of forms, depending on the complexity of value streams.[6] A corporation may have a dozen or so different types of value streams, each with its own management. The value-stream organization works well because each value stream has clear goals. It is customer focused; its purpose is to delight its customer (internal or external). It has clear measurements related to its goals, and it can be highly innovative in improving how it achieves its goals. In such an environment it is practical to build high-performance teams with employees excitedly striving to meet tough challenges.

The functionally oriented hierarchy wastes much energy running its own internal machinery—managing relations among departments, controlling problems caused by handovers, passing information up and down the hierarchy, and so on. The value-stream organization eliminates most of those tasks and focuses its energies on the value-stream customers.

Hewlett-Packard reengineered itself to minimize the time from having a product concept to having cash flow from customers. For new printers the concept-to-cash time was cut from four and a half years to twenty-two months, and then driven down to ten months. Products were redesigned so that they could be manufactured in the most automated way, cutting out as many manual steps as possible, and cutting out the possibilities for manufacturing defects. HP spent more money up front on good design in order to lessen the number of changes that would be made later, which would cause a chain reaction of delays. Such design needed a value-stream team spanning research, development, manufacturing, marketing, and interaction with suppliers. HP carved up its bureaucracy and created value-stream teams that could integrate cross-functional activities.

Even with a value-stream organization, central support functions are needed, such as financial control, human resources, and IT infrastructure. Some of the support functions should themselves be value streams. Exhibit 4-7 shows primary value streams and support activities in a typical cybercorp structure. These activities may span large distances in the world of cyberspace.

It is fashionable now to talk of nonhierarchical corporations, but some hierarchy survives. Top management must set the direction, establish the strategic vision, and design the enterprise. Financial control is needed of all of the activities. The different parts of the organization need to share a common computer network and services.

Each value stream needs somebody in charge of it even if it operates with self-managing teams. AT&T's Network Division, for example, reorga-

Exhibit 4-7. Cybercorp structure

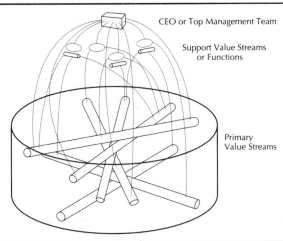

nized itself around thirteen value streams. Each value stream has an "owner" and a "champion." The owner focuses on the day-to-day operations of the value stream, and the champion ensures that the value stream is linked with overall business strategies and goals.[7]

The value-stream organization needs budgets based on value-stream operation rather than on functions and departments. It should have bonuses based on value-stream performance and, where possible, on customer evaluations of value-stream work. It makes sense to base a high proportion of employee compensation on results or on the satisfaction of the value-stream customer.

Kaizen Culture

The excellence of Japanese industry has to a major extent been due to a management philosophy called *kaizen* (pronounced *Ky'zen*). Management author Masaaki Imai quotes comments that there are three main religions in Japan: Buddhism, Shintoism, and *kaizen*.[8] Many intelligent Japanese practice all three!

Kaizen has no equivalent word in English, so it is desirable to use the Japanese word. Roughly, it means "everybody improves everything all the time." *Kaizen* is a form of enterprise learning vital to the modern enterprise. It means that *everybody learns all the time how to do things better.* The results of learning are recorded so that other people can be trained to use them. Much more learning can come from the people who do the work than from external designers or efficiency experts. The person who works with a machine all day, every day, understands its use better than head-office experts. A corporation with a *kaizen* culture encourages everybody to learn all the time.

If you constantly and relentlessly make small improvements to the way you work, you eventually become very good at what you do. Japanese industry evolved various methodologies for *kaizen,* with detailed techniques for constantly achieving improvements. The Japanese *kaizen* culture has been translated in the West into the TQM movement, but often TQM or ISO 9000 fails to capture the passion of Japanese *kaizen.*[9]

The passion of *kaizen* should pervade a value-stream team. The team should be avidly searching for better methods and ways to delight its customers. The customer focus of value-stream teams makes this attitude work well in practice. It should be management's job to build high-performance value-stream teams with a passionate *kaizen* culture.

Pictorial Decision Landscapes

The value-stream team, like the jungle creature, should have senses constantly alert, detecting anything that requires action. It should have instrumentation rather like a pilot's cockpit.

> **One of the reasons why organizing a corporation in terms of value streams, rather than traditional functions, is beneficial is that *value streams are clearly measurable.***

Computers and networks can produce a deluge of data. From 1975 to 1982 there was a massive drive to automate accounting. General Electric (GE), known for its superb financial management, had top executives drowning in data they could not possibly use. One GE business produced seven daily reports for top management containing product-by-product sales details on hundreds of thousands of items. Each report made a stack of paper twelve feet high. *Fortune* commented that such practices "emasculated top executives by overwhelming them with useless information, and enslaved middle managers with the need to gather it. . . . Briefing books had grown to such dense impenetrability that top managers simply stopped reading them. Instead, they relied on staffers to feed them 'gotchas' with which to intimidate subordinates at meetings."[10] Later, GE learned how to use computerized information very effectively.

Complex data represented by dozens of densely packed screens of figures are hard to digest and often too difficult to use in responding to fluid situations. A solution is to encapsulate information in graphical images. The best tools for doing this show three-dimensional landscapes that the decision maker can explore and zoom into. The human brain is designed to remember and react to images, and a decision maker familiar with a graphical landscape can quickly spot areas that need attention. A Canadian firm, Visible Decisions, applies such software to complex market trading, investment portfolios, and risk management. It makes anomalies, rogue positions, or dangerous situations jump out of the picture. It can display real-time "value at risk" pictures that show the probabilities of profits or losses from investment exposures.

Cybercorp managers need pictorial landscapes on computers that enable them to *visualize* their fast-changing environment, digest its complexity, interact with it in real time, and so make appropriate decisions.

The chief executive should be able to monitor all the value streams, in a highly visual way, and be alerted to any situations that need improvement. Corporate decision makers may explore alternative scenarios with software as events unfold, exploring with elegant graphics the probable results of alternative actions.

Value-Stream Use of the Net

Good use of the Internet and intranets has several important effects on the newly designed teams that operate value streams:

- The team can interact directly and constantly with its customers, including those that are far away. It can respond instantly to customer requests.
- The team is more able to be self-sufficient because it can access information, expertise, and special-interest communities. It usually does not have to pass work to other departments in the corporation.
- The team can use powerful tools and interact with distant people using the same tools.
- Given the available access to know-how and computer power, the team can be small and fast moving.
- The design of high-performance teams is a particularly important aspect of value-stream reinvention. The Internet and all its resources can greatly increase the capabilities of a self-sufficient team.

- The team can be geographically scattered if necessary.
- The team can be better informed and more aware of the competitive environment.
- Expert systems can be designed to improve the effectiveness of the team.
- Virtual operations can be designed in which the team uses certain external resources as though they were internal. It may use resources in countries with low salaries.
- Multicorporate teams can connect core competencies from different organizations.

Intercorporate Value Streams

If a value stream in a traditional enterprise has many delays and handovers, a value system that spans separate enterprises can be even worse. The relationship between two companies often needs rethinking to simplify the interaction, remove the queues and delays, and remove the sources of miscommunication. New technology, including the Internet and ISDN with video communications, enables fundamental reinvention of interenterprise value streams.

Business units, for example, may interact directly with vendors, each maintaining a database of information that can be accessed directly by the other. The vendor has computer access to the business unit's inventory of its product and is under contract to maintain the inventory. The business unit has computer access to the vendor's files showing details of shipments. The business unit and vendor interact on a regular and intimate basis. The business unit always talks to the same vendor representative, who tries to keep the customer happy.

There are examples of how procurement value streams can be dramatically simplified, with fewer people, less paperwork, lower costs, and faster interaction.[11]

Ruthless Simplification of Complexity

A danger of cyberspace is that complexities can multiply endlessly. Technology allows us to individualize products and offer customers a great diversity of choices.

> **Cybercorp managers need to be clearheaded and ruthless in simplifying operations, using tough management to eliminate *unnecessary* complexity.**

Much complexity is necessary. A car, for example, has 10,000 parts from many hundreds of suppliers and many different options; yet the most efficient plants assemble it with fewer than fifteen person-hours of work. Complex relationships with suppliers help to make this possible. However, many of today's complexities should not exist. They do because bureaucratic procedures have grown like weeds without adding value. The weeds have to be constantly and ruthlessly removed; otherwise they choke the garden.

Northcote Parkinson describes how the British Navy declined rapidly between 1914 and 1928. In 1914 it had sixty-two capital ships in commission; in 1928, fewer than twenty. However, during the same period the size of the Admiralty went from 2,000 to 3,569 officials and the number of dockyard officials and clerks went up by 40 percent. A magnificent navy at sea had become a magnificent navy on land.[12] Similarly, the British Colonial Office grew to its maximum size at the time Britain had almost no colonies.

If work expands to fill the available time, complexity expands to fill the available computer power.

A reason why the drive for simplification is so important is that cyberspace encourages new relationships among trading partners that are inherently complex. We need to spend our efforts on valuable complexity and eliminate activities that do not add value.

Most old corporations have structures designed for a world before cyberspace and value streams. Most employees are cogs in obsolete machines. Some are not even cogs; they are grit in a mechanism that itself should not exist. Clunky multidepartment work handovers of the old world should be replaced with value-stream teams designed to be tight, simple, and intensely focused on how to delight the value-stream customer.

References

1. Ross Ashby, *Introduction to Cybernetics.* (London: Pelican, 1951).
2. Value streams are discussed in more detail in James Martin, *The Great Transition* (New York: AMACOM, 1995).
3. Ibid.
4. Michael E. Porter, *Competitive Advantage* (New York: Free Press, 1985).
5. T. H. Davenport, *Process Innovation* (Boston: Harvard Business School Press, 1993).
6. James Martin, "Designing the Value-Stream Teams," Chap. 16 in *Enterprise Engineering,* 5 vols. (Carnforth, England: Savant, 1994).
7. "The Horizontal Corporation," *Business Week,* December 20, 1993.

8. Masaaki Imai, *Kaizen: The Key to Japan's Competitive Success* (New York: McGraw-Hill, 1986).
9. Martin, *Great Transition,* chap. 17.
10. Noel M. Tichy and Stratford Sherman, *Control Your Own Destiny or Someone Else Will* (New York: Double Currency, 1993), chap. 3.
11. See the Con Edison example in Martin, *Great Transition.*
12. C. Northcote Parkinson, *Parkinson's Law* (New York: Ballantine, 1957).

5
Predator Capability

Of all the value streams in a corporation it is likely that one (perhaps two) is of exceptional importance to the competitive position of the business. We refer to it as the *strategic value stream*.

> A *strategic value stream* is a unique capability that enables a corporation to move much faster or better than its competition. The strategic value stream should be reinvented in cybercorp form to make it superbly effective.

A primary way to add value, in most corporations, is to identify the most critical value stream and rebuild it with the creature-like alertness of cybercorp mechanisms. Sometimes the result is startlingly different from that which is traditional; it may, for example, use virtual or agile links to organizations with special skills (as described in the next two chapters).

As we discuss in Chapter 8, the cybercorp economy is changing the nature of competition. We are seeing collections of corporations form associations that link them into cross-industry ecosystems. The most profitable corporations are often those that establish a dominant position in the ecosystems they are part of. Understanding the evolving ecosystems is critical to determining what the characteristics should be of the most critical value stream.

> A critical question in the cybercorp upheaval is "Where do we focus our effort?" The answer should be "Focus intensely on that value stream which makes the strongest competitive difference, and make it into a capability which competing firms cannot emulate."

Extraordinary Success

What do you think enabled Wal-Mart to grow from a small American niche retailer in a Southern state where Bill Clinton was dating Hillary to the world's largest retailer? (If Wal-Mart meets its stated goals it will become the world's largest *corporation.*) Was it the charismatic personality of Sam Walton? Was it the use of "greeters" in the stores to welcome the customers?

As in all great corporate success stories many factors were aligned to contribute to goals that were held with relentless determination. But a particularly large factor was the determination to get goods on store shelves at a lower price than the competition. To do this the *inventory-replacement* value stream was critical. It needed to be reinvented with a simple and clear goal: *Get goods on the shelves at the lowest price possible.*

To achieve this simple and clear goal Wal-Mart needed a very complex logistics system. It needed to buy goods in bulk at minimum cost and distribute them so as to get the right goods in the right quantities at the right time to the stores. Information from cash-register bar-code readers was transmitted to a control computer. As a cross-check, inventory was monitored, also with bar-code readers. Wal-Mart built a system called "cross-docking" in which goods coming into a warehouse are selected, replaced, and quickly dispatched to stores. The warehouse was a switching yard rather than a storage facility. Cross-docking enabled Wal-Mart to buy whole truckloads of goods and so pay lower prices, but also to quickly dispatch these goods to stores without much inventory-holding cost.

Strategic systems that are highly publicized, as Wal-Mart's is, become widely emulated elsewhere. The strategic advantage lasts only for a time, and then the new mechanisms become common industry practice. The stragglers that are slow to adopt the new practice get hurt. To stay ahead, a corporation needs to ask what evolving mechanisms can enable it to maintain a leading position in cybercorp ecosystems.

Wal-Mart's system needed a continuous flow of information from every point of sale to the distribution centers and to 4,000 vendors. An elaborate computer network choreographed the rapid movement of goods, making sure that stores had the goods customers wanted to buy but that the holding costs were minimized. For a time, Wal-Mart replenished goods on its store shelves far faster than the industry average and achieved lower holding costs and bulk discounts. Rather than centrally *pushing* goods to the stores, which in turn pushed them to customers, Wal-Mart's computer network allowed customer purchases to *pull* the right goods to the stores. The computers provided store managers with detailed information about customer behavior from across the system so that they could make informed decisions about what to stock. Wal-Mart fine-tuned the system, constantly inventing improvements to its strategic capability for inventory replenishment. Then Wal-Mart went a major step further. It built computerized links to some suppliers so that those suppliers *themselves* could replenish the Wal-Mart shelves. Wal-Mart allocated shelf space to these suppliers and paid the suppliers only after customers bought the goods. For those goods Wal-Mart then had zero inventory-holding costs.

Key questions for every chief executive are: "Of all our value streams, which is the most important for competitive success? If any value stream is to be fundamentally reinvented to make it a world-beater, which one should it be? When it is reinvented, what are the most important results to achieve?"

A traditional value stream that clunkily passes work from one functional area to another, as in Exhibit 4-2, cannot move quickly. Because there is no "owner" or manager of the traditional value stream, it rarely moves with decisiveness and precision. Although commonplace, it should be regarded as hopelessly obsolete. Often the most valuable thing the IT organization can do is to identify the most important value streams and focus attention on reinventing them. These value streams must be creaturelike, constantly alert, responding like a tiger to their changing situation.

Core Competences

A core competence is a *critical skill or enabling technology* that is used in multiple different products. A goal should be to master the core competence at a level that the competition cannot emulate quickly. Once a corporation has mastered an appropriate set of core competences it can introduce diverse new products faster than its competition. Hamel and Prahalad described how core competences should be a central building block of corporate strategy.[1]

Canon was a much smaller corporation than Xerox when it took Xerox by storm in the early 1980s, and its main business was cameras, not copiers. Canon had carefully thought out how a common set of core competences would enable it to build multiple product lines. It entered, and sometimes dominated, diverse markets that used these competences. It repeatedly excelled in the camera and video camera market by using more advanced lens design than its competition. When it came close to destroying Xerox it had spent a tiny fraction of what Xerox had spent on copier research.

In the cybercorp age, where change is as fast and unpredictable as mercury spattering on glass, the planning and development of core competences is critical. First-rate competences take time to develop, but once the right set exists, new products can be introduced at lightning speed. The central planning of core competences for use in different business units enabled corporations such as Canon, Sony, NEC, Casio and Honda to expand in multiple volatile product lines much faster than their competition.

Some chief executives have a policy of focusing on core competences that are critical and eliminating other activities. Kodak, perceiving that photography was going to become digital, appointed George Fisher from Motorola as CEO. Fisher built up digital capability and helped pay for it by selling Kodak's chemical and prescription drug companies, which were unrelated to photography.

There are many types of core competences: component building, use of CAD technologies, production planning, software creation, brochure design, design of derivatives, skill in training—a great diversity. Products and services are becoming more complex and require a growing set of core competences. Increasingly, corporations do not have all the core competences they need in-house; they need to form partnerships to assemble a world-class set of competences. Cybercorp networks are coming into existence that give the ability to quickly assemble competences from different corporations, as described in Chapter 7.

Strategic Value Streams

Critical value streams usually require multiple competences. Senior managers should see their business in terms of *strategic* value streams and the competences required to perform them at a level of excellence that competing companies cannot easily match.

Core competences and *strategic value streams* are different but complementary aspects of the design of the cybercorp. They should be thought about carefully. Both change the design of the corporation and raise the key cybercorp question: What should be done in-house and what should be done using virtual capability?

A key part of strategic thinking is asking: "What are our strategic value streams? What can we do better than our competition? How in the future should we exploit these competences and value streams in new ways? What value streams should we be reinventing so that we delight our customers and create barriers to other corporations competing with us?"

Capability Predators

George Stalk, P. Evans, and L. E. Shulman used the term *capability predator* in their *Harvard Business Review* article to refer to a corporation that has built a strategic value stream to a level of excellence that is not quickly copiable and then uses it to move aggressively into new areas.[2] Different corporations in the same business may regard different value streams as strategic.

Wal-Mart used its computer-choreographed inventory-replenishment system to move aggressively into new retail sectors. It created Sam's Club, for example, to move into the area of warehouse clubs, which sell products in bulk at a deep discount. Price Club was the industry leader when Wal-Mart entered the business, but Wal-Mart grew to *three times* the volume of Price Club in a few years because of its "predator" value stream that could replenish stock cheaper than competition.

Different types of capabilities can provide predator opportunities. Toyota's development of lean manufacturing enabled it and then other Japanese companies to move aggressively into the car industry. Benetton expanded around the world at astonishing speed once its network, systems, and robotic warehouses enabled it to hit the accelerator. Microsoft built software for building software, established an ever-growing library of software components, and relentlessly improved its software development capability. Canon built core competences that made Xerox struggle for its life in the early 1980s. VISA International spent $50 million building a worldwide system for its card-processing value stream, which it believed would enable it to outgrow its competition.[3]

The American movie industry developed processes, technology, and special-effects capability so that it became an entertainment "predator," causing the rest of the world to complain about U.S. "cultural imperialism" and Europe to single out movies for exclusion from the critical General Agreement on Tariffs and Trade (GATT) treaties of 1993.

Banc One

Banc One, based in Columbus, Ohio, set out to reinvent its strategic capability. Its president, Donald L. McWhorter, said he wanted to reverse decades of banking tradition by being "in the information business, not the transaction business."[4] Instead of focusing on transactions, he wanted his bank to know everything there is to know about a customer. Most banks know remarkably little about their customers. Customer records with incompatible data structures exist on multiple computer systems, some for transactions, some for savings, some for home mortgages, and so on. Different systems record different types of loans. It is often very difficult to know whether a tycoon, like Donald Trump, is overextended on credit because he has borrowed from multiple sources. McWhorter set out to create computer systems to pull together all the relevant information about a customer so as to provide opportunities to cross-sell, help avoid bad loans, and provide better services to customers. Armed with such a system, bankers could spend their time deepening their relationships with customers. The system would also facilitate highly targeted marketing campaigns. Banc One's goal was that their bankers should have deep connections in their local community, backed up by the best nationwide information system—*the cybercorp should have the best combination of global and local capability.*

Local bank presidents in Banc One could run their operations in their own way, setting prices, making credit decisions, and serving their communities with the canniness and flexibility of the best small banks. The central organization provided automation support and constantly learned how to improve bank practices. Banc One set out to achieve the best mix of local employees and central support. Local bankers spent time learning how to serve their communities better; central management spent time learning how to automate, reengineer, and constantly improve the processes.

> **Many businesses should combine caring dedication to local customers with world-class global support.**

The Banc One system was very expensive to build, but once it worked well the bank could take over other banks and make them more profitable by putting into place its own hardware, software, and know-how and intensively training their officers. Banc One set out on an acquisition binge. In 1991, this strategic capability enabled Banc One to have its most profitable year ever— earnings were up 25 percent. Banc One became a capability predator.

Predator Computing

Making the strategic value stream unbeatable by the competition usually requires the development of highly complex technology. Wal-Mart made its distribution value stream difficult to beat because its elaborate computer network linked bar scanners in its stores to central planning computers where immediate information about sales was transmitted to key suppliers. Using data-warehousing and analysis systems, detailed estimates could be made jointly with suppliers about sales patterns to help get the right goods to the stores.

The software needed in order to be competitively different is generally not available from off-the-shelf packages. Ordinary operations are best done with software packages; unique value streams use unique software. The building of systems for unique predator capability is often the single most important activity for an IT organization. IT should focus its prime talent on the special activity that really makes a difference.

The executive in charge of the predator value stream needs a very close relationship with the IT organization because much invention is needed to make the new processes work as well as possible.

> **In some spectacular success stories, the head of computing and the head of the strategic value stream are the same person.**

Coca-Cola & Schweppes Beverages (CCSB) Ltd., Britain's leading soft drinks company, has six factories across Britain, which produce over 2 billion litres of soft drinks per year. The critical value stream is the capability to get the right drinks to shops, bars, and vending machines even though demand fluctuates greatly in unpredictable ways. CCSB needs elaborate real-time monitoring to enable its factories to vary and optimize their mix of products, warehouse them, and distribute them using trucks with satellite transponders and computerized control. The IT executive manages this logistics value stream and has the title *vice president of logistics and information systems.*

In 1995 Britain had a summer like Jamaica's, but CCSB, scrambling to hire trucks and extra-shift workers, managed to keep its customers stocked. The computer systems used to achieve this have been changed constantly in highly inventive ways. The IT/logistics vice president comments that an executive without *his* intricate knowledge of IT could probably not have built the control mechanisms that have proved so critical to CCSB.

An example of cybercorp thinking took place at the Harper group, a $430 million shipping company based in San Francisco, which distributes, ships, and tracks goods worldwide for customers, although it does not own ships or planes. Harper top management realized that the global trend toward just-in-time inventory practices combined with offshore manufacturing created a major new opportunity. Customers needed reliable worldwide just-in-time delivery. They needed electronic conversations with their shipper so that they could be fully informed of the whereabouts of all shipments. Harper set out to redesign its operations so that shipment waybills, bills of lading, insurance certificates, dock receipts, and so forth, could be sent electronically and all details of shipments, worldwide, could be gathered and put in a database that customers could inspect. All information about shipments must be visible to customers; there must be no surprises. Providing this strategic new capability was difficult because Harper had forty-five subsidiaries worldwide that all functioned independently. Each had different account codes for the same customers, different rules about the way it handled accounts, and different charging practices, so the software had to be custom built. Customers needed unified information so that they could plan production, respond to tariff changes or quotas, and switch to a supplier in a different country when such a change was beneficial.

This was a predator system; customers given on-line access to Harper's database would find it difficult to switch to a different shipper. Today, the access can be via the World Wide Web. Harper's software was complex and unique and needed to be built as quickly as possible. Building such IT capability was tough, but it was absolutely critical to Harper's strategy. So Harper freed its IT developers to focus all their efforts on the critical new capability by outsourcing all other systems housed in its headquarters at the time.

It often pays to outsource routine IT activities so that IT can focus intensely on the operations that make a cybercorp uniquely competitive.

Pareto's Law

In many business situations Pareto's law applies: 80 percent of the value comes from 20 percent of the effort. For example, 20 percent of a mailing produces 80 percent of the results; 20 percent of the research effort produces 80 percent of the innovations; 20 percent of the bus routes generate 80 percent of the revenue.

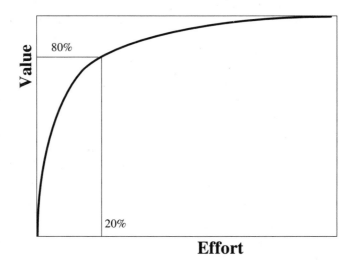

The tail on the right-hand side of the above diagram may generate losses. Management can cut the losses only if it knows *which 20 percent* will produce the good results and if the effort on the left-hand side can be conducted *independently* of the effort on the right-hand side.

Pareto's law applies to value streams: 80 percent of the value in a corporation usually comes from one or two value streams; most of the others don't make much difference.

The world of cyberspace sometimes produces a more skewed distribution. The customers who can be dealt with automatically may be very profitable, while ones that need much manual attention are unprofitable. The profitable ones may be the 10 percent that use cyberspace facilities:

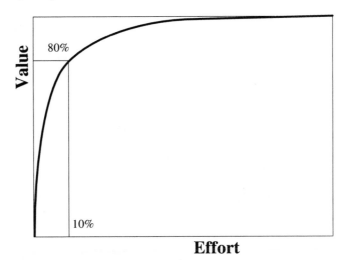

For example, retail banks find that the customers who exclusively use ATMs or electronic banking facilities are highly profitable, whereas customers who wander into the bank in person are mostly unprofitable. Customers who come into the bank in person are usually people with small accounts. Some bank executives have commented to me that 70 percent of their customers generate less profit than investing at fixed interest. What should the bank do? It may decide to close some of its branch banks. It may find other ways of discouraging unprofitable customers, such as increasing what it charges them. It may decide that it has to provide a banking service for the whole community, including the unprofitable customers, but then it will find new competition from companies setting out to lure away its best customers. Internet-based companies, possibly Microsoft, will provide electronic banking services of certain types, worldwide, and attempt to skim the cream of banks' profits.

Cream Skimming

For many corporations one of the most dangerous aspects of the cybercorp revolution is that new companies attack the high-profit part of their business and leave them with the low-profit part. In many industries there will be a battle between traditional companies and companies that master cybercorp operations that enable them to skim the cream of the traditional business's customers.

Ohio's second largest bank, Hamilton Bancshares of Columbus, found, like most banks, that most of its profits came from frequent users of ATMs.

So it replaced 40 percent of its branches with inexpensive unmanned branches, which used enhanced ATM-style machines but also allowed 24-hour video access to personnel at a central location if necessary. Customers could, by video, set up an account, ask for loans, or do other banking functions that needed human interaction. This worked well; there was no need for most people to go near the bank. However, future service organizations could provide such unmanned banking facilities for *any* bank. A relatively small bank could then have virtual branches worldwide, focusing on only the most profitable cream of the banking business.

Cream skimming by new companies using cybercorp mechanisms will be a threat to many old companies.

It is possible with software to make telephone calls over the Internet. Because Internet pricing is independent of distance, Net users can make long-distance telephone calls at a tiny fraction of their normal cost. In 1996 a small Canadian company, TheLinc, announced that it planned to offer 15 hours a month of long-distance telephone service for only $15 (U.S.), to anywhere in North America, through the Internet. This service, it said, was for "Ma and Pa" telephone users, not Net addicts.

The telephone industry reacted quickly to try to ban TheLinc's service. The actual cost of international calls is sometimes *only 1% of the charge* of those calls. Such a service could be very dangerous for large telephone companies because most of their profits come from long-distance telephone calls. The charge for international calls is sometimes *only one percent of the actual cost* of those calls. Telephone regulations in many countries provide that local telephone service is partially subsidized by lucrative long-distance fees. Some governments might succeed in preventing companies like TheLinc from skimming the telephone industry cream, on the grounds that it would hurt "Ma and Pa" local users. In this case, Ma and Pa would be prevented from making cheap long-distance calls, whereas savvy PC users would make them anyway.

Whereas regulations might succeed in preventing most cream skimming in telephony, there are no regulations that can prevent it among insurance companies, publishers, travel agents, banks, and so on. All service industries can be a target for a cyberspace cream-skimming attack.

Manufacturing companies can be similarly attacked in the marketing area. A company that makes excellent snowmobiles found much of its business slipping away to the Japanese because the Japanese had developed a worldwide set of relationships with dealers and were outmaneuvering their competition. The company needed to regard its worldwide dealer-support value stream as strategic and fundamentally reinvent it in a way the Internet made possible.

While excellence with a strategic value stream may enable a corporation to be a predator, weakness in a strategic value stream can cause a corporation to lose market share.

BHAGs

Some corporations have achieved greatness by setting a goal of audacious proportions. They "bet the company" on some spectacular achievement. If it works, the company will be way ahead of its competition; if it doesn't, it may be "goodbye."

Collins and Porras in their classic book about visionary companies *Built to Last* refer to such goals as BHAGs (pronounced *bee-hags,* short for big hairy audacious goals).[5] Two of the hairiest of BHAGs were IBM's building of the 360 computer and Boeing's entry into the civilian jetliner market.

The 360 was intended to replace all other IBM computers (in 1964). However, the development costs to make it work rose terrifyingly beyond expectations, reaching about twice IBM's annual revenue at that time. Only the most gutsy, single-minded, dictatorial top executive (T. J. Watson, Jr.) could have pulled off a gamble of such magnitude. Building the operating system for the 360 proved to be a nightmare; there was a time when IBM had difficulty meeting its payroll. The operating system eventually cost more than the building of the atomic bomb in World War II. But once it worked, the 360 became the most popular computer of its time, the standard for the industry.

IBM started similarly ambitious projects in the 1970s (FS, or Future Systems) and 1980s (Fort Knox), but Watson was no longer there. Both projects were abandoned before completion. One can only speculate whether they would have succeeded if the forcefulness of Watson had been behind them.

Boeing's building of the first jumbo jet, the 747, was as big a cliffhanger as IBM's 360 saga. Sales of the 747 were slow, and Boeing had to lay off about 60 percent of its workforce. Someone placed a billboard near Interstate 5 in Seattle saying, "Will the last person leaving Seattle please turn out the lights."

BHAGs need not be as hair-raising as the 360 or 747, but they need to set a firm goal that is inspiring, tough to achieve, and galvanizes everyone working on it. Collins and Porras emphasize that a BHAG must simple, clear, and exciting. It should not be something like "Let's beef up our space program" but "We will put a man on the moon by 1970."

When Ford was a small player among more than thirty automobile companies, Henry Ford proclaimed a goal of making a car so low in price that "everybody will be able to afford one, and everyone will have one." This ambition, which seemed outrageous then, inspired everyone at Ford to work at a ferocious pace on designing the Model T and the world's first mass-production line.

In 1952 the Japanese company Tokyo Tsushin Kogyo set itself the audacious goal of making a "pocketable" radio. When its designers visited Bell Laboratories and told them of their goal, five years after the transistor had been invented there, the Bell Labs staff looked at them in astonishment and said, "You've got to be joking." After enormous effort the company made its transistor radio work and then told its bank that it was going to change its name to Sony. The bank objected to their giving up such a fine name as Tokyo Tsushin Kogyo, but they said they had another audacious goal—to achieve worldwide sales—and Sony was a name that foreigners could remember.[6] Akio Morita had another inspiring goal: "To change the image around the world of Japanese products as poor in quality."[7]

A BHAG can be a *product* or *result,* or a *process.* The ones that are most remembered and talked about are *products,* "Build the first civilian jetliner" or "Create the Sony Walkman," or *results,* "Put a man on the moon by 1970" or "Achieve less than 3.4 defects in a million units." BHAG *processes* are less obvious, less dramatic, less likely to be talked about in the press, but they are often the BHAGs that make a corporation great: Toyota's lean manufacturing or Wal-Mart's distribution logistics. A BHAG process may require the creation of a very sophisticated IT system, like VISA's wiring the world with nine million miles of private superhighway going to two computer centers on different continents that back up each other with elaborate software to detect fraud and automate charge-backs.

Most products have to be right when first delivered, like the Boeing 747, but many processes should be designed with the expectancy of change; they should be designed for rapid evolution.

To build a strategic capability well beyond that of the rest of an industry takes dedicated effort and investment over an extended period. The computer systems needed to implement McWhorter's vision for Banc One took several years to develop and cost more than $100 million. PCs in a Branch Automation System acted as interfaces to a central system that had ten million lines of code. The new system replaced seventeen fragmented incompatible systems. Banc One teamed up with EDS to build the software, with a contract in which EDS paid about 80 percent of costs in return for the right to sell the software to other banks. Banc One managers did not worry too much about other banks' having access to the software because they believed that most banks would not compete effectively with it; they believed that other banks would not build the human expertise with the community that Banc One emphasized. The human part of the human-technology partnership is what creates true winners. The new system delivered a complete customer profile. It could produce a profile of an entire household, or of all the customers who work for a given employer. It could store as many as 12,000 pieces of information about a customer. It has substantially increased the accuracy of basic customer data.

Design for Constant Improvement

> **To stay ahead of the competition, a company must constantly improve its strategic value stream. It should be managed so that the value-stream teams do research and constantly search for improvements. It should be regarded as a learning laboratory, as described in Chapter 14.**

A strategic value stream that is operated like a jungle predator, with everyone alert to every possibility for improvement, can become a critical capability that is hard for competitors to imitate. It is a basis for repeated innovations that can provide sustainable competitive advantage.

In traditional corporations, strategic capabilities often straggle across multiple departments and functional areas. The strategic capability is a small part of many people's jobs rather than the explicit job of highly focused teams. *Because the strategic capability is scattered among different departments reporting through different branches of a hierarchy, no single executive is in charge of it.* To invest in the capability and improve it to the level where it is a major competitive resource would mean investing in many functional areas. This may be difficult to justify in normal accounting terms. Internal accounting and control systems miss the strategic nature of the scattered activities. For these reasons, many corporations do not focus tightly on a strategic capability and fail to develop and exploit the capability as they should.

Once the capability is identified as a value stream, it then becomes clear that the value stream should be carried out by cross-functional teams with cybercorp principles, using technology to maximize the effectiveness of the team. It should be designed to achieve the strategic goals as directly as possible.

To become unbeatable with such capabilities requires a constant flow of new ideas, experiments, and research. The value-stream teams should be constantly scanning journals, product catalogs, and new ideas and thinking about how they might be used to invent improvements in capability. IT professionals should be in constant communication with the value-stream teams, exploring the possible use of evolving resources such as smart cards, the Internet, pocket devices, image processing, cellular data transmission, and so on. Strategists should think in terms of strategic value streams using core competences and should establish a learning-laboratory environment in which the teams identified as strategic can experiment and search the world for improvements.

Once strategic value streams operate in cybercorp fashion, the value-stream teams should provide major input to strategic thinking. Value-stream teams can be a major resource in helping to anticipate trends and implement innovative thrusts ahead of the competition.

Strategic thinking should not be solely the province of senior management. It can be strongly contributed to by strategic value-stream teams. Such teams are often more alert to changing needs than top management, and more aware of the innovations that are possible.

Outsourcing?

To succeed, a corporation must be fully in charge of its core strategic capabilities. If it outsources part of them, it must be sure that it can make the partnership work as it wants. It is interesting to observe that Kmart was outsourcing its trucking fleet at the same time that Wal-Mart was buying a trucking fleet so that its trucks could have on-board computers and thus join its intricately controlled choreography of logistics. This was a key factor in enabling Wal-Mart to grow rapidly at the expense of Kmart.

When a corporation has a strategic capability that includes suppliers or other partners that cannot be owned, it should forge special relationships with those partners, with special contracts. The trading partners may be asked to change their own business processes in exchange for some benefit, such as guaranteed business or better payment terms. Many corporations need elaborate sets of world-class competences, some of which they own and some of which they do not. Complex ecosystems are evolving composed of many mutually dependent corporations, often with computer-to-computer links.

While it is desirable to manage strategic capabilities in-house, it may make sense to outsource capabilities that are not strategic.

If bread-and-butter activities are contracted out, management can focus corporate talent on those activities that make a competitive difference. Most of the corporate energy can be directed to strategic capabilities.

Summary

In any one industry, there is a wide range of profitability. Profitability varies far more among businesses within one industry than it does across separate industries.[8] To be at the upper end of the range, a corporation needs assets that are hard to replicate or skills that are hard to imitate. These assets or skills cannot be bought off-the-shelf; they must be acquired through investment, development, and learning.

Every corporation has one value stream that is more important than the others and that should be reinvented to achieve the highest level of excellence. Strategic value streams that give a major competitive advantage tend to have the following characteristics:

- They need fundamental reinvention.
- They take time to develop. Often corporations fail to develop them because they are impatient and do not persist for the long haul.
- To develop them needs substantial investment.
- They usually need the creation of major computer systems, sometimes with worldwide networking.
- If they are to give a unique competitive advantage they usually need unique software, not off-the-shelf software.
- They need small high-performance teams empowered by technology.
- Their value relates to the quantity and quality of learning that occurs. Everybody should contribute to the learning and be encouraged to search for innovation.
- Building a powerful knowledge infrastructure is necessary (Chapter 16).
- Top IT people and top business executives need to work together as a team.
- Strategic value streams must be managed at the CEO level. Their reinvention usually requires corporate restructuring.
- The reinvention is often hard to accomplish in an organization with an internal focus. An outside viewpoint is needed.

The next two chapters describe the importance of virtual operations and the role they may play in developing strategic capabilities.

References

1. Gary Hamel and C. K. Prahalad, "The Core Competence of the Corporation," *Harvard Business Review,* May/June 1990.
2. George Stalk, Philip Evans, and Lawrence E. Shulman, "Competing on Capabilities: The New Rules of Corporate Strategy," *Harvard Business Review,* March/April 1992.
3. "Visa International, Digital Credit," *Economist,* September 25, 1993.
4. "Files with Faces," *Computerworld,* December 14, 1992.

5. James C. Collins and Jerry I. Porras, *Built to Last* (New York: Random House, 1994).
6. *Genryu—Sony Challenge 1946–1986,* Collection of Sony Management Newsletters, 40th anniversary ed. (Tokyo: Sony, 1986).
7. Akio Morita, *Made in Japan* (New York: Dutton, 1986).
8. R. Rumelt, "How Much Does Industry Matter?" *Strategic Management Journal,* December 1991.

6

Virtualness

The term *virtual* means that something *appears to exist* and is used as though it exists when in actuality it does not. A computer may have a virtual memory of 256 megabytes when its real memory is 16 megabytes; the computer appears to have a larger memory because it quickly transfers memory contents from its disks when needed, like a conjurer producing coins. A virtual circuit appears to exist and is used as though it exists, but in reality it is derived by transmitting packets through a network. *Virtual reality* fills our senses with lifelike sights, sounds, and motion by means of electronics; we put a headset on, and it creates the sensation of being in a race car or moving through a three-dimensional structure.

A corporation may *appear* to own facilities that it does not own; it may use them *as though it owns them.* People who are not part of the corporation may be linked to it as though they are. Worldwide networks give us the capability for such linkages.

> **For every operation in a cybercorp we need to ask, "What should be done in-house and what should be virtual?"**

Virtual operations have caused some business partners to radically reinvent their relationships. Other companies have barely thought about the implications.

Very Fast Growth

Virtual operations can allow a corporation to grow very fast in an exploding market because they enable the corporation to use resources owned by other organizations. It would cost too much or take too long to grow those resources in-house. The corporation may need to use highly skilled designers, or complex software development, or manufacturing capability from another company.

We commented that Benetton was able to grow astonishingly fast in the 1980s because it did not own the 8,000 Benetton shops worldwide (except for a few prime ones). Benetton shop owners pay no fees or royalties to Benetton; they are licensees in an arrangement that frees Benetton from regulatory franchise laws. The shops agree to stock only Benetton merchandise; they obey Benetton's rules and are linked to Benetton's central computer. Similarly, Benetton does not own 450 factories that make Benetton clothes. It subcontracts labor-intensive production. Production that is automated and provides high return on investment is done in Benetton's own factories, for exmaple, dyeing sweaters with elaborate colors.

The worldwide Benetton system was designed to respond very rapidly to the fast, fickle changes in its marketplace. Buyers in big-name stores buy clothes that the store will sell in the next spring or fall season, nine months or so hence; Benetton shops can order clothes in *midseason,* when other stores are running out, and receive them in a week or so. Benetton achieves this capability by making many of its clothes without color. It dyes clothes with elaborate colors in its own factories at the last minute, based on customer demand. A robotic warehouse stores and retrieves 20,000 boxes of garments a day. (They describe its throughput in "garments per second.")

This setup needs the closest computerized cooperation between Benetton and its trading partners. Benetton uses the phrase "world transparency" to imply that its central computers in Italy have up-to-date knowledge of inventory levels, colors, and changes in customer demand. It monitors the wealth-generating process as it happens and constantly makes rapid adjustments.

As with most highly successful corporations, many factors were involved in Benetton's success. It had a flair for advertising that was always eye-catching, sometimes outrageous, and often played on sensitive social issues. One morning Paris awoke to find a giant plastic purple condom draped over the large needle in the Place de la Concorde. The authorities removed it by helicopter with much cheering from the crowd. It was put there by Benetton amid worldwide publicity allegedly to demonstrate Benetton's concern about safe sex. Benetton's teenage customers around the world gleefully showed one another the pictures of it.

In 1987, General Motors built most of the parts used in its cars in-house; Toyota contracted out most of its parts. However, amazingly, GM had 6,000 employees in its parts-purchasing operations, whereas Toyota had only 337.[1] (GM made only twice as many cars as Toyota.) The reason for this enormous difference is that GM provided suppliers with detailed drawings of the parts it needed whereas Toyota usually allowed its suppliers to do the detailed design because they were supposedly expert with that type of part. The key to low-cost manufacturing is to have the manufacturer, not the user, of the part design the part for automated fabrication and assembly.

Even though GM's assembly plants used mostly parts made inside GM, these plants have an inventory of parts immensely greater than Toyota plants. Toyota's Takaoko plant had two hours' inventory, whereas GM's Framingham plant had fourteen days inventory, on average.[2] *Toyota had reinvented the supply value stream so that it was vastly better than GM's even though Toyota used mainly external suppliers whereas GM used mainly internal suppliers.*

Virtual Offices

> There are basically two types of corporate virtualness. The first relates to *virtual space*. Employees in the same company may be scattered geographically but linked with electronics as though they were in the same building. The second relates to *virtual business*. Employees in different companies may be linked as though they were in the same company.

Virtual space has given start-up companies more flexibility in hiring critical people. They can work in different cities but be closely linked electronically. Salespeople do not need a desk in a branch office that they visit once a week; instead they need their notebook computers and modems. Phoenix Designs Inc., a subsidiary of Herman Miller Inc., sold office furniture with a salesperson in a branch office who gathered ideas and worked up a draft. It used to take six weeks of back-and-forth interaction to produce a proposal, and the customer often became exasperated. Now the salesperson works up designs *in the customer's office,* interacting directly with the customer. This change has greatly increased sales.[3]

Compaq closed its sales offices and instructed its salespeople to work out of their homes instead, with computers linked to comprehensive databases. It also cut the size of its sales force by a third. These moves were part of a cost-cutting campaign that allowed it to drastically lower the price of its products. Compaq doubled its revenue in two years, with each salesperson selling six times as many computers.[4]

At Oticon, a Danish company making hearing aids, the CEO banned all paper. He decreed that paper must be shredded after its contents had been scanned into the computer system and that every employee (with a handful of exceptions) must have the same standard workstation. Employees could then do the same work from any desk at any location and would not be tied to one office. The employees moved, not the equipment. This gave great flexibility in changing work processes and was part of a business redesign activity that cut the product development cycle time from two and a half years to eleven months.

A virtual team may be far apart physically but linked as though they are in the same office. They may need to share computer resources with software designed for a LAN. Today's networking technology allows the installation of virtual LANs that look like a LAN to the software but are not "local." A virtual LAN can link members of a team with high bandwidth when some are in Singapore and some in Bangalore.

Today, some corporations are designed so that employees rarely come into the office. This may cause a lessening sense of company identity, so it is desirable to have physical get-togethers periodically, such as Friday night parties or monthly meetings at which management describes what is going on.

Virtual Board Meetings

Most boards of directors operate under the assumption that their members must be physically present at board meetings. This severely restricts their choice of board members, especially in corporations that operate globally. Many individuals who would be highly valuable on the board want to avoid any increase in their jetlag.

Today's technology makes a *virtual board* practical. Before the board meeting, the board members can be linked with secure e-mail and "chat" lines so that debate of issues, queries about finances, and so on, can be thorough. The board meeting is then shorter and goes to important points quickly. The actual meeting can use video conferencing connections; ISDN makes video connections reasonable in cost. There is less travel involved and less time required from people who are intensely short of time.

Virtual Research Organization

A cybercorp should be constantly searching beyond its own walls for ideas and new ways to do things. The term *virtual research organization* is used to refer to a far-flung network of affiliates that provide ideas and information and possibly do contract research or outsourced design. Drug companies and leading-edge high-tech companies need a big-budget R&D laboratory, but most companies can obtain more cost benefit from a virtual research organization than from their own internal laboratory.

A virtual R&D organization can tap a much larger variety of knowledge sources than an isolated laboratory. It may pay for specific problems to be researched, prototypes to be built and tested, or specific designs to be done in external organizations. The virtual research organization may have a collegiate network, organizing visits to universities and monitoring relevant research at universities. Universities are only too anxious to talk about their research and to exchange ideas, often hoping for research sponsors. The corporation may participate in multiclient research done by consulting firms.

Some corporations have a joint arrangement with customers or suppliers to share results from a network of research sources. Improvement of products, parts, processes, or services often needs to be done in conjunction with a supplier or customer.

Virtual Value Streams

We have stressed that the cybercorp should be thought of in terms of its value streams. Many value streams can be reinvented with virtual operations. A *virtual value stream* can be tightly knit with computer networks, but scattered to the winds geographically and organizationally.

In looking at a value stream you ask: "What is its purpose? Who is its customer? How do we delight the customer?" and "How do we do that in a cost-effective world-class way?" In finding answers to these questions, you should ask: "What should be done in-house, and what should be done by a partner firm?" Where a partner is involved—for example, a supplier—you should ask: "What can our partner do best, and what can we do best?"

Can Proctor and Gamble plan inventories and deliveries better than Wal-Mart? Is it better to test for quality at a vendor's location before goods are shipped? Can dealers do better forecasts than manufacturers? Salomon Brothers may be better at setting prices for aviation fuel than oil companies because of their experience and their computer models of futures markets. Otis may be better than insurance companies at giving insurance covering elevator failures in a skyscraper because they know more about their elevators.

> **When a value stream spans two (or more) enterprises, the question should be asked, "Where is the work best done?"**

Goodyear's tire factories receive raw materials from Third World countries with rubber plantations. Goodyear used to check the quality of the materials when they arrived. Quality varied greatly. Some materials were rejected; others could be used in lower-grade products. Goodyear decided that it would be better to have the materials checked at the source location and use a worldwide network to transmit the results to their factories. This prevented out-of-spec goods' being shipped, and it enabled earlier production planning because the factories knew the characteristics of the material as early as possible. It reduced waste and simplified the payments mechanism.

Navistar International arranged for Goodyear to manage its warehouses of truck tires. Goodyear has more experience managing tire warehouses and knows more about tire failures. It manages Navistar warehouses that contain tires made by other tire companies. This shifting of work to the partner in the value stream simplified operations for Navistar. Goodyear succeeded better than Navistar at tire warehousing—it dropped the inventory from twenty-two days' supply to five.[5]

Navistar saved $167 million with its first eighteen months of using electronic data interchange because it fundamentally reinvented its value streams.

What Should Be Outsourced?

Because modern communications make virtual operation practical, the cybercorp will increasingly be a cluster of common activities in the midst of a vast fabric of relationships. It may be a nerve center linking many resources where few resources are wholly owned. The activities may change rapidly in response to customer demands or changing capabilities.

Some operations in a corporation are critical to its competitiveness. They may include the creative design of the product, proprietary manufacturing techniques, or careful attention to customer service. These are operations that would not be outsourced. They are what makes the corporation unique. Other operations are bread-and-butter activities that can be done elsewhere if that is easier or cheaper. A corporation should maximize value-added by having all employees make contributions that are special and that help build unique strengths. Exhibit 6-1 indicates which activities might be outsourced and which should not be.

In the cybercorp world, virtual operations using intercorporate computer linkages will increasingly be a way of life.

The corporation's management needs to ask: "What are we exceptionally good at? At what activities do we want to be world-class so that competition can't touch us? What should be our unique strengths? If another corporation does something better than we can, shouldn't we employ its services and focus our own efforts on what makes us unique?"

Components Built In-House

Components or software that cannot be bought off-the-shelf may be built in-house or outsourced. Components that have a major effect on the competi-

Exhibit 6-1. What should be outsourced?

Activities that *should* be outsourced are those that

- A partner would do better
- A partner would do cheaper
- A partner would do faster, where speed is critical—for example, in moving into an explosively growing market
- A parnter would be more successful at selling
- Need operations in a distant land with a different culture
- Need special capability, such as obtaining government funding
- Need expensive resources but may decline suddenly as the result of fashion swings
- Are too risky to do in-house
- Give low return on investment

Activities that *should not* be outsourced are those that

- Make the corporation unique or competitive
- Are a strategic value stream that the corporation needs to control
- Are core competences that the corporation needs to develop
- Can be done exceptionally quickly or cheaply in-house
- Need complex integration with other activities
- Need careful interaction with customers
- Need in-house quality control
- Give high return on investment

tiveness of the product may be designed and developed in-house. However, components that are less critical vis-à-vis competition may be given to trusted suppliers to design. For example, a car manufacturer might do its own internal design of engines, transmission, body panels, and electronic management system but outsource the development of brakes, seats, wheels, and windows.

The supplier may be told to develop and deliver an entire subsystem. For example, to build seats for a top-of-the-line car, General Motors often deals with about twenty-five suppliers who build the different components of the seats; Nissan has *one* supplier to build the complete seats. A Japanese car manufacturer in the United States asked an American supplier of seats for a price bid. The seat manufacturer requested a detailed set of engineering drawings so that a bid could be prepared. The Japanese manufacturer said that it had little knowledge of the details of seats and could not supply drawings— it was the job of the supplier to design and deliver complete seats.[6]

Should IT functions be outsourced? It usually does not make sense to program bread-and-butter applications in-house. These should be obtained from software packages if possible. Where unique programs have to be created, the IT organization needs to ask: Can they be built faster and cheaper in-house? Would the in-house resources be better deployed doing something else?

Close Cooperation

A vitally important part of cybercorp thinking is reinventing the relationships among corporations. Electronics makes possible fast, intricate, and highly detailed interaction between corporations, and such interaction is needed to make virtual and agile relationships as valuable as possible. New forms of cooperation are being forged with intercorporate computing, CAD, videoconferencing, Internet facilities, and cybercorp webs designed for agility. New relationships have resulted in more complex products, lower costs, higher quality, and more capability to enrich customers.

The airline industry changed drastically as networks of SABRE-like systems linked travel agents and airlines worldwide. Boeing created one of the most complex machines ever built by using hundreds of contractors interlinked with the same design software. Such innovations deal serious blows to competing corporations that do not make similar changes. *Corporations that do not change are sometimes crippled or put out of business.*

Some virtual relationships are simple. Swissair's accountants in India carry out straightforward tasks; Swissair does not ask for creative accounting. Other virtual relationships are highly complex, with both sides contributing original and creative ideas.

The mature cybercorp is likely to have many virtual partners. It needs very close relationships with many of these partners. To throw jobs over their walls and say, "Now it's your problem," does not work. Often there needs to be close and intricate cooperation made possible by computer-to-computer interaction, shared tools and databases, and videoconferencing. Partners should climb a joint learning curve together, cooperatively learning how to improve their operations. Often cross-corporate teams are formed and are the basis for joint learning.

Antagonistic Relationships

Junior executives often have an urge to appear macho and tough. They think they should bully vendors to create tough deals, constantly threatening to move to their competition. The buyer who does not threaten his suppliers is seen as weak. Often this attitude rules out intimate cooperation in which both parties work together creatively to lower costs and provide better service. Instead both parties keep their detailed operations and costs secret, saying, "What happens in my facility is my business."

To succeed in the future, trading partners need computerized relationships for intricate cooperation. Reinventing the relationship can make both parties stronger. It is a win-win improvement. In partnership, corporations are better able to weather the fast-moving storms of competition.

Government contracting often achieves the worst of both worlds. It is bureaucratic and expensive, it discourages the best companies from bidding, and its regulations prevent the invention of mutually beneficial relationships.

Joint Learning Curves

When reinventing a value stream, we put an entirely new learning curve into place. With intercorporate value streams it is desirable that the partners reinvent the value stream jointly, although one may be an aggressive leader in this. The reinvented relationship should be designed so that both parties recognize that there is a steep learning curve to be climbed and both benefit from together climbing the curve as fast as is practical. There are often massive benefits to be gained from climbing the curve jointly.

Relations that corporations have with their suppliers are being fundamentally reinvented in such a way that there is a much higher level of cooperation. To climb a joint learning curve, both sides have to reveal much about their operations instead of maintaining the secrecy that often accompanies competitive bidding. Both sides "open their kimonos" (not a Japanese expression!). Close and intimate cooperation need not destroy the value of competitive pressures because the reinvented sets of rules that link corporations are designed to provide a high incentive for excellence, cost reductions, and quality improvements. The new relationships can usually avoid sole-source suppliers, and new contracts create high pressures for cost reductions and performance.

Fewer Suppliers

Corporations of many types are shrinking the number of suppliers they use. If you want a close and elaborate relationship with suppliers, you can afford to do this only with a small number.

It is better to have close relationships with a small number of suppliers than antagonistic relationships with a large number. The following are examples of cuts in the number of suppliers:

	Number of Suppliers	
Company	Cut From:	To:
Control Data (Cyber Division)	800	150
Sun Microsystems	450	150
Harris (Electronics Systems Division)	2,500	270
Harley-Davidson	320	120
Xerox	5,000	400
American car companies	2,000–2,500	1,000
Japanese car companies	400–600	200–300

If you are one of the suppliers that gets axed—too bad. As corporations everywhere cut their number of suppliers, this adds to the pressures that force companies out of business. The survivors are often those who reinvent ways to add value to their partner, use information systems that span the partnership, and nurture the human side of the relationship.

Low-Income Countries

Wages around the world differ astonishingly. Factory workers in Germany are paid fifty times as much as factory workers in Indonesia. Programmers in Russia (who are often brilliant) earn less than one-tenth of what programmers earn in America. Cyberspace has a slow equalizing effect around the planet. We have to ask: Are German workers worth fifty times more than Indonesian workers who have been carefully trained by the Japanese, or are they like the aristocracy of the 1930s—doomed to forces of equalization?

To use foreign programmers or designers great discipline is needed. CAD technology enforces discipline. Multiple component suppliers can exchange information electronically so that components will fit precisely into a completed product. Parallel development may be done with multiple corporations creating different parts of a product simultaneously. Similarly, computer-aided software engineering (CASE) allows a software developer to create software that exactly meets a computer-represented specification. The discipline that CAD and CASE imposes has enabled corporations to use low-cost developers in India or the Philippines. Cities like Bangalore are full of skilled software developers, but there is almost no Indian software product selling in high-income countries. The developers are working as virtual extensions to corporations in high-income countries.

Together with the discipline that computerized tools help to provide, caring human attention is needed. Video person-to-person communications can help to achieve that. Switched ISDN circuits are now available to much of the world at fairly low cost. The tool users can talk to each other face-to-face on their PC screens.

In some countries there have been outcries in the press and on television about moving work offshore. Ross Perot's most famous claim is that the North American Free Trade Agreement (NAFTA) would produce a "great sucking sound" as American jobs moved to Mexico. However, in the long run, if foreign competition can produce quality goods at lower cost, the great sucking sound will be business and profits going abroad.

References

1. Toshihiro Nishiguchi, *Competing Systems in Automotive Components Supply*, IMVP Working Paper (Cambridge, MA: MIT, May 1987), 15.
2. James P. Womack, Daniel T. Jones, and Daniel Roos, *The Machine That Changed the World: The Story of Lean Manufacturing* (New York: Harper Perennial, 1991).
3. "The Technology Payoff," *Business Week,* June 14, 1993.
4. "New Paths to Success," *Fortune,* June 12, 1995 (an article adapted from the book *Harmony* by Arno Penzias [New York: Harper Collins, 1995]).
5. M. Hammer and J. Champy, *Reengineering the Corporation* (New York: Harper Business, 1993).
6. Nishiguchi, *Competing Systems,* 15.

7

Networks for Agility

We should think of virtual operations as being *static* or *dynamic*. Chapter 6 gives examples of *static* virtualness in which two or more partners cooperate on an ongoing basis. This chapter discusses *dynamic* virtualness in which the mix of partners can change in a fluid manner in order to deal with rapidly changing situations. Dynamic virtualness is more difficult to organize but presents greater opportunities. It may become essential in many areas of business as the rate of change continues to accelerate.

Increasing Complexity

Products and services are becoming steadily more complex. The complexity is hidden under the covers as it is in a car or camcorder and gives the customer valuable features and greater reliability. It allows products to be customized. Most products no longer have one standard model but a large number of variations. Seiko markets 3,000 different watches. Creating today's products requires an immense array of skills—research skills, mechanical design, microelectronics, programming, factory engineering, marketing, professionalism with a great diversity of technologies. While the skill requirements are increasing, the windows of opportunity are getting smaller. Product life cycles are shorter, and less time is available to get products to market.

As competition intensifies worldwide, products must be excellent in order to survive. Customers have become used to quality and increasingly demand it. A key success factor in corporations is having the set of core competences needed for excellence. That set of competences is often too much for one corporation, so we are seeing more and more partner arrangements where competences in different corporations are linked. Even the largest corporations today are using external partners, sometimes large numbers of partners, because they cannot maintain world-class capability in every aspect of their business. Computers facilitate partnering, and worldwide networks are linking core competences in multiple corporations. It is increasingly necessary to synthesize new competitive capabilities quickly.

> **Pooling core competences is very different from using other vendors' components or products. With a rich mix of competences, corporations can create more interesting or complex products and services.**

Pooling competences is essential in an age of complexity. It is particularly valuable for small companies becuase it greatly extends the market opportunities available to them.

Agile Manufacturing

The term *agile manufacturing* is used to describe manufacturing done by networks of partners who share core competences, rather than merely supply components. The term was popularized by the Iacocca Institute.[1] Agile manufacturing is replacing both mass production and Japanese-style lean manufacturing. It is a response to the changing marketplace in which customers want more choices, customization, and solutions rather than off-the-shelf products. Information processing is permitting companies to offer individualized solutions while maintaining high production volumes. The goal is to create better value for customers.

> **Agility is concerned with the dynamic assembly of core competences from different corporations to react to a fast-changing marketplace that demands excellence and very flexible capabilities.**

Agility should apply to all types of corporate activities, not just manufacturing. In the best cases the assembly of core competences from different companies enables corporations to build all-star capability, selecting the best from different organizations. The cocktail of combined competences can achieve results that no single corporation can. This is becoming essential for world-class competition.

The groupings that are assembled may have short or long lives. The group might stay together only for the creation of one proposal; it might exist for the duration of a short-lived product; or it might have a long ongoing relationship. There may be dormant partnerships waiting to spring into action when needed. Some of the best products reflect a stream of improvements that have evolved though many variations over many years. A virtual group may stay together throughout the product evolution.

> **Agility is about shifting patterns of virtual relationships. Competition on a planet laced by electronic highways is turbulent, fast-changing, and unpredictable. Agility is needed to respond to the turbulence and make money out of it.**

Unlike corporations of the past, the cybercorp must be designed to *thrive* on change and uncertainty.

Pooled Resources

Sometimes small companies in the same business form a network that allows them to bid on large jobs. For example, the Kentucky Wood Manufacturers Network links companies none of which employ more than forty people. As a result they won a $2.5 million Disney World contract that they divided up on the basis of their capabilities.[2] It makes sense for small companies to pool their resources so that they can obtain lucrative contracts.

Sometimes the pooling is entirely informal. For example, a small company that builds corporate software applications may sometimes need skills that it does not have in-house, so it makes informal agreements with companies having those skills. It may have one associate good at designing Web pages, another skilled at process modeling, another that specializes in security, and so on. It calls on them when it needs to assemble a set of talents that enable it to bid on a lucrative job.

Some such networks have a fixed membership; others have a floating membership or have loosely affiliated associates who can join in when needed. Some have a formal structure; others have little or no structure. There needs to be a clear agreement on the ways in which companies are prepared to work together. Networks of companies doing *physical* craftsmanship may be in the same local area; networks doing *knowledge* work may extend around the planet.

Eleven British chemical manufacturers that are normally highly competitive formed an umbrella organization called UK Fine Chemicals so that they could market themselves, primarily in the United States, as a single virtual company. They combine whatever skills or capacities are needed in order to obtain a contract and then farm it out among themselves on a previously agreed basis. The customer is effectively dealing with a single supplier.[3]

Seven Canadian health care institutions around London, Ontario, are linked by a fiber-optic cable system called LARG*net so that they can share medical image databases, access to specialist consultation, video teaching, and other resources. The seven institutions seem like a single health care facility. Increasingly fiber optics will link large numbers of facilities separated by large distances, even worldwide. Clinics in remote locations can have access to world-class expertise.

Much pooling of resources is done by small companies. Sometimes, however, giant companies cooperate to create facilities that they can share. In the 1970s the U.S. auto industry had to develop catalytic converters in order to conform to government regulations. Each company spent over $250 million to achieve the same result. Today, GM, Ford, and Chrysler have a consortium, USCAR, that develops new technologies or components that the car companies can all use.

Cybercorp Webs

Cybercorp webs are groups of companies with an agreement that they can quickly form a virtual company in order to seize a market opportunity by pooling competences that they collectively possess. The companies in the web may be intensely competitive with one another, except when they pool resources. The web has an umbrella corporation with which customers interact and may have its own presence on the Internet. A cybercorp web is *greater than the sum of its parts* because it can achieve results by synthesizing diverse competences that the individual companies could not achieve alone.

A *virtual company* is a combination of resources from different places assembled and managed so as to behave like a real company. A *cybercorp web* is an association of companies organized with the capability to quickly assemble and disassemble virtual companies on an opportunistic basis.

The web must have a way of knowing the collective core competences available to it and how they change with time. It needs to *prequalify* the capabilities of members of the web and to keep this information up-to-date. The web needs a computerized knowledge infrastructure. It should continually assess what new competences should be added and what other potential partners could be approached if necessary.

Precision in communications can be achieved by using common computerized tools such as CAD, CASE, a common software repository, bulletin boards, groupware, or other means of cooperation. Chrysler provides training to its suppliers so that they can employ uniform CAD software, linked over networks. The U.S. government computer-aided logistics system (CALS) initiative requires that technical specifications, drawings, manuals, and other documents be computerized and follow standards that enable them to be transmitted over networks. These standards are being adopted in much of the world.

In the advertising industry, associations of agencies existed long before cyberspace. Today, such associations are becoming linked on the Internet. The members can then share competences and troll for business worldwide.

A small agency in Kuala Lumpur, for example, can use talents from Britain or France in order to obtain key contracts in Malaysia. Specimens of copy and artwork can be edited and worked on jointly in multiple locations with face-to-face conversations on PC screens.

AgileWeb is a network of machine shops in Pennsylvania linked by a computer network so that they can create mix-and-match combinations in order to bid on large contracts. AgileWeb was created with federal funding to gain knowledge about how to operate shifting patterns of virtual companies. As AgileWeb marketed its joint competences it found that there was much to learn about doing business in this way. It established a set of guidelines for forming temporary virtual organizations in response to opportunities and established rules for how profits would be shared.[4]

From the customer's point of view there must appear to be one organization with whom the customer has a single contract. When things go wrong there must be no finger-pointing among the companies in the web.

AgileWeb created a fourteen-step methodology for identifying opportunities, qualifying the customer, making a go or no-go recommendation, and then developing the virtual organization that will carry out the work. Memorandums of understanding among the participating companies are filled in, and then a memorandum of understanding is established with the customer. There may be several iterations of these memorandums, and then the customer contract is signed. AgileWeb developed generic agreements that can be used repeatedly by changing some of the details for each virtual organization that is set up.

Emergency Room

A hospital emergency room receives a call, and a helicopter races to the scene of an emergency. After assessing the situation, the staff members on the helicopter radio information about the resources needed.

In some ways an agile cybercorp is like a hospital emergency room.[5] It does not know what situations will arise or what resources will be needed. It has a variety of resources available to it, human, technical, and institutional resources, some of which it owns but many of which it does not. The hospital ER needs access to medical specialists from elsewhere. It may need specialized equipment, or access to data located anywhere in the world. General hospital facilities may be brought into use that are not part of the emergency room. The staff of the emergency room responds to unexpected situations with a great sense of urgency and rapidly assembles whatever teams or resources are needed, many of them coming from other organizations. It sometimes has to use resources from direct competitors. Similarly, a cybercorp web should be able to deal with unexpected situations, linking together partners so as to minimize the concept-to-cash time. When new opportunities arise, the ambulances race out.

In medical emergencies, people from different organizations expect to work together intensively, joining their different expertises to achieve a common goal. Personnel are given the authority to command resources and to reprioritize the allocation of these resources as situations demand. The efficient cybercorp web is similar.

The structure of the emergency room is deliberately designed to deal with the unpredictable. Similarly, the cybercorp web should be designed for fast unpredictable change. The strategic goals of the emergency room are clear. The strategic goals of the cybercorp web should be spelled out clearly, and the structure should be designed to meet those goals.

Prime Contractor

An important distinction exists between *democratic* webs and *prime-contractor* webs.

AgileWeb is a democratic web; any corporation in the group may or may not participate in a virtual operation. In some situations, however, a prime-contractor approach is better. When most people build a house they deal with a general contractor that hires other companies to do work. The general contractor is delivering a solution rather than selling a product. Many types of customers today want solutions, not just products. A prime-contractor approach is needed when the company delivering a solution needs to be totally in charge. Hollywood studios, for example, make a film by farming out work to numerous contractors but retaining creative control. The prime contractor need not be the largest company. A small company can employ IBM, AT&T, giant consultants, and others. A cybercorp web linking many companies can operate by appointing a prime contractor to head each virtual company that is formed. The customer then deals only with the prime contractor.

Reasons for Agility

Agility, the ability to dynamically assemble and disassemble core competences from different companies, can have the following advantages:

- A corporation can tackle far more complex tasks by assembling the necessary core competences. It may be able to create products or services not otherwise possible.
- The corporation can latch onto an exploding marketplace trend and assemble the capability needed to ride up the curve.

- Speed can be achieved by having different partners in different places work *concurrently,* using computer tools for coordination. Concept-to-cash time can be minimized, and the corporation can play in the earlier, more profitable, part of a window of opportunity.
- A small company can be part of a group that gives it access to more customers or new markets, as was the case with UK Fine Chemicals.
- The corporation may appear to have larger size or greater capability and hence be more likely to gain a sale.
- Customers increasingly want a *solution,* not merely an off-the-shelf product. Multicorporate linkages are often needed to provide skills, information, and services along with the product.
- Risk can be minimized by avoiding ownership of expensive resources. If an initiative does not work out as planned, the corporation is not saddled with facilities it cannot use.
- Costs can be lowered when multiple companies share infrastructure or resources.
- Low-cost resources may be used in countries with lower salaries.
- Much more brainpower can be made available for research, development, and design.
- Multiple companies needing the same facilities may develop them jointly, as the U.S. car industry is doing with its joint USCAR corporation.

New Problems

The above reasons for agility are so important that cybercorp webs are likely to become a major component of twenty-first-century business. Operating with dynamic, agile linkages brings many new problems, but groups of corporations that solve these problems will have major competitive advantages.

We are in the early stages of a historic transition from mass production to agile production, and single-company operations to cybercorp webs. Like other transitions of this magnitude, like the coming of mass production in its day, this transition will take many years, perhaps decades, to progress from the early pioneering to a time of well-established guidelines, methodologies, laws, accounting practices, and training and a well-prepared workforce. During the uncertainties of the transition the companies that go first will often be the winners and those that do not change will be pushed into the low-value-added end of the economy. Future cybercorp webs will need methodologies and models of how to operate. Organizations such as the Agile Manufacturing Enterprise Forum[6] and the Iacocca Institute[7] in the United States and the Fraunhofer system of institutes in Germany[8] are concerned with establishing guidelines, practices, templates of contracts, and so on. Guidelines and templates are evolving for establishing such methodologies and for making them work well. With experience, the language of generic agreements will be better established. Some of the issues will be difficult to resolve at first but steadily a modus operandum will become established, which the participants will understand and agree to. The Iacocca Institute has listed barriers to agility and set about finding ways to remove the barriers.[9]

Customer Participation

Involving the customer in specification, design, and production is essential in agile operations.

An old-line manufacturer of hydraulic valves, Ross Operating Valves, created a facility at its plant in Lavonia, Georgia, for making customized valves where the customer could design the valve jointly with Ross engineers using CAD software and Ross's library of digital valve designs. Ross engineers transfer the design to numerically controlled machine tools and fabricate a prototype that is tested and shipped to the customer. The customer can request modifications to the prototype. As soon as the prototype is approved, the valve can be put into production. Ross reduced the time needed to design and create prototype valves to one day. Ross does not charge extra for this custom-design process; it is part of their marketing strategy. Ross still makes off-the-shelf catalog valves, but since this Ross/Flex operation was introduced business has increased dramatically, and Ross has extended it to plants in Frankfurt and Tokyo.

Ross then went a step further. Reacting to customer desire to save time and be yet more flexible it allowed customers to make valves themselves on numerically controlled machine tools, or have them made at a facility near their own location. For a fee Ross downloads proprietary design software, specimen designs from the library, and instructions for the numerically controlled tools. What used to be a mechanical operation making catalog products became an information-dominated business giving a higher return on investment. The Internet can make computerized customization like this available worldwide.

The Pricing Ritual

In much of the world's car industry a ritual game takes place around supplier pricing. Winning a major contract is very important to the suppliers because in addition to the large volume the follow-up business may last for ten years. The car manufacturer is under great pressure to reduce costs, and bidding suppliers know that cost will be a major factor determining whether they win the bid.

Under intense competitive pressure suppliers sometimes make a bid below cost. They understand that once the car is in production they can raise the price, with appropriate excuses, and the car assembler will probably have to live with the increase because it would be very expensive to switch suppliers once production with its heavy investment in production tooling is under way.

Often low-price bids win contracts and realistic bids lose contracts. The supplier calculates the chance of being able to raise the price later. The manufacturer knows that this is going on because it has happened so many times in the past, and so expects the supplier to raise its prices. The manufacturer would like to understand the supplier's costs in order to estimate possible price increases, but the supplier keeps the costs secret, hoping to hide eventual profit figures from the manufacturer. A similar game goes on in other industries, for example, with building contractors and their suppliers.

When the bids are awarded, the suppliers make prototype parts and the manufacturer's early attempts at assembly reveal many problems. Parts do not fit; the car squeaks; parts expand differently in hot weather; and so on. The problems are steadily worked out. Sometimes, after fine-tuning, the car manufacturer goes to other potential suppliers with the information that has been learned and tries to drive the price down. The original bid winner is upset about this because it invested in the joint development. It is all part of the battle for price reduction.

This battle between manufacturer and suppliers causes the suppliers to guard information on improved production techniques. They often find ways to lower production costs, and they do not want competitive bidders to find out. Because of this there is little communication between manufacturer and supplier when it would benefit both of them to learn from one another about potential joint improvements.

Running Changes

When this ritual was a way of life in Detroit, Japanese car companies were developing more intricate relationships with suppliers. Instead of the tight secrecy and mutual suspicion of the competitive bidding process, Japan's lean manufacturers and suppliers worked intimately together to find ways of mutually reducing costs. This benefits both sides.

Once the car is in production an ongoing succession of changes have to be made. Modifications in parts are required to make production easier or to solve problems discovered when the cars are on the road. The assembler and suppliers have to work closely together to make many hundreds of these "running changes." The more they make, the more likely customers are to be pleased with the car.

Both manufacturer and supplier expect to see the cost and quality steadily improve as each climbs the learning curves. A contract exists between the manufacturer and supplier that establishes the ground rules for determining the supplier's prices. The manufacturer and supplier may agree on cost reduction curves over the life of the contract, based on their experience. If the supplier achieves more cost reduction than the curve, it can keep the resulting profits. The contract also spells out the rules about quality requirements, proprietary rights, and mechanisms for ordering and just-in-time delivery. This contract is the basis for a cooperative relationship instead of the Western adversarial competitive bidding relationship.

The manufacturer establishes its market goal and target price and then works with suppliers to establish how this price can be met with an acceptable profit for both sides. The manufacturer and supplier together analyze the costs of each step of the production process and identify any factors that could lower the cost. The cost may be lowered by redesigning the part, combining it with other parts, perfecting its manufacturing process, introducing new tooling, and improving computer-to-computer links between manufacturer and supplier. The manufacturer and supplier work out a formula for sharing profits from their joint cost reductions.

It is in the interest of the manufacturer to help the supplier reduce costs if this lowers the price of the goods supplied, and it is always in the interest of the manufacturer to help the supplier improve quality. Working as a team they can jointly improve the end product.

Not Sole Source

The myth exists in the West that Japanese manufacturers are able to cooperate so closely with their suppliers beause they have an incestuous relationship with a sole-source supplier; the supplier is like a member of the family. This is not the case. On the contrary, the manufacturer has more than one supplier of the same part whenever practical.

Surprisingly, sole-sourcing is more common in Western car factories than in Japan, as the following table shows:

	Japan	Europe	U.S. Factories in the U.S.
Percentage of parts sole-sourced	12.1	32.9	69.3

From the IMVP World Assembly Plant Survey, 1990.

The view of the mass-production world is that sole-source vendors can achieve larger production volumes for a part and hence can make it at lower cost. The view of lean manufacturers is that, above a certain size, volume has little effect on unit cost and that competing sources of supply are needed in order to keep suppliers on their toes. Lean manufacturers like to have multiple sources so that each supplier tries harder to improve quality, meet just-in-time schedules, and climb a learning curve that will result in lower costs.

Those parts that *are* sole-sourced tend to be those for which massive investments are needed in tools. They are the complex systems such as transaxles, engine computers, and so forth. Simpler parts tend to have multiple suppliers.

When a manufacturer has two suppliers of a part, if one fails to meet delivery schedules or produces parts with defects, the manufacturer can shift *some* of the volume to the better supplier. Japanese car assemblers rarely dismiss a supplier who defaults, as Western assemblers might; they move a fraction of the business away from the supplier for a given period of time as a penalty. This can seriously affect the supplier's profit, so it provides a very strong incentive for suppliers to perform well. It maintains rather than destroys the complex long-term relationship between the manufacturer and supplier in which both try to climb mutually reinforcing learning curves. Lean manufacturers do occasionally dismiss suppliers, but this is an extreme measure.

Rules and Measurements

The view in the West is often that business relationships in Japan are based on familylike coziness or on some uniquely Japanese culture of cooperation. In reality Japanese manufacturers and suppliers have no more affection for one another than manufacturers and suppliers in the West. The relationship is based on skillfully designed processes, logical sets of rules, and appropriate measurements. The same rules and measurements can work in any country.

Although trust is essential in virtual relationships, the relationship between producers and suppliers must be based on sets of rules, procedures, and measurements that are spelled out in contracts. These rules and procedures are designed to benefit both sides mutually to the maximum extent, recognizing that both sides benefit if they jointly strive for improved performance. The rules are designed to encourage constant attention to zero-defect performance and continuous effort to reduce costs.

As we increasingly use cybercorp webs, measurements that can be monitored in real time will be important for making agile associations succeed.

Virtual BHAGs

As discussed in Chapter 5, some companies lead exciting lives by setting Big Hairy Audacious Goals (BHAGs). The term "BHAG" seems to have high appeal to the cybercorp generation, and many conversations take place about what BHAGs are appropriate.

When cybercorps are designed to link together core competences from different companies, this extends what is possible.

With cybercorp mechanisms, audacious goals can be much more audacious.

The building of the Boeing 777 was an extraordinary example of corporate cooperation. It was the first commercial airliner to be designed and put into production without paper. All partners shared the same CAD software and could interchange designs worldwide over networks. Every part of the plane was modeled with this software. As the components were "assembled" with three-dimensional modeling, many design changes were made. Designers and potential customers could "walk through" the plane in virtual reality, check every aspect of it, and request modifications. Many designs were done concurrently in different organizations, and the software ensured that they would work together. By the time the physical components were ready to assemble they fitted with few problems. The software greatly reduced the time and cost of development, and it facilitated better design. Boeing scoured the world for the best capability. Because everybody used the same CAD software Boeing had great freedom in building an alliance of designers and manufacturers in the United States, Japan, and Europe. Some of the partners were competitors—manufacturers of competing aircraft or aircraft components. There were many *cross-enterprise teams* linking suppliers, consultants, and potential customers.

The Boeing 777 will have a long life, and during its life enormous numbers of changes will be made to it. When the plane at last became physical reality, a most dramatic test was done on it. It was subject to steadily increasing stress, measuring every aspect of it. The forces on the plane were increased until the plane finally disintegrated with explosive violence. It survived much greater stress than the maximum the design called for, which indicated that new models can have a stretched fuselage and greater capacity. There will be different engines, new control systems, and many models customized for different airlines. The CAD software will help the partners participate in the changes throughout the life of the plane.

Global Networking

Internet tools give their users an extraordinary ability to search for information that may be anywhere in the world on hundreds of thousands of bulletin boards. A report from the Iacocca Institute, *21st Century Manufacturing Enterprise Strategy: An Industry-Led View,* envisioned a resource called Factory America Net (FAN) that would provide immediate access to detailed information about hundreds of thousands of companies, their capabilities, expertise, and facilities, and their terms for participating in collaborations.[10] The IT industry research consortium Microelectronics and Computer Technology Corporation (MCC) developed the Enterprise Integration Network (EINet), a platform for similar commercial directory services on the Internet, along with funds remittance capabilities. Although EINet's databases are steadily expanding, EINet has national competitors such as CommerceNet and more local competitors such as ECNet, which is aimed at small and medium-size manufacturing companies in the Southwest. Such systems can help in the formation of virtual partnerships. Like everything else on the Internet, these resources will become worldwide, thereby expanding the market of both the participants and the information provider.

In the cyberspace world all manner of agile and virtual relationships are possible. As we move into the twenty-first century there will be numerous shifting patterns of affiliations. Some organizations may be nerve centers linking together virtual partners for different purposes. There is much to learn about what types of affiliations are best and how to make them succeed. What forms of contracts are needed? How will they work in countries with different cultures such as China? Could the highly successful Japanese *keiretsu* become multinational? What will be the effect of different national behavior patterns? How will high-salary and low-salary countries interact? Will the Internet create one melting pot, or will there be different cyberspace strata around the planet?

Relationships will take many forms, the successful ones being designed to create maximum customer value in a marketplace that is changing in fast and unpredictable ways.

References

1. S. L. Goldman, ed., *Agility Intial Survey,* Working Paper no. 94-03 (Agility Forum, Iacocca Institute at Lehigh University, Bethlehem, PA, 1994).
2. Steven L. Goldman, Roger N. Nagel, and Kenneth Preiss, *Agile Competitors and Virtual Organizations: Strategies for Enriching the Customer* (New York: Van Nostrand Reinhold, 1995).
3. Ibid.

4. AgileWeb was formed by the Lehigh Valley office of the state-supported Ben Franklin Partnership, Bethlehem, PA.

5. The emergency room analogy was first used by Phil Weinzimer, a consultant to Unisys, and was used in Goldman et al., *Agile Competitors.*

6. Agile Manufacturing Enterprise Forum (Agility Forum), Iacocca Institute, Bethlehem, PA, fax: (610) 694-0542.

7. Iacocca Institute, Lehigh University, Bethlehem, PA, fax: (610) 758-6550

8. There are many Fraunhofer Institutes for different types of industry, for example, for production systems and design technology: Fraunhofer-Institut für Produktionsanlagen und KonstruktionstechniK (IPK), Berlin d-52074, fax: 49 (0) 2 41/89 04-198.

9. S. L. Goldman and K. Preiss, eds., and R. N. Nagel and R. Dove with fifteen industry executives, *21st Century Manufacturing Enterprise Strategy: An Industry-Led View* (Bethlehem, PA: Iacocca Institute at Lehigh University, 1991).

10. Ibid.

8

Ecosystems in the Cybercorp Economy

As corporations become creaturelike, with nervous systems and cybercorp mechanisms, they live in a jungle with electronic links to other creatures, all jockeying for position and struggling to make a profit. The jungle, like jungles in nature, evolves its own ecosystems. Cybercorps of immense diversity are synergistically dependent on one another, with rapidly evolving codependencies. Some corporations in an ecosystem are connected in *virtual* relationships; most are not. Some corporations become king of their territory; others carve out a lucrative niche; some become victims. Cybercorp mechanisms change the relationships among corporations in complex ways, and to survive it will be desirable for managers to understand the ecosystems they play in.

James Moore, in a seminal book, illustrated how the classical view of competition has become too simplistic.[1] Instead of merely competing head to head within their industry, corporations are becoming linked into ecosystems that often span multiple industries. There are many such ecosystems, each with its own synergistically dependent flora and fauna. New ecosystems are being invented fast and change fast. In the cyberspace age they increasingly span the world. Moore points out that much insight can be gained by studying biological ecosystems and how they evolve and learning where business ecosystems have behavior patterns similar to biological ecosystems. In business, as in nature, diverse organisms struggle for survival and growth within an overall environment, but that environment is being drastically changed by cybercorp evolution, which makes it global, electronically networked, automated, fast reacting, and capable of high complexity.

A *biological ecosystem* is a community of organisms interacting with one another and with their environment. Similarly, a *cybercorp ecosystem* is a community of cybercorps interacting with one another and with their environment.

During its great period, Apple Computer was successful because a large number of application developers made the Macintosh their platform of choice. Apple encouraged this by aggressively building relationships with colleges, publishers, advertising agents, communities that benefited from the Mac's superior graphics, and, particularly important, with software developers. Apple created a fiercely loyal ecosystem and gained more strength from this ecosystem than it did from merely its own virtues. Apple stumbled in 1995, not because competing products were better, but because the PC community led by Intel and Microsoft had built a larger ecosystem that poured much more money into software, networks, notebook computers, and so forth, so that the PC rather than the Mac became the platform of choice for many product developers because they could achieve higher sales.

In the 1990s the environment of the pharmaceutical industry changed as public concern grew about the escalating costs of health care. The United States focused on managed care systems (the "health maintenance organization" concept) that link doctors, hospitals, cost controls, and health insurance. Some of the drug companies set out to examine the overall health care problems of society to see what new roles they might play. They might be able to empower the public to take charge of more of certain health care problems themselves, with appropriate education, medical equipment, and access to doctors when necessary. There are various ways in which pharmaceutical companies could take a leadership role in a broader health care ecosystem.

Business ecosystems range from small to gigantic. A flower shop might be linked to international florist services, a nearby computerized greenhouse, local gardeners, restaurants, hotels, organizations that provide banquet services, and so on. At the other extreme, the world's vision of information superhighways needs to link telephone, television, satellite, cellular radio, and computer network providers with companies that provide films, television, magazines, electronic books, and libraries of information of all types. The U.S. telephone deregulation of 1996 enables these companies to battle or converge in an ecosystem that will exceed $1 trillion in annual sales. In the future it will no longer be clear what is a news magazine, a cable TV company, or a telephone company.

Many business ecosystems link corporations in multiple industries. To bring the benefits of the "information highway" into the home, telephone companies link to film studios, television set manufacturers to computer vendors, software companies to sports management companies, and all of these will vie for synergies and supremacy in the same jungle. Traditional ideas about vertical or horizontal integration within one industry break down. Successful corporations need to build and manage relationships across multiple industries.

In the cybercorp economy, with virtual and agile linkages, businesses *coevolve* rather than simply *compete.* There is a complex interplay between competitive and cooperative business strategies. The best strategic managers think not just about products and competition within their industry, but about how they might play a profitable long-lasting role in a cross-industry ecosystem. Relatively few managers have adopted this ecosystem thinking as yet, but as it becomes widely accepted it will bring very fast change and many surprises.

Ruinously Intense Competition

In the cybercorp world certain types of competition will become ruinously intense. If you are buying a music disk with your personal computer you can use a software agent that searches the Internet looking for the lowest price for that disk. The use of such agents is just beginning today, but as they mature their use will become widespread. When people who buy goods use computers to search for the lowest price, vendors' profit margins will be cut to the bone (especially as the Internet goes to cheap-labor countries).

The cream skimming described in Chapter 5 presents major opportunities to entrepreneurs but will have a devastating effect on companies whose cream is skimmed. Telephone companies make a fat profit on long-distance calls but almost no profit on local calls. Internet operators are rapidly improving their capability to provide telephone calls over the Internet, and this could skim the cream of telephony. Similarly, cybercorps can skim the cream of retail banks, publishers, stock brokers, insurance brokers, mail-order houses, and other service industries. Deregulation will make protected cream skimable. Middleman organizations of most types can be bypassed.

In the early 1990s U.S. airlines went through a period of intense competition triggered by deregulation and electronic booking systems, and they piled up losses of $13 billion—equal approximately to all the profits in the history of American aviation. "Open skies" policies for international airlines, combined with electronic booking, will be a disaster for many tax-payer-supported national carriers. Deregulation of the electric utilities will bring fierce competition from independent power plants made in countries such as South Korea.

Many high-margin products are being reinvented as commodity products. The computer business, for example, evolved quickly from very-high-margin mainframes to cutthroat competition in PCs. The customers wanted open systems with plug-in components. I used to pay $400 for eyeglasses (which I lose regularly), but now I pay $10 at Walgreens and find them more satisfactory. Commodity products can be easily copied. Copycat products are made in vast quantities in cheap-labor countries, and such competition has wiped out whole industries in the West. The United States, more than any country, is the land of television; the first competing networks spread there and the TV industry took off with feverish enthusiasm. Yet America lost all its TV set manufacturing to foreigners, at first to Japan but then Japan was hit by the same problem; Japan now imports nearly three times as many TV sets as it exports. No videotape machine of any type is made in the United States, although video recording was largely invented there. In the next ten years vast fortunes will be made as television becomes digital, but this time with understanding and management of the complex ecosystems of the digital media business.

Most new software tools are easy to imitate and can be built in India or Russia, where skilled programmers earn peanuts. The companies that remain highly profitable in the computer or software business are those that understand the ecosystems they operate in and discover how to play a dominant role in them, like Intel and Microsoft. These companies spend a large amount of time understanding, building, and nurturing relationships with the other members of their ecosystem.

The *Encyclopedia Britannica,* the grandest of encyclopedias, felt it was immune to competition because of its reputation and hernia-giving size. For over 200 years *Britannica* was the world's best-selling encyclopedia, but in 1994 its sales went over a cliff. It suddenly became number three, overtaken, not by its traditional competitors, but by Microsoft and Grolier. People didn't want to buy their children a dry twenty-volume set of books that didn't change for ten years when the children wanted a PCs, and for less than a tenth of the *Britannica* price you could buy up-to-date CD-ROM encyclopedias with music and pizzazz. The CD-ROM seemed an ideal medium for an encyclopedia, not only because it can hold hundreds of thousands of pages but also because software is so effective at searching and interrelating facts. *Britannica*'s North American president, Joe Esposito, concluded that it would probably be impossible for him to make a profit with either books or CD-ROMs.

Esposito set out to create an entirely new type of business in which *Britannica* was on the World Wide Web linkable by mouse-clocks to any knowledge accessible on the Web. This facility could potentially grow into a directory of all electronically stored human knowledge. *Britannica* would charge a subscription fee for it, and success depended on *Britannica*'s being able to establish business agreements with vast numbers of copyright owners. *Britannica* decided that it could not survive as a conventional product company; the only way it could survive was to *invent and control an entirely new ecosystem.*

Avoiding Ruinous Competition

> **Under what circumstances do cybercorp mechanisms drive down profits, and under what circumstances do they lead to sustainable high margins? Managers everywhere need to understand the answers to this question.**

Unfortunately most managers still think in terms of the old paradigms of business; they are concerned with product-to-product competition within their own industry, which can lead to computer-aided price war. When profits turn to losses many corporations react by downsizing. They cut employees and slash expenses, sometimes on a grand scale. This temporarily restores profit, but morale sinks, the infrastructure is damaged, it becomes more difficult to move into new areas, and unless a different strategy is put into place the brutal effects of cybercorp competition will return.

> **A cybercorp should try to sustain high margins by making itself unique.**

It may be unique because of special skills or art, as with a fashion designer, top architect, or movie director, or because of the way it looks after its customers. It may be unique because of an unbeatable mix of competencies. Sometimes patents protect uniqueness, as in the pharmaceutical industry, but increasingly uniqueness comes from creating, or playing a leading role in, a corporate ecosystem.

Value-stream teams should be designed to constantly pay attentive care to customers and to determine how they can delight the customer. Rather than selling a product, it is often desirable to think in terms of providing a solution to a customer's problem. Complex solutions often need a diversity of skills from different organizations, but the customer wants to deal with *one* organization, so that organization should use virtual linkages. Sometimes the virtual linkages are assembled quickly from prequalified partners in the agile manner described in the previous chapter.

Often the key way to avoid profit destruction from commoditization is to learn how to play a dominant role in an ecosystem. Unlike biological ecosystems, a business ecosystem has an intelligently planned purpose and vision for the future. Each member must examine what role it wants to play within that vision and to what extent it can influence or manipulate the overall ecosystem. Some corporations maneuver themselves into a dominant role in their ecosystems. Managers everywhere need to understand the ecosystems they play in, the jostling for position within these ecosystems, and how the ecosystems evolve in a cybercorp world.

When Intel made memory chips it was initially very profitable. But memory chips became a commodity, with aggressive competition from Japan and the Asian "tigers." Prices collapsed spectacularly in the mid-1980s. Intel could not make a profit in simple price competition with chip makers in the Pacific Rim. However, from 1991 to 1995 Intel was one of the world's most profitable companies because it made the 386, 486, and Pentium chips, which were the heart of Intel-compatible PCs and as such dominated a vast ecosystem of hardware and software vendors. In a brilliant campaign of managing relationships, Intel succeeded in getting its *intel inside* branding mark on both PC advertisements and on the machines themselves.

A memory chip has a simple structure that is easy to replicate, but the structure of advanced processor chips is exceedingly difficult to copy. Intel spent a fortune on chip design and innovation to keep ahead of would-be clone makers. In a gutsy role of the dice it spent over a quarter of its revenue on design and fabrication facilities, and this huge expenditure enabled it to maintain its controlling position in the PC ecosystem.

Microsoft had a controlling role in the same ecosystem becaue it made the operating systems and office software that the ecosystem depended on. Microsoft struggled to create de facto standards and ensure that software vendors everywhere created software that was Microsoft compatible. It kept its prices low to ensure sales in large enough volume that Microsoft dominated the industry. Microsoft's software, such as Windows 95, burnt through computer power even when running simple applications. It would have been possible to run spreadsheets and word processing with far less power. There might as well have been a conspiracy between Microsoft and Intel because as Microsoft expanded its sales there was ravenous demand for the power that Intel could provide. Intel constantly redesigned its chips to make them faster than Intel "clones" and drove its prices down as production volume soared. Microsoft took advantage of the soaring processor power to add new features to its software that, like real-time spell-checking, needed ever more power from Intel. A galaxy of hardware vendors, software vendors, service firms, and consultants evolved to play in the ecosystem dominated by Intel and Microsoft. Some of them established profitable niches.

The big winners will increasingly be those who work out how they can play a controlling or dominant role in the ecosystems they are part of. Microsoft, while less than a tenth of the size of IBM, led and shaped the behavior of many hundreds of associated companies, and so did Benetton when less than a tenth of the size of the clothing giants, and Rupert Murdoch when his operation was much smaller than Time Warner. As in all business, power brings antagonisms, and there are intense anti-Microsoft and anti-Murdoch feelings. While companies co-evolve in ecosystems, there will be constant struggles for supremacy among the ecosystems.

When executives think in terms of ecosystems rather than one industry, they can play a grander game, often with higher return on investment.

The Cybercorp Gardener

Competition is essential to society; it keeps corporations on their toes and trims the fat. By synergistic interactions within a business ecosystem can strengthen the parties involved. For example, to build the 777 jetliner, Boeing assembled an international ecosystem in which hundreds of corporations had to learn how to develop a plane in a fundamentally better way, using CAD tools linked to global networking.

In a contrary example, many software companies have created tools to help develop software. Unfortunately, tools from different vendors did different parts of the job but not all of it. What was needed was a high level of cooperation among the vendors to integrate design tools, code generators, templates, libraries of application objects, and so on. But competing software companies copied each other's tools rather than attempting to create such an ecosystem. Most of the companies had an arrogant "not invented here" attitude about embracing software from other vendors. Instead of standing on each other's shoulders, they stood on each other's feet.

In Boeing's new ecosystem, corporations that were bitter competitors cooperated, and all companies that were part of the ecosystem were strengthened by it. The software tool companies, on the other hand, largely failed to strengthen one another, and in many cases destroyed one another.

The ecosystem leader is like a flower gardener selecting species, weeding, and fertilizing, with a vision of the future. This intelligent guidance is very different from uncontrolled competition between species. Adam Smith expressed the view that free competition is an invisible hand guiding capitalist society. In the best ecosystems the invisible hand is replaced by the intelligent hand of a gardener. In the complexity of the cybercorp economy, competition between ecosystems will tend to replace competition between simple products because electronics can make simple competition ruinously intense. There will be competition among gardeners who know how gardens can delight their customers, rather than uncontrolled competition between species.

Couturier Ecosystems

The garment industry has equipment that does quick-and-easy three-dimensional body scans of customers. The results can be transmitted to equipment that designs clothes that fit perfectly. Cloth that the customers has chosen is cut and sewn by computerized machines.

High-tech selling and production of clothes will require new ecosystems in the garment business. TC², the Textile/Clothing Technology Corporation, a 200-company consortium, demonstrates at the Bobbin show how a designer in New York can be linked by video to a booth with a customer where unique clothes are designed. Computers prepare screen-print color separation data and send instructions to laser-controlled cutting machines. Perfectly fitting clothes are delivered overnight. Many shops that charge $1,000 for ill-fitting men's suits will probably not survive.

The results of your body scan can be stored on the Net (or on your own disk or smart card). Customers will be able to choose clothes from a vast computerized collection of fashions, select the style, the cloth, the colors and pattern, buttons, and other items. They may explore fashion photographs, assembled digitally, of themselves wearing the clothes before they buy.

My wife assures me that many women will not buy clothes that way because clothes buying is a therapeutic recreation where the fun lies in trying the clothes on. As rag-trade ecosystems evolve, a viable part of the market will be shops for people for whom clothes shopping is fun. It will be desirable to distinguish clearly between shopping-as-entertainment and minimum-effort buying—between customers who love shopping and customers who won't go near a shop.

As cybercorp ecosystems evolve there will be much to be learned about adapting virtual operations to market realities.

Coopetition

Fierce competition brings prices down. However, mutual cooperation and joint learning can cut costs even more and raise the quality of what is provided. Can one have both? The goal in reinventing relationships between corporations should *definitely be to achieve both.* Cybercorps are often competitors and cooperating partners at the same time. This relationship is referred to as *coopetition.*

James Martin & Co. (JM&Co.) competes intensely with LBMS in the development of business systems. JM&Co. has a client-server methodology implemented with an LBMS project-management tool. Although competitors, both companies sell this combined product in order to make it dominant in the market and generate funds for its improvement.

James Moore points out that many *mutualisms* in nature (in which species have mutually dependent symbiosis) evolve from antagonistic relationships. Some predators play the vital role of dispersing seeds over long distances. Your antagonistic relationships may be convertible into mutualistic ones. Nordstrom and J. C. Penney collaborated on an interactive home shopping channel on television. The agile webs described in the previous chapter often link together companies that are otherwise intensely competitive.

The evolution in Japan of lean manufacturing, which so changed the car industry, was the successive invention of an ecosystem with intricate relationships between a manufacturer and various partners. The relationship was concerned not only with cutting costs by just-in-time delivery but also with close cooperation going all the way from the initial design of the product, through manufacturing planning, to eventual after-sales service. Chrysler, following Japan's lead, has completely reinvented its relationships with suppliers in order to achieve an extreme degree of cooperation. They learn together how to improve their joint design and manufacturing process, often modifying the component supplied to make it easier to manufacture or easier to assemble in the car. Each visits the other's plant so that they can jointly investigate and eliminate problems and suggest improvements to one another. The manufacturer gives the supplier advanced information about changes in models or production volumes. The cooperation extends all the way from planning to after-sales service.

Rather than having a sole-source supplier, the car manufacturer often has two or more suppliers for each part and can adjust the amount purchased among these suppliers. The suppliers are rated with an agreed-upon formula, and each supplier strives to achieve the best rating and progressively cut costs so as to preserve or increase its share. The contract is thus written to keep the supplier constantly on its toes. In this way, it is possible to achieve the best of both worlds: intimate cooperation with trading partners at the same time as intense competition among trading partners. Combining the best of both worlds should be a goal of cybercorp design. Different forms of it are found in different industries.

Complex Relationships

> **As business ecosystems evolve and become more complex because of cybercorp mechanisms, a major key to business success will be the invention, development, and nurturing of business relationships.**

To avoid ruinous price wars, corporations need to search for win-win associations in which there is intricate cooperation among different contributors. The allies need to understand the ecosystem they play in, form alliances with a shared vision, negotiate appropriate contracts, and then manage the aliance with much human attention. There are many types of alliance that avoid antitrust implications.

Exhibit 8-1 shows the evolving emphasis from head-to-head competition within one industry to development of strength within an ecosystem.

A variety of companies have put into place *cross-corporate teams* in order to solve production problems, speed up operations, lessen inventory costs, and enhance product design. Some value streams span business partners and should be designed accordingly.

In the early months of production for a new model of car the supplier

Exhibit 8-1. The changing emphasis from simple head-to-head competition to positioning within an ecosystem

Characteristic	Industry Focus	Ecosystem Focus
Competition:	Product vs. product	Ecosystem leadership or control
	Company vs. company	Being a company of choice within the ecosystem
Linkages to:	Suppliers, customers, agents, etc.	Diverse companies within the ecosystem
Determinants of economic performance:	Sales and profit within industry	How well the company manages alliances and relationships
		Performance within those relationships
Growth concern:	Individual company growth	Ecosystem growth as well as position of company within the ecosystem
Primary unit of strategy making:	Company	Community of co-evolving ecosystem participants

often has an engineer working at the assembly factory so that when problems occur with supplied components he can investigate, deal with the problem, and prevent the problem from reoccurring. Bose, the half-billion-dollar manufacturer of audio equipment, went further and offered to enter into long-term contracts with selected suppliers if they would station a senior excutive at Bose who would identify ways in which her company could enhance Bose products or production processes, sharing expertise as appropriate. These executives had access to Bose inside information, including production data and reports on concurrent engineering, and could place orders with their own companies. This innovative level of cooperation helped Bose because of its very short windows of product opportunity.

> **Recognizing the importance of establishing ecosystem leadership quickly, corporations should ask, "What can we give away free in order to establish a dominant position?"**

Netscape became the fastest growing start-up in history because, at the time the World Wide Web was coming to life, Netscape gave away its "browser," making it the Web browser that most people used. At Sun Microsystems a new programming language had been created, Java, that Sun realized could become a language common to all Internet computers. To make this happen, Sun gave it away free, with massive publicity about its future potential for making Web pages come to life. What might have been just another forgotten language swept through the Internet community, quickly establishing itself as a de facto standard that other vendors had to support. As Sun poured free fuel on the Internet fire its stock appreciated and hardware sales rose.

In a digital world there are many valuable items that may be given away free because reproduction costs almost nothing—software, education products, anything that can be transmitted over the Internet.

The Jungle Master

The reason why Bill Gates is so successful is that he always thinks in terms of the ecosystems that Microsoft plays in. He meets the key thinkers of the corporations in these ecosystems and spends many hours with them, exploring their views, sitting up into the early hours of the morning talking like a fascinated academic, oblivious to the surroundings, discussing the other ecosystem players, chewing over new ideas, and delving into as much detail as he can on their strategies. Gates makes himself the ecosystem's number one guru. He sets out to learn all he possibly can about its possible directions, research, and tactics. He absorbs the ideas of all the key players and is prepared to adopt any idea as his own.

Gates constantly works out in his head all the ways in which Microsoft might dominate the ecosystem. A form of dominance may need a large expenditure; it may be an uphill climb sometimes taking years, but once it is established the money flows in. Sometimes dominance is aided by mutual cooperation with other companies, often not in the same industry. Gates debates what mutual relationship might be avantageous, sometimes converting antagonistic relationships into thrusts of mutual benefit. Bill Gates's determination is to be master of the jungle.

Gates asks, always, "What de facto standards does the ecosystem need, and how can Microsoft establish and own those standards?" What has to be given away free in order to make the Microsoft standard permeate the ecosystem in such a way that it cannot be dislodged? How can Microsoft undermine any alternative standards, or any attempts by other players to achieve forms of ecosystem dominance? When other ecosystem players, like Intel, cannot be dislodged, Gates cooperates with them and helps them, working out how he can share in their success. Sometimes he cooperates with them until he has obtained all the benefits possible and then moves into competition with them, as he did with IBM. PC ecosystems are littered with ex-Microsoft partners where only Microsoft acquired a long-term benefit. Gates is a dangerous bedfellow.

This ecosystem leadership is in sharp contrast to the tunnel vision of many executives and strategic planners who ask, "How do we sell such-and-such a product?" They look only at directly competing products in their own industry and are consequently often trapped in the intensifying competition of the cybercorp age, forcing down their margins.

Trust

Complex relationships between corporations depend on a high level of trust.

Some corporations are incapable of being trustworthy. They regard a business handshake the way Hitler viewed a peace treaty; if the other party believes that they must honor the handshake or treaty, that puts them at a disadvantage. The dishonorable company claims to honor the handshake while knowing that it will violate it when expedient. Many corporate lawyers get their thrills from perverting rather than upholding justice. In the cybercorp age, dependence on such lawyers can be immensely damaging in the long run.

> **Trust needs to operate at a much deeper level than what is expressed in contracts. It is almost like the relationship that you might have with your doctor. It is about deep ethical caring.**

In car factories in Japan, incoming parts are often not inspected, whereas they are most carefully inspected in Western factories. In Japan the suppliers are trusted to deliver parts without defects, on time, and in the right sequence. Violation of this trust would be a serious breach of the supplier's responsibility.

Joint Development

To be as efficient as possible the relationship between partners needs to start in the early stages of product planning and development. A supplier, for example, can simply supply components or can propose new ideas for components that could improve the overall attractiveness, cost, or quality of the product. It is valuable to have this input during planning. In film production, cooperating companies do much brainstorming to explore creative ideas, and the mutual stimulation results in new possiblities.

A key to cutting manufacturing cost is to design a product so that its components can be assembled with as little human work as possible. Automated assembly requires that the manufacturer of the product and the manufacturer of components work very closely together in designing the product and designing how it is assembled. In an age of CAD tools, this cooperation can become very intricate and can take place anywhere in cyberspace.

Cooperation during planning results in lower-cost products and often products that are more reliable and easier to maintain, but it raises a dilemma. The supplier needs to be selected, at least tentatively, long before any competitive price bidding for the component can take place. The supplier's development team may need to do detailed development work in conjunction with the manufacturer long before the design is finalized. Suppliers are selected because they have a record of good quality, reliable delivery, and good relations.

Combined Intelligence Data

Information can be collected in new ways with new technology. Business partners should jointly invent how to collect valuable information and cooperate using the information to help customers, improve products, or maximize profits.

Large retail chains collect much information that is of value to their suppliers, and suppliers collect much information that is of value to retailers. In general, partners in a business relationship can help each other by exchanging information, especially when it can be collected electronically and immediately transmitted to where it is most useful.

Staff in some stores use a handheld laser device that reads bar codes on goods and has an in-store radio link to the store's inventory system. The system shows whether fresh stocks have been ordered. It can show whether the current price should be lowered to sell slow-moving items. If a large store has too much stock, that is expensive; if it has too little, it may lose sales and make customers unhappy. Some stock moves in spurts that may be difficult to predict, often related to the vendor's television advertising. Large national vendors have computer models of their product usage patterns and how they are influenced by advertising. They collect data on retailer orders from across the nation and have a nationwide system for tracking and predicting sales. They associate sales with customers' zip codes to establish demographic patterns. *If the retail chain's database is combined with the supplier's database, the combination is especially valuable for planning advertising and increasing sales.*

There are several types of information here that need to be combined:

- The store manager's insight about local sales patterns and the effects of local advertising
- The store's central tracking of nationwide trends and measurement of the effects of national advertising

- The supplier's analysis of its nationwide sales patterns
- The store's computerized correlation of product sales with zip codes
- The supplier's analysis of the effects of its own advertising

If the retail chain's data is combined with the supplier's data in a joint data warehouse designed for data analysis and data mining, the combination will probably be very valuable for planning advertising and increasing sales.

A retail chain's goal ought to be to move beyond an obsession with sales per store and work out how to maximize sales per customer. This can be done by advertising in the store and by forging links between different products that one buyer could purchase. A person who buys a luxury item like a cellular phone, for example, might buy an electric toothbrush. Soft toys may sell if placed next to infants' clothes. Computer data shows that shoppers buy certain items together more often when they are displayed together. A supplier might decide that it should manufacture items that sell together.

When the oil in a truck is changed, the old oil is thrown away. The old oil, however, is a source of valuable information. It has many tiny particles in it caused by wear and tear in the engine. If it is analyzed correctly, actions can be taken that prolong engine life or give better engine performance. Some Japanese car companies have suggested that their cars should use oil designed for that car, and that the oil should be changed in their service stations and analyzed there. This would produce information that could help the car owner, and it would help the car manufacturer by providing detailed engineering information from their cars worldwide. Used oil contains valuable knowledge!

Information can be collected in new ways with new technology. Different players in an ecosystem collect different data and can often help one another by sharing them.

Companies should jointly invent how to collect valuable information and cooperate in using the information to help customers, improve products, increase sales per customer, and maximize profits. The mass of data may be taken into a common data warehouse. Each player then uses its own analysis and visualization tools for exploring the shared data.

The Dangers of Protectionism

South America's rain forests have vast numbers of competing species, each of them tough—a survivor of countless millions of years of lush ecological battle. Midocean islands have a much smaller number of species, less hardened in battle. When new birds or plants are introduced into such a protected environment, they may attack and displace existing species. Bermuda in 1945 had only one car, and tourists came only by boat. The island was covered with Bermuda cedar trees, many of them ancient and beautiful, a unique species of cedar that had evolved only in Bermuda. For the first time, landscape gardening catalogs became available. Bermuda residents ordered plants from California, which unfortunately came with a bug that attacked the cedar trees. This bug would not have done much harm elsewhere, but in Bermuda it multiplied furiously because it had no natural predator. In a few years all the Bermuda cedars were dead. The windbreak they provided was gone, and so the fierce ocean gales that swept the little island killed many other plants. Foresters rushed to plant thousands of fast-growing casuarina trees from Australia to restore the windbreak.

Businesses that have survived the full force of competitive pounding tend to be tough, whereas businesses that have evolved with artificial protection from competition tend to be vulnerable if the protection is removed. When deregulation occurs in a regulated industry, or when a country with import restrictions, like Brazil, removes those restrictions, tough predators move in and the previously protected organizations have deeply embedded cultures that are inappropriate for competition and extremely difficult to change. When protection ends, a new ecosystem evolves. There are entrepreneurial opportunities like the selling of windbreak trees in Bermuda.

It is dangerous for countries to adopt protectionist policies, with high tariffs or bans on using foreign labor, because in the age of cyberspace, protection cannot last and when it ends the protected companies fare badly.

Summary

Every manager ought to ask and seek to understand answers to the following questions about business ecosystems:

- In what ways is your business vulnerable to cream skimming or overintense cybercorp competition? What means of protection are available?
- What ecosystems does your corporation participate in?
- What different ecosystems *could* it participate in?

For each such ecosystem, ask:

- Who are the major shapers of its future?
- What visions and strategies do they have?
- What do you need to learn about the ecosystem and its players? What research should you do?
- In what ways can members of the ecosystem help one another and develop mutually beneficial long-term relationships?

- What de facto standards would enable its players to work together better? Could you be involved in creating or owning these standards?
- What common templates or processes does it need? Can you create, acquire, or gain access to those templates or processes?
- What tools do corporations in the ecosystem need to achieve disciplined cooperation (such as CAD, CAM, CASE, Web servers, repositories, groupware, presentation tools, computer-based training, etc.)? Could you create, acquire, or control any key tools?
- In what other way could you play a leadership role or occupy a key niche in the ecosystem?
- What other computer systems are desirable to make the ecosystem work well?
- What knowledge infrastructure (Chapter 16) is desirable for the ecosystem?
- What intercorporate relationships would you need to manage well in order to be as successful as possible in the ecosystem?
- What new ecosystems could provide a needed customer service?
- Could you initiate a *new* ecosystem in which you would play a dominant role?

Reference

1. James F. Moore, *The Death of Competition, Leadership and Strategy in the Age of Business Ecosystems* (New York: HarperCollins, 1996).

9

The David
Syndrome

The cybercorp revolution is bringing many David and Goliath stories. Small and nimble corporations can attack old and arthritic corporations and win. The old corporation, like Goliath, often reacts with scorn to the newcomer rather than with appropriate caution. There are many new opportunities for entrepreneurs.

The Biblical David was taking a risk that would not have looked good in the strategy meetings. A cybercorp newcomer needs less raw heroism; it can plan how to use new ideas to exploit the old company's weaknesses. It may use newer technology, virtual mechanisms, excited value-stream teams, and cybermarketing; it may build a cozier relationship with customers. Cybercorp networks enable newcomers to overcome the main advantages of large corporations—access to resources. And technology often eliminates the advantages of economies of scale. Goliath is loaded down with the baggage of an earlier era. Old corporations often have old cultures, inappropriate to the mercurial cybercorp age. They have cumbersome hierarchical structures and politics. Their computers are snarled up in old spaghetti-like software that is murder to change. They pay lip service to reengineering themselves but make only mechanical changes within the present structure when that structure ought to be scrapped.

Before the 1970s almost no corporations grew to $100 million revenue in their first ten years. In the 1980s the fastest-growing corporations grew to a billion dollars revenue in a decade. Some, like Compaq, grew to a billion in five years. In the 1990s the fastest growth is ten times faster. McCaw Cellular Communications sold for $12.6 billion six years after it was started by McCaw and his brother. Netscape, which makes the popular Internet browser software, went public when the company was only sixteen months old, with a valuation of $2 billion. Jim Clark, its cofounder, a former Stanford University professor, had shares worth $565 million at the end of the first day's trading. Marc Andreessen, his twenty-four-year-old colleague, who originally programmed the software, had shares worth $58 million. A few months later the market valuation of Netscape had tripled.

For every billion-dollar story like Netscape there are many thousands of small successes. Many Net entrepreneurs work from home. An entrepreneur who subscribed to Prodigy dreamed up a service for allowing other subscribers to order flowers from their PCs. He relayed the orders automatically to an international florist network and billed the user's credit card. His company, PC Flowers, never deals with a customer by phone, but it has grown quickly to $10 million a year.

An Irishman with a hacker son built an Internet site called World Golf so that golfers could explore what courses they might play at, see pictures of the courses, check green fees, and make bookings. The entrepreneur makes money from the golf courses that pay to be displayed at the World Golf site. In all types of business, cybercorp mechanisms increase the potential for innovation dramatically.

David in an Old Company

New corporations are evolving with radically new types of organization. They grow from the start with virtual office space, e-mail not snail mail, value-stream teams, a "boundaryless" culture, and electronic links to trading partners. They employ virtual mechanisms designed for fast growth. They make use of the Internet. They are cybercorps from the beginning.

In many cases the best policy for an old company is to start new spinoffs. Where an established corporation is proving resistant to business reengineering, its best chance of moving into the cybercorp age is to give birth to new cybercorps. The dog may be too old to learn new tricks, but it can have puppies. The puppy has advantages that a new start-up does not, such as access to its parent's money, services, skills, and customers, but needs to be isolated from the culture that makes the old dog sluggish.

Teddy Bears

A quaint little company in Vermont makes teddy bears. Its amusing chief executive, John Sortino, first sold his bears from a cart in the street. He admonished his employees, "Be a teddy bear person and don't let anyone in who isn't." Nothing can be further from the high-tech world. It seemed most unlikely that Sortino could make a dent in the giant toy companies. But Sortino invented "Bear-Grams." The public could dial an 800 number on Mother's Day, or any other day, and send a greeting message that had a teddy bear packaged with it. Sales shot up thirtyfold and kept growing. A computerized system was set up to market directly to the million or so people who have sent bear-grams, most of whom have never seen the bears. Analyzing the responses, the computer indicated that the mailed brochure should emphasize the Pregnancy Bear and the Bride and Groom Bears. The bears the company thought people would buy were quite different from what the computer showed customers wanted. Design and manufacturing changed fundamentally because of the computerized analysis of bear-gram responses. The company went public and had a frenzied first day of trading. Now it is planning worldwide bear-grams.

The bear company went on to use the Internet. Many people as they explore the Net find a subject "teddy bears," and many click on it. They find the opening Web page of the Vermont Teddy Bear Company and text that tells them why big folks need teddy bears. Bear-grams, computerized follow-up, marketing on the Net, and electronic feedback about customer needs are all *cybercorp thinking*. They enabled the bear company to grow at breathtaking speed, astonishing its founder.

But the bear company also contained some *anti-cybercorp thinking*. Sortino insisted that his bears *must* be made in Vermont. He said, "We don't want any damned Indonesian bears around here." However, bears can be made in Indonesia at a fraction of the cost, with tight quality control. The *design* could be done in Vermont with Sortino's sense of what bears ought to be, but the *manufacturing* done at much lower cost elsewhere. Sortino's expenses in Vermont became too high to support the revenue, and Sortino was removed by the board.

If the bear company had taken cybercorp thinking to its logical conclusion it would have had *worldwide* bear-grams adapted to *local* markets, computerized follow-up and marketing constantly adjusting to *local* customer demand, *local* design reflecting local stuffed-animal tastes, minimum-cost manufacturing in cheap-labor countries with rigorous quality control, and *global* computerized logistics of bear shipping and warehousing. The company might have evolved into a global bear ecosystem.

Insisting that bears be manufactured only in Vermont might have made business sense ten years ago, but today the world is becoming interconnected rapidly. Successful products and ideas are copied rapidly. Other companies can have bear-grams and Internet marketing. Global corporations are creating whatever the world wants in low-labor-cost countries with tight quality control.

Small, Bright, Fast, and Virtual

A motto of the David corporation might be *Small, Bright, Fast, and Virtual*. A small company need not have expensive offices; some employees can work from home. Key players may live in different cities but be linked electronically. A small company can be a virtual company.

A start-up may want to build something unique and interesting but cannot do it all by itself. It may outsource part of the design; it may work jointly with component suppliers; it may use students to create brochures or software. The founders may have the view that they hire only the brightest, most dedicated people with unique talents and outsource everything that does not need much skill. The company focuses all of its efforts on what it is brilliant at. It may have a policy of *owning everything that is high return on investment and outsourcing everything that is low return on investment.*

Start-ups should expect a turbulent ride. They often don't do the right thing the first time and need to cut back and switch direction fast. They should plan for this by avoiding fixed or expensive resources.

Start-ups may benefit greatly from being members of cybercorps groups such as those described in Chapter 7. They may need much trial and error before they put together an act that really takes off.

Intellect Amplifiers

The best computerized tools greatly amplify the skill of professionals. They give David the weapons to attack Goliath. A relatively small firm of architects can design the most elaborate buildings. A publisher or television editor can produce sophisticated results with desktop equipment and work with colleagues on different continents as though they were sitting at the same desk. With the right power tools, small teams can handle highly complex processes. Professionals can off-load the easier tasks to nonprofessionals and spend their time on the tasks that really need their special skills. Conversely, technology can enable nonprofessional staff to handle those cases that are easy and pass difficult cases to professionals. A nurse, for example, can use a computer to screen patients, know what tests to perform, analyze the results, and decide whether the patient needs Alka Seltzer or a session with the doctor. Software can help a businessperson generate legal contracts for straightforward situations and avoid legal expenses except where the software says that the results need to be checked by a lawyer.

An important result from some of the best expert systems is a major increase in the capability of people who are already expert. Some startling improvements in the productivity of professionals have been recorded. Canon, for example, had eighty highly skilled lens designers and built an expert system that enabled them to produce fourteen times as many designs in the same time.[1] A zoom lens is complex. It has many different glass surfaces that can move relative to one another, different glass surface shapes, and different refractive indices. There are at least seventy variables to control in the design. Lens designers use CAD software that traces rays through a possible lens and simulates its behavior. Canon found that some of its lens designers were exceptionally good at certain aspects of the design. The expert system attempted to capture such skill and suggest different configurations that should be tried (or avoided). It contains rules that relate to manufacturability, intersurface reflections, glass that might break, and so on. Designers could explore many more options and were more likely to discover a breakthrough design.

Soon, however, start-up companies acquired similar capability. Today many of the best lenses in the mail-order catalogs come from companies the buyer doesn't know the name of—David companies.

Lower-Size Profit Threshold

Production equipment is evolving rapidly to provide greater functionality with smaller units. This cheaper equipment is enabling small companies to compete in niche markets, often with a high level of innovation. Small, bright companies take advantage of CAD and cheaper numerically controlled tools. The days when a large lot size was the key to low-cost production have largely gone. Many manufacturing companies have shifted to small lot sizes to achieve the product variability and customization that customers are asking for. Toshiba assembles its portable computer models in batches of twenty per model and can afford to do it in batches of ten.

> **Small companies can join forces in partnerships or cybercorp webs and often establish capabilities that older corporations do not have. Small members of such partnerships need less capital and hence can become profitable earlier.**

Stealth

It is good idea to avoid attacking the establishment overtly. The establishment bands together to protect its own. The shrewd David starts a separate operation that the establishment feels unthreatened by.

Wal-Mart spent many years opening stores in small towns where no similar stores existed. It overcame the weak local retailers and easily became the best-stocked least-expensive store in the region, but it felt little threat from other discounters because the town was not large enough. It was able to develop the systems that would eventually make it so powerful without alarming its big powerful competitors. Hewlett-Packard had a similar policy: "Attack the undefended hill."

ESI, Ltd., a British start-up in the shadow of the Goliath 250-year-old London Stock Exchange, set out to become "the world's first cyberspace stock exchange," but Goliath made a murderous attack on it. ESI had remarkably little capital. As a step prior to full regulatory approval it created an Internet-based service for private investors, due to start on September 8, 1995. Four days before that launch the London Stock Exchange cut ESI's lifeblood, the real-time feed of stock market data. This was the only source of up-to-the-minute stock prices, and ESI was totally dependent on it. ESI held a press conference, and its demise became a public issue. The British Office of Fair Trading began an investigation about whether canceling its contract with ESI was "intended to distort, restrict or prevent competition." On September 28 the dispute ended, and the London Stock Exchange renewed the data feed. While ESI was waiting for regulatory approval as a recognized investment exchange, it made its presence known on the Internet and received many inquiries from groups in other countries interested in franchising its virtual stock exchange model for worldwide use.

Cybermarketing

Chapter 3 describes how today's electronics are creating a trend from mass markets to fragmented markets. Instead of broadcasting to the masses you can target highly specialized communities on the Net. Cyberspace provides marketing facilities that are being used by small companies that cannot afford to do the promotion that large companies do. Small companies with little or no advertising budget can take actions such as the following:

1. Establish a home page on the World Wide Web. Use a service firm with good skills in designing Web material with color pictures and sound.
2. Display the Web page address on all business cards, brochures, product packages, and other advertisements.
3. Find innovative ways to attract people to the Web site. A consulting firm may operate a bulletin board of consultant jokes; a food company may provide recipes and entertaining cooking lessons. There may be competitions, lotteries, prizes, free gifts.
4. Make sure as many potential customers as possible know the address of the Web site and why they should visit it.
5. Put appropriate information in Internet special-interest bulletin boards, and allow potential customers to drill down into great detail when they want to.

6. Create a news bulletin board containing stories about the products.
7. Do highly focused marketing targeted at narrow communities with specific interests.
8. In a company that sells information, books, music, or anything that can be transmitted, allow prospects to download snippets free.
9. Allow customers to buy things with e-cash or credit cards.
10. Send information about new products or features to customers by e-mail.
11. Solicit knowledge of customer wishes—for example, color and features; ask for market research data.
12. Create an electronic suggestion box. Invite all customers to send comments and suggestions. Prompt customers for comments on specific items ("We've just added a new option on . . . Is it useful to you?").
13. Set up conferences or bulletin boards shared between marketing or sales and engineering or manufacturing, to facilitate communication.
14. Create an electronic fan club where fans can trade information and tell other fans what they like. Ask fans for testimonials.

Joe Boxer sells men's boxer shorts with fanciful prints. It publicized its Internet address in advertisements and received about 300 responses a day, 80 percent of which asked for catalogs or product information.[2] The company set out to compile an entertaining book about boxer shorts and invited people to send in funny stories over the Internet. This attracted the type of customers the company needed for its gimmicky products.

My favorite single-malt scotch is James Martin scotch (no kidding), but they don't advertise on the Net. The Vermont Teddy Bear Company, on the other hand, gets many new customers from the Net. Digital publishing media can be linked automatically to the Internet. A travel guide CD-ROM, for example, could contain thousands of photographs but also enable its user to make hotel bookings, check restaurant menus, and examine changeable information via the Net.

New Media

Today's thesaurus products seem obsolete and unimaginative; the user can easily think of better phrases than those in the thesaurus. A more interesting type of thesaurus would be one that asks all of its users to contribute; their suggested words and phrases would be accumulated in a bulletin board and periodically edited and published. A thesaurus would quickly grow to many times its present size and would be much more inventive. There are many other types of products to which a publisher could invite the cyberspace community to contribute continuously.

Publishers have some interesting choices ahead because of new media. Toshiba's superdensity digital video disk can hold almost 5,000 novels or 85 hours of music in the compressed form used on the Sony minidisk. Like CDs it can be mass-produced for much less money than a book. How will publishers use such a medium? How will they use the Internet? New types of publishers will grow fast, and others will be devastated because of obsolete thinking. There will be many David and Goliath stories in publishing.

Arteriosclerosis

John Akers, the chief executive of IBM at the time of its great crash, had a mission statement that was known to every employee:

1. To match or beat the growth in all segments of the information industry during the coming decade
2. To exhibit product leadership across our entire product line
3. To be the most efficient at everything we do
4. To sustain our profitability, which funds our growth

This mission statement could have applied to the 1960s or any other decade. However, by the Akers era the computer industry was different in a fundamental way: It had an extreme rate of change. New corporations were springing up and growing faster than ever before in history. The world of small machines, hacker networks, and software stores was very different from the staid world of the mainframes. To survive in the computer industry you had to be fast, fluid, and flexible. The Akers-era IBM mission should have emphasized *speed, fluidity, and adaptability to fast-changing markets.*

The management style that had made IBM so successful in the past had become a liability. Its size, centralization, and high level of discipline caused it to respond too slowly. The winners in the computer industry were now companies with fast reactions and the ability to improvise.

Although it had the world's best computer research IBM repeatedly fell behind its competition in introducing new products. Many of its brilliant developers were frustrated because their ideas never reached the marketplace. IBM's developers would have contributed far more if they had been working for small Silicon Valley companies.

IBM's technical visionaries knew all along that IBM should have moved much faster and more aggressively into client-server technology, peer-to-peer networks, object-oriented software automation, and open systems. While

IBM was trying to swing around an ocean liner, large numbers of small nimble powerboats were racing to its customers.

In the cybercorp world it is not only the computer industry that is affected by mercurial change. What happened to IBM will happen to many corporations in different ways. Many old corporations have arteriosclerosis. The comfortable folks in the middle of a bureaucracy are not ready to admit that they are part of the problem. This makes restructuring difficult to accomplish. New start-ups run rings around the old corporations.

Gates of Hell

In the 1980s IBM was confronted with a fabulous opportunity. The computer industry was about to go through a massive discontinuity. Personal computers would be on every desk and be linked together with networks. PC operating systems and office software would sell in huge numbers. Computer customers everywhere would need a leader that would establish industry standards.

IBM's initial move into personal computers was spectacularly successful. In 1984, the third year of the IBM PC, the PC division had revenues of $4 billion. If the division had been a separate corporation it would have been the fastest growing corporation in history, and the third largest computer company (after Digital and the rest of IBM). *Time* magazine picked the IBM PC for its "Man of the Year" cover (rather than Reagan or Gorbachev). *Time* commented that the IBM PC "has set the standard for excellence for the industry."

Bill Gates, in those days, with his owllike spectacles, nerd clothes, and habit of rocking backward and forward in a chair when he talked, looked an unlikely person to be able to attack the stately starch-collared IBM. His parents had banned him from playing with computers because they interfered with his studies, but Gates dropped out of college anyway. IBM needed to acquire an operating system in order to move quickly into the mushrooming PC market. Bill Gates didn't have an operating system, but when he saw IBM shopping he quietly purchased the rights to one called Quick and Dirty Operating System (QDOS) and changed its name to MS DOS (Microsoft Disk Operating System). This became the operating system with which IBM drove into the PC business. The big battle between Bill Gates and IBM came a few years later. Gates wanted to be more than a minor partner of IBM, he wanted to own the dominant PC software. Gates pushed his Windows operating system while IBM pushed OS/2.

In a movie it would have been an improbable plot. The Goliath was one of the most successful and toughest corporations of all time. Quiet-spoken Gates looked anything but tough. The fight was about establishing standards for the new PC industry, and IBM was a past master of setting standards. It seemed improbable that it would let a small start-up company beat it with such an important issue at stake. Gates had learned from IBM the value of owning the standards in computing. He comments, "It's an expensive uphill battle to own the standards, but once you own them the money pours in." Gates wanted his software, Windows, to be a standard for other computer companies as well as IBM.

IBM said to its customers, "Trust us and we will lead you steadily to the next generation of systems." For decades IBM had demonstrated that it was worthy of that trust. As a symbol of the trust IBMers dressed like bank presidents. Microsofties had earrings, jeans with holes at the knees, and T-shirts with messages like "FYFV." When IBM software developers asked what FYFV stood for, the Microsoft person had to explain the meaning of "Fuck You, I'm Fully Vested." Microsofties had to be accompanied by chaperons whenever they went to the bathroom, and IBM lawyers lectured IBMers about not going out with Microsofties after work.

David sized up Goliath and carefully assessed his weak spots. IBM sold OS/2 as an "enterprise-friendly" design, which meant that it helped link PCs to mainframes, rather than giving maximum desktop ease of use and power. Gates judged that most PC customers were not interested in the mainframe. Gates said that IBM stands for "Install Big Machines." He targeted his software at stand-alone PCs. IBM built its Office Vision family of products with the mainframe in mind, and it could barely compete with Microsoft office products.

IBM and Microsoft developed the first version of OS/2 jointly, so there were many detailed negotiations. Bill Gates often found it easy to outmaneuver IBM at various points in the negotiations because he knew exactly what he wanted *technically*, whereas IBM had a more complex and political agenda. The game was won not in one battle but slowly throughout a prolonged journey, with Gates paying attention to detail at each step.

A decade after the battle began Gates became the world's wealthiest person (except for royal families) with a net worth over $14 billion,[3] and IBM had made no money in the market for PC software.

Ecosystem Thinking for Start-ups

Ecosystem thinking is necessary for today's entrepreneurs. There are far more opportunities for corporations participating in cooperative relationships than there are for go-it-alone companies. Innovation is limited, not by the availability of good ideas, or technology, or capital, but by the ability to command cooperation among the existing ecosystem players. Many entrepreneurs create brilliant inventions but they get nowhere, just as many writers create brilliant books or film scripts that get nowhere while mediocre ones are produced and hyped.

Suppose you devised a machine-readable business card that could contain much information about the card giver and his company, and you thought that these would catch on fast so that businesspeople everywhere would carry them. If you wanted to succeed in introducing such a product what would you do? To achieve wide acceptance the card should be like today's business cards but with machine-readable codes (perhaps like supermarket bar codes but smaller) printed on the back. Software for creating and interpreting the codes should work with the main forms of PC office software such as Microsoft's Office. Success would depend on getting a standard design for the card coding accepted worldwide as fast as possible. To achieve this you might plan to give the software away free and make money licensing the scanner design. In the beginning, software working with existing scanners might be given away free. The scanner could be a cheap device, no larger than a mouse. It might be built into a handheld organizer. Such a venture would need its own ecosystem; you would need to identify the players in the ecosystem and understand their strategies. If the venture succeeded, it might quickly be bought by a major company, and so from the start you should plan alternative exit scenarios.

Some greeting cards play music when you open them. Such a card could be designed to transmit a brief radio signal and receive a personal recorded message on a cellular radio link. At the right price this could be a high-selling product. What ecosystem members would need to cooperate to make this business succeed?

Often there are opportunities in an existing business ecosystem for a small company to establish a niche that is sustainable and profitable. James Moore describes how a bug that is smaller than a pinhead uses hummingbirds as taxis. It waits patiently on a flower until a hummingbird visits, then hops on to the hummingbird's beak and travels on the beak until it reaches a flower with suitable food; then it hops off. Many start-up companies have hitched a ride on existing companies. For example, some have created educational products, software, or consulting services for existing ecosystems. They key to such opportunities is to identify important customer needs or problems and find solutions, while at the same time building good relations with the established players so that you can help them improve their sales or customer service.

Entrepreneurial BHAGs

By using agile networks of companies, or by using relationships in ecosystems, audacious goals can become more audacious. What kind of BHAGs could an entrepreneur initiate? Today's entrepreneur needs to ask what existing corporations it makes sense to partner with. Many opportunities exist for entrepreneurs to play a role in business ecosystems, or in some cases to tackle a real customer concern by trying to asemble a new ecosystem. Some young corporations have found a way to dominate a new ecosystem, as Microsoft did, for example.

Entrepreneurs or relatively small companies can create ambitious plans achievable by linking the right virtual partners.

There are millions of hackers accessible via the Internet; suppose that you could devise a project in which large numbers of them cooperate. This has been done to break encryption codes that were considered so safe that it would take thousands of years to break them. Tasks were farmed out to vast numbers of volunteers around the world who all worked on their part of the problem and together eventually broke the code in months. Could software that would otherwise take hundreds of years to build be tackled in a similar way? What entirely new capabilities could be built by a central architect farming modules out to the world's Internet community? Could a fabulous computer game be devised where thousands of hackers around the world contribute to building it, each receiving e-cash compensation? Could a massive artificial intelligence capability be grown organically by thousands of Internet users trained on-line how to contribute? Doug Lenat, for example, has dedicated his life to a BHAG of giving a computer common sense, but this requires a huge amount of work to create millions of rules.[4] (Common sense is very complex.)

Entrepreneurs should think in terms of BHAGs they might achieve by assembling competencies in a virtual organization. Suppose you believe that there is a vast market for unattended baby lawn mowers that spend their day manicuring lawns. A group of partners might be assembled for designing such devices and raising the money to build them. If the money is raised, the group would be expanded to manufacture and market the product.

Around the planet there are over a billion non-English speakers anxious to learn English, and their number is growing. Learning English with CD-ROMs could be made fun by using great songs and dramatic clips from movies. A market of such size is rare.

Very Fast Growth

In the forests of Finland, Nokia, a company that had made forest products for 130 years, demonstrated how different the 1990s are. The company was in deep trouble. Its CEO had committed suicide. In 1991 and 1992 it made terrifying losses. In addition to wood, pulp, and paper, it made mundane products such as rubber boots and electrical cables. In the 1980s it had diversified into television manufacturing but lost money with its television set factories; it made small computers but sold its computer operation. To make matters even worse, the Finnish economy started a nosedive because it was substantially linked to the collapsing economy of Russia. In January 1992, a new CEO was appointed, Jorma Ollila. It became clear to him that Nokia must focus on entirely new markets with high growth potential.

In the early 1990s it was clear that a new generation of cellular phones would sweep through that market and greatly increase worldwide sales. The new generation was digital, not analog, and it opened the prospect of very appealing pocket telephones. The giant telephone companies expected to dominate the cellular telephone marketplace and spent vast fortunes on it.

Ollila decided that the new cellular telephone was one of the best growth opportunities available. He built a mobile phone division like a virtual cybercorp. He outsourced much of the design, chip production, component production, and selling of a new line of cellular phones based on digital technology. Nokia stayed lean and mean, buying most of the technology from the outside. It advertised its featherweight phone worldwide as "the most portable phone." Nokia quickly became No. 1 in Europe in cellular phones, and second only to Motorola in the United States. It far outstripped the Japanese at their own game in Japan. As well as marketing in industrial countries, Nokia targeted countries like China where almost no homes have phone lines and digital cellular technology enables telephone services to be provided at much lower cost. It left the giant phone companies standing at the gate. In two years it rose from being a tiny operation to having revenues of $2.25 billion in 1993 and 20 percent profit on its phone manufacturing.[5]

Nokia demonstrated that in new markets today, speed is much more important than size. A virtual operation can be designed to move with lightning speed.

The Goliath telephone companies had spent a vast fortune on research into digital cellular telephony but completely missed the market for pocket phones. Their conventional wisdom was that their size was critical because of the capital intensive nature of the telephone industry. But Nokia's new cybercorp rose almost overnight to become the world's twelfth largest telecommunications manufacturer.

The cybercorp can streak past giant corporations with slow-moving hierarchies and fossilized mainframes. Lightning speed is possible in global markets with innovative products, built with purchased components and outsourced know-how. The virtual cybercorp can grow or change direction very fast compared with the corporation with fixed desks, permanent employees, and everything done in-house.

Amoebas

The Nokia phone story, an archetypal illustration of virtualness giving explosive growth, took place in an old corporation, not a start-up, but stories like it will become the legends of future entrepreneurs.

Some corporations have created a solitary David; others have created hundreds of them. The Japanese technology company Kyocera created 800 small companies, which it called "amoebas," and expected them to trade both internally and externally.

In 1987 the Swiss Brown Boveri and the Swedish Asea corporations merged, and CEO Percy Barnevik split the resulting company into 1,300 separate companies. He set out to establish an entrepreneurial culture with a goal of 25 percent return on capital and cut the headquarters staff from 4,000 to 200.

Sir John Harvey-Jones, ex-chairman of the giant chemical company ICI Ltd., reflects on a lifetime of beating organizations into shape: "Although everyone complains of overmanagement and obsolete controls, it is extraordinarily difficult to fight free. Over time a sort of cat's cradle is devised, so that as one frees oneself from one entanglement, it is only to find oneself in another."[6] It is much easier to start new David operations than to change Goliath.

We are entering an age when many executives realize that instead of attempting to "reengineer" arthritic corporations it is far better to create brand new cybercorps, designed for fast growth.

References

1. Edward Feigenbaum, Pamela McCorduck, and H. Penny Nii, *The Rise of the Expert Company* (New York: Times Books, 1988), chap. 5. This is an excellent description of the creation of many leading-edge expert systems.
2. Seth Godin, *eMarketing* (New York: Perigee, 1995).
3. *Forbes* estimate, July 1995.
4. Douglas Lenat worked on computer "common sense" for many years at the MCC, Dallas, TX.
5. William Echikson, "How Nokia Wins in Cellular Phones," *Fortune International*, March 21, 1994.
6. John Harvey-Jones, *Managing to Survive* (London: Reed, 1993).

10

Agents and Intelligent Documents

I have sometimes watched with fascination the process by which Arabs negotiate the price of rugs in Middle Eastern shops. The process follows a remarkably fixed pattern. The seller gives an outrageous description of the special nature of the thing to be sold. None of this has any effect on the buyer; a rug is a rug. The seller asks a price much higher than what he expects to get. The buyer laughs hysterically and describes the places where he could buy rugs at a small fraction of that price. This has no effect on the seller, who knows exactly what his competition is selling rugs for. The buyer makes an offer that the seller laughs at with a matching sense of theater. After a protracted series of offers and counteroffers the two agree on a price roughly halfway between the starting prices.

Could computers do the same negotiation? Could we build electronic Arabs?

Electric power companies sell electricity to one another, transmitting electricity between different companies and different countries. Computers in some utilities set the prices automatically with competitive bidding as the current races through the grid.[1] In some parts of the world, electric utilities have been deregulated and dynamically negotiate prices. Some generators are more efficient than others. Prices are lower at off-peak times or when there is excess capacity. Loads vary from one place to another and off-peak times differ in different time zones.

Programmed trading is used by investment managers so that computers buy or sell shares, currencies, future contracts, derivatives, and so forth, or carry out arbitrage automatically when prices change. The programmers of such computers have to embed the rules of the dealing process into their programs. Each program is trying to maximize the profits it makes, taking into consideration the existence of other automated trading programs and human traders.

Increasingly, computers in different organizations interact with one another, sometimes replacing actions that used to be done by people. In a simple example, a supplier's computer may be linked to a manufacturer's computer to monitor inventory, so that as inventory is used up, the supplier's computer arranges for the delivery of more parts. In a somewhat more complex example, the manufacturer's computer may use alternative suppliers. It recommends periodically which suppliers to place orders with and how large the orders should be. The supplier's computer may try to influence the manufacturer's choice by adjusting the price. If the price is too high it loses orders; if the price is too low it loses profit.

Better Allocation of Resources

As telecommunications are made competitive, people are given the option of selecting among alternative phone companies. In the United States subscribers choose their long-distance supplier, and all calls are made via that supplier until the customer changes the choice. This is a somewhat primitive competitive mechanism. It has been proposed that phone competition should be made more dynamic by having subscriber phones select the carrier they use for a call each time a call is placed (an idea that horrifies monopolistic European Telecoms). There would not be fixed rates. Long-distance carriers would quote prices and change these prices as the traffic varied.

If the price quoted could change dynamically, it would depend on many factors such as line congestion, trunk outages, and switching center repairs. The competing prices would be stored in the subscriber phone, and the phone would have a microprocessor to select which carrier to use. The choice might be based on quality as well as price, especially when high-speed modems are used for data or fax transmission. The choice would also be based on avoidance of circuit-busy signals. To achieve competitive prices, phone companies would automatically lease circuits from other carriers. Allocation of resources would be more dynamic.

Automated competitive pricing can be used in various industries and is likely to benefit the customer. It also benefits suppliers when it enables them to allocate resources better. When communication circuits have little traffic on them, dynamic pricing can try to attract more traffic. When power lines are congested, computers can cooperate to balance the load. The price of purchased computer time can vary with demand. Airlines can allocate equipment or schedule crews better. Today's telephone pricing is static and has to be simple so that the customer can understand it. The phone company has to stick with its prices even when switching computers are down or circuits are jammed. When buying and selling are handled by machine, the interaction can employ rate structures much more complicated and changes much more dynamic than is possible with manual systems.

Sometimes when you buy a house you have to make one price bid in an envelope that is sealed until the decision time. In a simple phone company bidding scheme, the phone companies would each offer one price and the user machine would choose. Usually house buying is more complex; you can make multiple bids along with competing house buyers. In a more complex telephone scheme, the user machine might tentatively choose and then give the phone companies a brief time to make better offers.

In general, when a service is expensive, computers might make multiple bids like competing house buyers. There are many ways in which software can be designed to obtain the best results from the bidding process. The complexity of the process is completely hidden from the buyer.

Rules of Encounter

When Arabs negotiate the price of rugs they are following certain protocols. The rules that computers use when they interact are referred to as protocols. Many protocols relate to low-level mechanisms such as file transfers. Increasingly, high-level *rules of encounter* are needed for cybercorp interactions such as automatic just-in-time delivery, selecting vendors, resource scheduling, program trading, selling electricity, and so on.

Rules of encounter are needed in the running of communications networks. A U.S. carrier sends data packets through Germany, and the computers of the two organizations must immediately decide how the packets are to be routed given the current queues and congestion. They may route them via Swiss or French networks. Computers owned by different companies have to come to agreements about dynamically sharing trunks.

In some situations, the rules of encounter are fixed. The rules may be negotiated between trading partners when they decide to do business and are reflected in a business contract. In more complex cases the rules change dynamically.

There are several possibilities:

When the rules of encounter do not change dynamically:

1. The rules are fixed by one party.
2. The rules are jointly agreed to by both parties.

When the rules of encounter do change dynamically:

3. Each party determines its own rules.
4. The parties agree to dynamically changing rules.

Automated Decisions

As the cybercorp world spreads, computers are making more decisions in a more autonomous fashion. Many automated decisions are made by one machine; some require intermachine protocols in which machines of competing companies must decide how to cooperate, for example, to determine which flights will be delayed during airport congestion.

We need to understand clearly what decisions can be entrusted to software and what decisions must remain human decisions.

Decisions that are best left to machines include:

- Simple decisions (such as when to reorder goods)
- Decisions that need complex but precise logic (such as the allocation of gates to incoming flights at a large airport)
- Decisions that require logic so intricate that the human cannot compete with the computer (such as the rescheduling of equipment after failures and delays on a large airline)
- Decisions that must be made too rapidly for human involvement (such as which trunk to use when routing packets over the Internet)

Decisions that must be human decisions include:

- Decisions that are too subtle to program and need the special skills of human intelligence
- Decisions that need creativity, originality, and intuition
- Decisions where human sensitivities predominate
- Business negotiation, including negotiating rules of encounter that can *then* be programmed

Many decisions should not be made by humans alone or by software alone, but by a combination of the two. They are too complex for a human to do well but need human intelligence or negotiation in the decision-making process (such as the scheduling of work in a factory). The human ought to use sophisticated computerized tools in conjunction with his or her own intelligence.

Expertise at American Express

American Express has a worldwide system that, like most such systems, came into life a stage at a time. American Express built databases of information about customers. Authorizers used this information via a worldwide network to decide when to refuse authorization of purchases with American Express cards. The amount of information about customers steadily grew.

American Express wanted a new marketing drive in which it could advertise the fact that American Express cards carry no spending limit. If you are on vacation and discover outrageously expensive antiques, you should be able to charge them on your American Express card. However, credit card theft had been rising alarmingly. How could American Express tell that such charges were collectable and nonfraudulent?

Making the decision to authorize an American Express purchase is a difficult job. The knowledge and rules for doing it are encoded in a training manual four or five inches thick. Sometimes authorizers say yes when the charge is in fact fraudulent or uncollectable; sometimes they say no when the customer is genuine and has the money to pay. Some authorizers become uncannily good at sensing the false use of an American Express card. Like a detective they develop a nose for trouble.

A thief with a stolen card usually exhibits patterns of use that are detectable. The authorizers try to apply rules that they have been taught indicate concern. They cannot apply rules as thoroughly as a computer, but they have common sense and instinct, which the computer does not have. It was desirable to take rules learned from the experience of the best authorizers and encapsulate them in software. American Express built a worldwide system for capturing this learning experience.

When the American Express Authorizer's Assistant system was built, the authorizers worked with it, understood its rules, and constantly thought about how they could improve its rules. They often developed new human skills because they worked in conjunction with the rule-based system. The system gave them the capability to tune and improve the decision-making process.

The system handled some transactions automatically and sped up the authorization on others. The customer had less waiting time. The system improved the productivity of authorizers, so that transaction volume could grow without adding more authorizers. However, both of these savings were small compared to the main benefits: less approval of fraudulent or uncollectable charges and fewer rejections of acceptable charges. The system resulted in a 50 percent reduction in credit and fraud losses and 33 percent fewer denials of valid charges. It was estimated that the expert system added $27 million per year to American Express profits.[2]

Documents Are Dumb

Conventional purchase orders are pieces of paper without any intelligence.

Being paper, they have to be laboriously filed, searched for, and sent by snail mail. It does not make much sense to have a computer print paper documents and then have humans stuff them in envelopes, deliver them to the postal system where people sort them, put them in sacks, deliver them to planes, sort them again, missort some of them, and so on, until eventually they reach a destination where they are manually keyed into another computer system with a one percent error rate. Instead, purchase orders should be digital. They should be transmitted electronically from the purchaser's computer to the supplier's computer. They then travel at electronic speeds with electronic checks that no errors occur. In corporations around the world the documents of commerce have steadily become digital so that they can be filed and transmitted digitally, leaving electronic audit trails. The world of paper documents is as obsolete as the Dickensian world of clerks in top hats sitting on high stools.

We commented that the first horseless carriages looked as though they were designed to be pulled by a horse. Similarly, when documents first become digital they are usually replicas of the paper documents they replace. Such design misses the main point of becoming digital: *Digital documents can have intelligence.*

For every business document we need to ask, What should this document do if it is made intelligent?

When Documents Become Intelligent

A digital replica of a paper purchase order is *dumb*; an *intelligent* purchase order would behave differently, as described in Chapter 1. An intelligent purchase order can monitor inventory and spring into action when needed, executing preprogrammed behavior. Some purchase orders may be allowed to travel to the supplier on their own initiative.

If goods are supplied repetitively there may be no need for the buyer to send a flow of purchase orders. Instead, the supplier's computer monitors the inventory of the purchaser and initiates the delivery of goods. As cybercorp mechanisms evolve, the supplier's computer monitors more than just the inventory. It is aware of the customer's changing production schedule and sends the right mix of goods at the right moment in time.

We may thus progress through five levels of automation:

1. Computers produce paper purchase orders.
2. Paper purchase orders are replaced by digital purchase orders with equivalent functionality.
3. Dumb digital purchase orders are replaced by intelligent purchase orders.

4. No purchase orders are needed for repetitively supplied goods because the supplier's computer sends goods automatically when they are needed.
5. The supplier's computer monitors the customer's needs or production schedule and supplies goods appropriate for a changing production mix, in the correct sequence, just in time.

In many different aspects of corporate activity a broadly equivalent progression can be observed.

Digital Creatures

Object technology is important to the cybercorp. A software *object* contains certain *data* and *methods that can manipulate those data*.[3] Paper documents, such as dumb purchase orders, contain only data. When they become digital objects the game changes; instead of being dumb they have programmed behavior of their own.

A digital object may be thought of as a simple little creature that has only one purpose in life: to apply certain methods to a specified collection of data. The creature protects its data with a vengeance, not allowing anyone to access the data except with the creature's methods. The data is "encapsulated." The creature goes into action only when it receives a request, correctly formatted. The request tells it what method to use and may specify parameters. The creature performs its function and sends a response back, sometimes over a network. In a complex system many different creatures interact, each doing its own thing. Some creatures work in the same computer waiting to become active. Some work in client-server systems where a *client* creature may send a request to a *server* creature and wait for a response. The creatures may send messages over networks or may themselves travel over networks.

An object type may have many subtypes that behave in slightly different ways. For example, an insurance contract may have many subtle variations for different customers. Object-oriented programming makes it relatively easy to create these variations. Analysts draw a taxonomy of objects rather like botanists drawing a taxonomy of plants.[4]

As we design the cybercorp we ask: What operations does it need? How should digital creatures or groups of creatures be organized to perform these operations? The creatures can reside in Web sites and be downloaded from the Internet (programmed in Java applets, which can be executed on any computer). They can travel the world at electronic speed. They may be intelligent documents; they may be packets of electronic cash; they may be agents that search for information on the Internet; they may be agents who can negotiate with rules of encounter. As cybercorp design advances, such electronic interaction will become widespread and change the way operations are designed. As it becomes mature, the cybercorp will bear little resemblance to traditional corporations.

Agents

Object technology may be used to design *agents* that carry out clearly specified tasks.

Personal agents will be a part of PC software in the future. A personal agent should steadily learn more and more about its owner's preferences. It may gather news items of possible interest to its owner, or reviews of films or books that match his or her tastes. It may carry out tasks such as making restaurant bookings, trying to obtain theater tickets with preferred seats, or suggesting what television programs its owner might like it to record. CD-ROM encyclopedias or reference disks ought to have built-in agents. When the user searches for something and does not find it the agent sets off into the Net to try to find more satisfactory information.

The Internet contains a deluge of information that is becoming more overwhelming by the day. Users will increasingly need agents to search the Net or to help them use it. A search agent can replicate itself and produce many subagents all of which search in different places simultaneously.

There will be many types of business agents designed for different purposes. Most of them, at first, will do simple tasks such as searching for products or finding information on subjects of interest. However, agents will steadily become more intelligent and may use rules of encounter. If you buy a camera lens you might phone multiple mail-order firms and negotiate the lowest price. Some agents on the Net search for best-price items, for example the lowest price for a music CD. This may become one of the most popular uses of agents.

Automated Reasoning

Software tools can perform *inferential reasoning* with a collection of knowledge stored in the form of facts and rules. For example, there might be two assertions: "All A is B" and "All B is C." These together produce the conclusion "All A is C." The computer may employ a large collection of rules that it uses in this way to come to conclusions. The rule-processing software searches for rules that apply, uses them to produce an interim assertion, then again searches for rules that apply, and so on until a result is achieved.

Computers have always been able to do *calculations* beyond the capability of humans. With rule-based processing, they are able to do tasks that require *reasoning* beyond the capability of humans, such as scheduling, diagnosis, planning, design, reconfiguring, selecting investments, and improving the yield in a factory. The most advanced systems for automated reasoning far exceed human capability and sometimes improve the productivity of a knowledge worker many times. Once this ultrahuman capability becomes trustworthy, we can build more complex products and more complex operations. Products of greater complexity can be designed knowing that computers will diagnose their problems. Factories can be designed for automated planning. Worldwide logistics can be complex knowing that computers will do the rescheduling.

Systems can be built to do inferential reasoning of great complexity at great speed and so solve problems too hard for humans. However, software has no flicker of common sense. The minutest step beyond its domain of knowledge is a disaster.

A story is told of an aging mathematics professor who was found pumping up a tire on his bicycle. The front tire was flat, but he was pumping up the back tire. A student asked him why, and he said, "Oh! Do they not intercommunicate?"! That is like software taken one step beyond its domain of knowledge. Software for some types of decision making needs to be used to aid a human who *does* have common sense.

Human vs. Machine Intelligence

"Artificial intelligence" was always a misleading term because it gave an unwary person the impression that computers could be intelligent in the way humans are intelligent. This is far from reality. In spite of the proliferation of androids in science fiction, we have no idea how to build such machines. The human brain is exceedingly complex, and in the foreseeable future, we will not come close to emulating its capabilities. However, it is slow, lacks precision, and lacks the computer's capability to handle highly complex calculations and logic. Fortunately, perhaps, what we are good at machines are bad at, and vice versa.

Exhibit 10-1 contrasts the capabilities of the human brain and the computer. Most processes in corporations need both the human and the computer. Some processes can be completely automated. Few processes can be done in an optimal fashion by a human alone.

Expert Systems

An *expert system* stores knowledge in the form of facts and rules and uses that knowledge with computerized reasoning to give advice that would nor-

Exhibit 10-1. Comparison of human intelligence and computer capability

> *Machine enthusiasts have always wanted to believe that we will build machines like humans. When Babbage created mechanical calculators in the nineteenth century, a firm trying to sell this technology ran advertisements saying, "BRAINS OF STEEL." Computers, and networks of computers, have immensely powerful capabilities that humans, and networks of humans, do not have. However, human intelligence remains unique. Most corporate processes need both human and machine capability.*

Capability	Human	Computer
Common sense	Yes	No
Ability to set goals and to think about meaning and purpose	Yes	No
Ability to recognize patterns familiar to humans	Yes	Limited
Ability to recognize complex abstract patterns	No	Yes, with neurocomputing
Ability to draw analogies and associated diverse ideas	Yes	No
Very high speed logic	No	Yes
Accurate storage of a vast amount of data and rules	No	Yes
Ability to apply a vast number of rules with precision	No	Yes
Ability to do complex calculations	Limited	Yes
Absolute accuracy	No	Yes
Precise replication in many locations	No	Yes
Immediate communication with many locations	No	Yes
Originality	Yes	No
Ability to inspire or lead other humans	Yes	No
Wisdom	Sometimes	No

mally require the abilities of human experts. Expert systems provide a person doing a job with knowledge and guidance so that work can be done better.

Sometimes the knowledge is intricate, and the reasoning done by the software is complex. The system should be able to explain its reasoning when asked to. The users who work with the system should be able to add to its knowledge, so that its knowledge steadily improves. It thus acts as an accumulator for corporate learning. Expert systems are often linked to other powerful tools so that in combination there is a major increase in capability. The best expert systems have given breakthrough results.

Unfortunately, expert systems were associated with artificial intelligence, which conjured up images of machines with humanlike thinking skills. Expert systems are very dull by comparison. They do mechanistic reasoning by applying multiple rules, just as a spreadsheet tool fills in its cells by doing multiple calculations. In the late 1980s, artificial intelligence hype collapsed like a burst balloon, and people said, "That didn't work. The shares went through the floor. The peddlers of expert systems sold us snake oil." In reality many expert systems functioned well and demonstrated that they could help humans do much better work.

This unfortunate history caused many corporations to neglect a useful technology. Some corporations continue to build valuable expert systems but decline to talk about them because the systems give them a unique competitive advantage. Some consider that their expert systems contain trade secrets that must not be shared or copied.

The Amplifying of Expertise

Corporations succeed because they have greater expertise than their competition—design expertise, management expertise, marketing expertise, or other forms of expertise. Human expertise can be greatly amplified by computers. Computers provide knowledge workers with a diversity of powerful tools and assistance in using them well.

The knowledge and expertise that are stored in computers steadily accumulates and improves with time. Some expertise enables actions to be taken automatically; some guides humans in processes that require human intelligence. Many processes in corporations can be automated *only partially.* Expertise stored in corporate computers is steadily refined on the basis of experience in using it. Such systems are a vital asset of a *learning* enterprise. Exhibit 10-2 lists characteristics of expert systems.

Exhibit 10-2. Characteristics of expert systems

- They operate in a narrow domain of knowledge.
- Within that narrow domain they can apply complex reasoning and have the potential of solving problems too hard for humans.
- They have no trace of common sense.
- If they take a small step beyond their domain of knowledge, they can give idiotic answers.
- For the above two reasons they are usually used to *assist* humans; the human is in charge and knows the system's limitations.
- Humans should be able to question the system and instruct it to explain its reasoning.
- When linked to other computerized tools, expert systems can achieve breakthrough improvements in productivity.

By 1990 there were several thousand expert systems in use. Most of them had been designed to enhance existing processes. This use missed the big opportunity with the technology, which is to invent radically different processes where an expert system or rule-based processing allows you to operate in a fundamentally different way.

Well-designed expert systems can enable small teams to handle far more complex processes, so they are especially valuable for the reinvention of value streams, where a small team is focused on delivering results to the value-stream customer.

Many early expert systems captured the expertise of one person. More-complex systems capture the expertise of many people and distill it into one collection of facts and rules. Such multi-expert systems can tackle problems too hard for individual humans. They are used to help manage and optimize chaotic processes such as rescheduling the worldwide operations of an airline when problems occur. They are used for such tasks as diagnosing problems in complex systems and recommending corrective actions, validating complex configurations, or aiding in the design of products requiring high levels of design expertise. Some corporations have built factory expert systems that collect data about the entire production process and can reason about the process to optimize the flow of work, make rapid changes, solve problems, and bypass bottlenecks. The system uses knowledge from many specialists and factory workers. When factory processes are redesigned, the new process contains the expert system knowledge as an integral part.

O'Hare

O'Hare Airport in Chicago is one of the world's busiest. It is common to land at O'Hare and wait for half an hour before reaching a gate. A small staff carries out the exceedingly complex task of allocating gates to flights. They used to use a magnetic board with gate allocation staff putting magnetic counters with flight numbers into position on the board. Occasionally, a magnet would drop off the board while a long line of 747s shimmered in the heat, waiting for gates.

Some of the gate allocation staff become very knowledgeable about subtle requirements, problems that cause gate changes, and so on, but the complex reasoning needed for optimal gate allocation needs the help of a computer. O'Hare installed a rule-based system for gate allocation. The computer knows the incoming flights, their requirements, and problems with tight connections. The system contains many rules, and the rules can be changed quickly. The gate allocation staff constantly makes changes as problems occur, such as instrument failures, breakdowns, thunderstorms, medical emergencies, or the mayor of Chicago needing priority. The computer examines the rules and recommends optimal gate allocations.

Expert Systems "Owned" by Their Users

A lesson repeatedly learned with expert systems is that the team using the system must be able to add to the system's knowledge. They must believe in its rules and be able to contribute to them. The expert system must be a living thing that evolves as the know-how of its users evolve. The users may be able to enter rules into a PC or to sit down with a facilitator who enters rules. The rules may be adjusted or added to in workshops.

An expert system should represent knowledge in the way that its users represent knowledge. The users can then become more confident about the system and, particularly important, can continuously add to or improve the knowledge in the system. The expert system should be a valuable part of the learning process. It steadily accumulates and refines what is learned. Its knowledge becomes a basis for users to record what they learn. It is an accumulator of human learning.

Many early expert systems slipped into disuse because they did not talk the language of their users. They were often built by brilliant technicians but failed to communicate. They seemed to be created by academics for academics, and they sat on the shelves like unread books. The primary requirement of an expert system is that the users like it, "buy into the concept," and can steadily add their own knowledge and learning to the system. The expert system, in effect, should be "owned" by its users.

Exhibit 10-3 lists observations about expert systems in practice.

The Intelligent Net

When the World Wide Web first came into use, it was mostly used for transfers of messages and pictures; it was dumb in the sense that paper purchase orders are dumb. Soon it evolved so that applets of program code could be transmitted to PCs and agents could be used for exploring the Internet. The applets could be chunks of expert systems or other uses of artificial intelligence. "Intelligent" uses of the Net will be invented by developers worldwide and put to use worldwide. The Net will evolve into not only the world's largest library but also a gigantic collection of expert systems, agents (some of which will interact worldwide), and code for an infinity of purposes. Nobody can predict the eventual consequences of a hundred million computers interacting in this way.

Exhibit 10-3. Observed effects of expert systems in practice

☹ Many expert systems have fallen into disuse.
☹ Intended users did not "buy in."
☹ To succeed, the system has to communicate well; many did not. It must be an integral part of the users' daily working fabric.

☺ The best expert systems have greatly increased the capability of people who were already expert.
☺ They produce a major increase in the productivity of professionals.
☺ Nonskilled staff are able to execute some tasks that previously required experts.
☺ Expert systems improve the quality of work.
☺ They improve consistency and help avoid failures.
☺ A process team can handle far more complex processes.
☺ The best-conceived expert systems have added substantially to corporate profits (e.g., American Express's Authorizer's Assistant).

> **To succeed the system must be part of the user's daily working fabric and its users must be able to update its expertise continuously.**

Some typical benefits for designers using expert systems linked to design tools:

- Time is saved.
- Many more options are explored.
- Undesirable options are avoided.
- The design is better optimized.
- Limitations are detected earlier.
- Multiple parameters, such as those concerned with manufacturability, are considered.

> **Whatever the long-term consequences, corporations should be asking how they can put "intelligence" in the Internet to work today.**

References

1. N. R. Jennings and T. Wittig, ARCHON: Theory and Practice. In N. M. Avouris and L. Gasser, eds., *Distributed Artificial Intelligence: Theory and Praxis* (Dordrecht: Kluwer, 1992), 179–95.
2. Edward Feigenbaum, Pamela McCorduck, and H. Penny Nii, *The Rise of the Expert Company* (New York: Times Books, 1988), chap. 5.
3. James Martin, *Principles of Object-Oriented Analysis and Design* (Englewood Cliffs, NJ: Prentice-Hall, 1993).
4. This taxonomy is called a *class hierarchy* (discussed in ibid.).

11

Computerized Choreography

As dawn breaks in Africa an awesome sight is a cheetah stretching itself after sleep, looking casually around at distant movements, then suddenly racing at seventy miles per hour. A small buck leaps with astonishing agility and evades the cheetah for twenty seconds twisting and turning, and then the cheetah grabs the buck by its throat and holds on. The movements of the cheetah are exquisitely choreographed to achieve a precise purpose.

Choreography

As events happen in a cybercorp, certain sets of actions need to be choreographed with computer networks so that they relate to one another in an optimal fashion.

When customers place orders, these can be transmitted immediately to computers that plan manufacturing, so that production is scheduled to achieve fast delivery. This may be done when a diverse mix of products is manufactured. Delivery of parts and components for these products should be choreographed so that they arrive just in time and in the right sequence for the manufacturing schedule. The different steps in manufacturing can be linked electronically, and electronics tells the supplier when to deliver the next batch.

A computer-controlled assembly plant is like a complex theater performance, with the actors coming in on cue, the scene changers operating the stage machinery, and hundreds of lights being adjusted with perfect timing. A chassis floating down from above meets a power train gliding along the floor. Parts are bolted by robots, and a master cylinder is welded by a robot. The brake lines move into position at the right moment to connect them. Every person checks the work done by the previous person. Defects are found immediately so that the *cause* of any problem can be pinned down and corrected. It is everybody's job to make the choreography work as smoothly as possible.

The choreography squeezes down inventory costs and eliminates other forms of waste—space, time, money, or manpower. Every problem is recorded and analyzed thoroughly to try to prevent it from happening again. When problems occur, they have to be solved quickly, or the system will stop. Every worker understands that he or she has a critical role in keeping the system running. Everything in the factory needs to work together; such choreography needs computers. All teams, including those at suppliers, can observe the progress on their computer screens and make sure that their own activities happen on time.

Lean, just-in-time operations with computerized choreography can be applied to many aspects of business, not only assembly plants. Airlines have put much thought into choreographing their worldwide operations, maintenance, and crew scheduling. Only with complex computing can they reschedule and rechoreograph when breakdowns occur, storms delay flights, or crew members become sick. Many of the world's distribution systems are using computer networks to eliminate delays, close some warehouses, and lessen the capital tied up in inventory. Most organizations need better computerized choreography.

No Purchase Orders

General Motors' Saturn factory has computerized links to car dealers. When a customer places an order for a car with specific features, this order is entered into the factory's production schedule database immediately. The intent is to deliver the car to the customer as quickly as possible.

The suppliers are on-line to the same production schedule database. They are under contract to deliver parts needed for the production schedule on time, without receiving any purchase orders. They are contracted to deliver the right components for the right cars on the right day, palletized in the sequence of car production. The suppliers can plan their own production better by knowing the forecast schedules in the Saturn database. The supplier's computer informs the Saturn computer what has been shipped. The person who receives goods scans the bar code on them, and this information enters the computer for automatic checking. The computer initiates payment to the supplier.

In time, probably most corporations will eliminate invoice processing and adopt a rule that receipt of the correct goods automatically triggers payment (possibly after a calculated delay). Ford, at some of its plants, has gone further and adopted the rule that it pays when it *uses* the goods. As vehicles roll off the production line, payment to the suppliers is triggered. In effect Ford is saying to the supplier, "Until we use the goods, they're yours." This simplifies the payment process because if the goods are found to be of unacceptable quality, or wrong in some other way, or if production is changed so that the goods are returned to the vendor, then payments do not have to be reversed. And it dramatically improves cash flow!

The vendor with this arrangement is, in effect, financing Ford's inventory. Why would the vendor agree to this? It would agree in order to obtain *all* of the plant's business for that product, instead of a part of it, and to be reasonably sure of continuing sales. The sales are more predictable because they are geared to Ford's production. The predictability allows the vendor to schedule its own production better and reduce its inventory.

Wal-Mart pioneered the idea of allocating self-space to some large suppliers so that the vendor assumes responsibility for maintaining its own inventory on those shelves. Just as Ford pays some of its suppliers when their components are used, so large stores pay some suppliers when customers buy the goods. The store pays with cash it has already received, which has a wonderful effect on its cash flow. The supplier, not the store, bears the main inventory-carrying cost. The store enables the supplier to track its sales electronically and to replenish the inventory based on its own decision-support computing and marketing database. The stock may be managed more effectively because the supplier has a better knowledge of its nationwide sales patterns than the store.

This arrangement violates the basic principles of how stores have dealt with their suppliers in the past. But it is good for both parties. The store needs less working capital, has better use of shelf space, and suffers fewer out-of-stock situations. The supplier is assured of shelf space. It may be able to negotiate preferred end-of-aisle displays. It is more in control of its distribution and is better able to forecast product demand. It can avoid large shipments and use continuous replenishment, thus lowering its own product inventories. A manufacturer can know exactly what is sold by retail stores and hence be alerted immediately to changes in sales pattern. A supplier can supply parts or materials at just the right time. A CAD department can link to the subcontractor's design department so that they cooperate intimately in developing a new product.

Instead of battling suppliers, an enterprise joins forces with them to bring products to market faster, or to achieve other mutual advantages. Relationships between enterprises need to be reinvented. This involves major changes in philosophy and attitude.

Distribution Choreography

In 1988 the U.S. food distribution industry had about $80 billion worth of products sitting in stores and warehouses. The figure is less than half of that today. Some stores and supermarkets have introduced electronic systems for responding more efficiently to consumer demands. They monitor shelf stock with scanners and do computer-aided ordering with orders going electronically to manufacturers. In some supermarket chains, products now leave the warehouse in twelve hours, on average, and this is being driven down to three hours.

> **With today's electronics, the warehouse should be regarded as a *switching yard*, not a *holding yard*.**

Robotic warehouses are used to achieve faster turnaround of goods. Sales are monitored electronically at cash registers, and the sales are cross-checked with shelf inventory counts using bar scanners. This information is transmitted immediately to distribution warehouses and often to suppliers. There is electronic ordering and electronic payment.

> **There is no need for three levels of storage—retailer, distributor, and factory warehouse. With electronic systems, either the factory or distributor warehouse can be eliminated in many organizations.**

The acronym CAO is used for computer-aided ordering. Such systems use scanners to help determine what has been sold and to cross-check that with what is on the shelves. This information is often used with a forecasting technique based on historical sales of the product. A computer places orders based on what has been sold and what is expected to sell. The orders should be sent electronically to vendors. When goods are received at stores this should trigger electronic payment to the vendor's bank. The whole process should be paperless.

Many companies need to reengineer their distribution logistics. Distribution, factory warehousing, and marketing should not be separate isolated functions; they are part of a computer-controlled process. When retailers, wholesalers, and factory warehouses are considered part of one system, major simplifications can be made, and often one level of warehouse can be closed down.

Hill's is a pet food manufacturer, but unlike other pet food manufacturers it does not sell its products in grocery stores; they are sold instead by veterinarians, pet shops, and special pet food shops. Hill's sells food for sick animals, dogs and cats on diets, a few orangutans, and police dogs. Pet shops and veterinary clinics place orders with wholesalers; wholesalers place orders that go to factory warehouses; four factories manufacture pet food to fulfill warehouse orders. Hill's reorganized itself to create a continuous flow system to supply vets and pet shops. The factory warehouses were eliminated. The factories now ship directly to forty-eight service centers that are owned either by Hill's or by independent distributors. Many steps in inventory management were eliminated. Much time and money was saved.

Before the redesign, market executives worked on promotions to move the factory inventories. Now marketing efforts are focused on customer need and demand. Jim Keebler, the executive who achieved the reengineering, comments, "We reversed the polarity." The tension is now a pull, based on what's happening in the marketplace. Before it was a push: the company would make forecasts, fill the warehouses, and push the product on its wholesalers.[1] The new choreography saves about $7 million per year in logistics costs. It cut the order cycle time from two months to two weeks, and could cut it lower. It enabled the factory to react much more quickly to changes in demand and to serve customer needs better.

Britain's Coca-Cola & Schweppes Beverages had a different problem: extreme unpredictable peaks in soft drinks consumption when summer heat waves occurred. The soft drink company persuaded its can and bottle suppliers to store containers in their warehouses that were *full* rather than empty, to help cope with the extreme peaks. The drink company needed to decide which factories should make and ship which products, and which warehouses should be used, in order to meet the fast-changing demands. It employs *linear programming* to optimize such decisions. As its logistics decisions tightened up it found a need to use powerful "server" computers to do such computations very quickly while goods were being shipped.

To facilitate fast, choreographed business machinery, government needs to avoid any unnecessary hold-ups. Singapore reduced the time to clear goods through its ports from four days to ten minutes. The government changed the regulations to allow electronic clearing and a system called Tradenet was created, which linked the information systems of shippers, freight forwarders, banks, and customs officials.[2]

Breakdowns

It is generally true that the overall efficiency of a process is much less than the efficiency of each operation.

Suppose that ten sequential operations are needed on ten machines in order to complete a process. Each operation takes one hour, so the time needed to complete the process would be ten hours if every machine is working. However one-sixth of the time, on average, a machine is broken and being fixed. The efficiency of any one machine is then 83.3 percent. It might be tempting to think that the efficiency of the overall process is 83.3 percent. In reality, it is much worse because when a machine is idle it does not feed the next machine in the line, so it makes that machine idle also. The idle time cannot be recovered. If it takes an hour to fix each breakdown, the overall efficiency of the process is about 50 percent, but it is often much worse because some of the breakdowns take longer than an hour to fix, and then they cause multiple downstream machines to be idle.

Factory planners since the days of Henry Ford have wrestled with how to maximize the efficiency of production lines when machines break down. Much choreography of work today is far more complex. It relates to processes that span long distances and often span separate corporations. It is usually competitively desirable to minimize the elapsed time. The far-flung processes can be simulated by computer and engineered so that computer networks are used to optimize the overall choreography.

Out of the Software Straitjacket

The cybercorp needs to be a dynamic creature, constantly alert to changes in its situation, constantly adapting its actions and learning. Although it is dependent on complex software and may have complex choreography, it must be able to change its behavior very quickly and continuously determine what behavior is best.

The computer is the most flexible machine ever invented because software permits infinite variations in its behavior. But hand-coded applications can be so difficult to change that attempts to make a seemingly trivial modification set off a chain reaction of unexpected problems. Changing complex applications can be so difficult that an IT organization is often reluctant to try and users realize that they have to live with what the software does today. While business pressures demand ever more rapid change, software puts many businesses in a straitjacket.

Unchangeable computer systems have been a major contributor to businesses' decline and fall.

Corporations of the future have to be fluid and flexible or they will not survive, but the software that supports them will be ever more complex.

It is essential to design and build software that it can change as fast as the business needs to change.

Not only are programs difficult to change; it is often difficult to know *which* programs to change. Business people have rules and policies about how to deal with situations. The policies change, and should change, all the time in the search for constant improvement. A policy might, for example, state how to deal with customers who are bad payers. It must define when a customer becomes categorized as "bad payer" and may say that when this customer places orders, they are put on hold until previous payments arrive and the customer is automatically notified. Rules such as this are often buried in the spaghetti of more than one program. This rule might be inherent in the code of the payments program, the accounts receivable program, the customer order processing program, and several others. Often such a rule is not stated *explicitly* in the specifications of these programs; it is *implicit* in the code. Business people might decide to change this rule, but when they change it it is not clear what programs have to be changed. The programs often fail to reflect the desired business policies.

In the cybercorp world the rules are likely to change often, and the changes need very fast implementation. It is necessary to build software with tools that not only facilitate fast development but also express business rules explicitly so that they can be clearly understood and can be changed quickly and easily. Some modern development tools enable us to state business rules explicitly and generate code that executes the rules.[3] This is a vital step in making cybercorp operations fluid and flexible—the rules can be changed and code regenerated to implement the rules. We must be able to regenerate software very rapidly when business policies and rules change.

A business should be run in such a way that its policies and rules can be changed quickly and experimented with. There is all the difference in the world between business policies being buried in incomprehensible program code and business policies being clear, explicit input to tools that generate code.

The deeper we go into the cybercorp revolution, the more business policies and rules will be encapsulated in software.

Dynamic Changes in Choreography

The ability to translate policies and rules directly into software is changing the way some organizations are run. Just as a plant controller can turn a valve and adjust a manufacturing process, so should business people be able to modify the rules of the business and make a direct change in the software used for running the business. It is desirable to constantly adjust the rules to optimize how the business is conducted.

This dynamic controllability is a vital cybercorp characteristic, but it is quite different from the way most corporate computing works today.

When computers were first used for inventory control it was discovered what a mess stores were in. When computers require that business rules be made explicit, it is usually found that the rules are badly thought out. Today, many business policies are not explicit. The attempt to identify them and state them with enough precision to simulate their effects causes much debate.

We are moving into an era when the rules for running a business must be precise and explicit because they are implemented in software. Their effects are repeatedly simulated as conditions change, and the software that determines the behavior of critical operations can be adjusted the way a missile is steered to its target.

Brainlike Organization

It does not make much sense to compare a computer with the human brain; they are too different. However, we can compare a cybercorp with the brain because a cybercorp requires a high level of *human* intelligence throughout its organization to make it work well.

The brain has an intricate organization that enables it to perform in an amazing way. Like a corporation, it has to interact with a complex and ever-changing environment. It has many components with diverse functions, which must work together, but which must be flexible enough to constantly learn and adapt. Peter Schwartz, a key player in the planning that helped Shell to prosper through the OPEC shocks to the oil industry, comments: "An organization of the scale and complexity of Shell functions very much like a brain. Research in cognitive science might help people who want to make large organizations operate more effectively."[4]

The brain is not organized hierarchically; it has many parts that have specialized capabilities. Surgeons have explored the brains of animals, and sometimes people, with electrical probes. They have located small nodules of brain tissue that are concerned with specific skills. Some nodules deal with physical behavior, some with spatial perception, some with logical-mathematical skills, some with music, and so on. These areas are relatively independent, like departments or teams in an enterprise. Cognitive psychologist Howard Gardner discusses these brain mechanisms in his book *Frames of Mind*. He describes "the existence of several relatively autonomous human intellectual human competencies. . . . These are relatively independent of one another, and they can be fashioned and combined in a multiplicity of adaptive ways."[5]

Each component of the brain learns to improve its functioning as the human learns. Marvin Minsky sees the architecture of the brain as a dynamic, very loosely integrated collection of specialized learning agents—similar to what organizations must become.[6] Minsky developed a theory of learning based on how these agents do their individual, simple tasks in ever more complex alliances. Many of the functions of the brain require more than one agent to work in tight cooperation. The cooperating agents are usually in separate parts of the brain. They become interlinked in complex and dynamically changing patterns. Much of the power of the brain seems to stem from the messy way its agents cross-connect.[7]

Today, most people still think about organizations using spatial metaphors—the boxes and lines on an organizational chart, managers who are "higher" in the "chain of command," the number of people "in" a particular function. Spatial metaphors and language shape how people behave in organizations. Lines on organizational charts limit how people communicate—they say "one ought to follow the organizational lines"—organizational boxes define "turf" to be protected.

When empowered teams are used, employees become knowledge workers using computer networks that pervade every nook and cranny. We need new metaphors. The old spatial hierarchical metaphors block real organizational change. The cybercorp, like the brain, needs many separate competences that are linked, not hierarchically, but with a multiplicity of parallel channels that adapt to changing needs. In the cybercorp world these parallel channels will increasingly span separate corporations.

The cybercorp, like a creature, needs a mixture of tight coupling and loose coupling. A tightly coupled organization can be engineered and tuned for a specific purpose so that it carries out that purpose as efficiently as possible. A loosely coupled organization is more flexible and adaptable; it can exploit unpredictable changes. Tight coupling can produce high leverage and economies of scale, but it does so at the expense of adapting less well to changing needs. Loose coupling makes it possible to build localized teams with high creativity and energy.

> **The technology should mirror the human architecture with both tightly coupled systems optimized for specific purposes and loosely coupled systems that facilitate unpredictable change.**

Webs of Activities

An enterprise has many interconnected activities. An action in one place causes an action in another place: Activity A causes event B, which causes events C and D; event D affects activity A. There are feedback loops with varying time delays. A factory orders more material; several weeks later the material arrives. A sales manager lowers a product price, and some time later sales volume increases; this requires the production rate to be increased, but production cannot be increased beyond a certain level without establishing a second shift, which is expensive. These collections of interconnected activities can be referred to as a *system*.

> **The enterprise has a certain behavior determined by its system, referred to as** *systemic behavior*. **Complex webs of interrelated activities have behavior patterns of their own. Often these behavior patterns are contrary to the intuition of managers who make decisions and create policies. It is only too common to observe policies that had quite different effects from those that were intended. The system seems to have an agenda of its own.**

In many corporate situations, individuals, no matter how hard they try, can make things happen only to a limited extent. Like driving across a city in rush-hour traffic, they cannot achieve fast results. The *system*, represented by the city streets or the corporate organization, exhibits a behavior of its own. To speed up rush-hour travel across the city would need a fundamental redesign of the system. The corporate system represented by corporate policies and procedures not only puts a speed limit on the achievement of results, it sometimes has the opposite effects from what was intended.

The fault is not in ourselves, it is in the system.

Systemic behavior in a corporation is complex because it links together software and people. Human decision making is part of the system, and the effects of this are subtle. When we reengineer a business, we fundamentally change human decision making by building cross-functional teams and eliminating much of the hierarchical control of the past. This changes perceptions, rules, and culture. We may build a cybercorp with fundamentally changed webs of activities. We change systematic behavior and interactions. Sometimes, the consequences of the change are not what our intuition would expect.

Senge, after much study and simulation of corporate behavior observed: "Systems cause their own crises. Different people trying to maximize profits produce similar results. The cause of the problem is not external forces, such as customer behavior, and not mistakes by individuals; the cause is the system. The systemic mechanisms need to be redesigned."[8]

Long-Span Activity Webs

Where a web of activities takes place fairly quickly, managers observe it, learn about it, and try to improve it. Where the web has long time delays or causes effects in remote places, managers cannot directly observe the effects and so often do not learn about them. We will refer to webs of activities that span long distances, span separate organizations, or have long time delays as *long-span activity webs*.

It is becoming increasingly common for an action and its results to be far apart. Long-span activity webs are becoming far more common because of computer networks, global operations, intercorporate linkages, tighter relationships with trading partners, and corporate complexity. Activity webs span separate enterprises. Customers buy goods from retailers; this causes retailers to place orders with distributors; distributors then order shipments from a manufacturer; the manager consequently plans his production schedule; the manufacturer's marketing executive decides how much to spend on advertising; the advertising changes the rate at which customers buy goods, and so on. The dynamics of this entire corporate food chain are changing as the Internet and other computer networks speed up interaction.

Webs of activity might be easy to understand if they were linear; but they are not. They are filled with feedback loops.

An enterprise has many people taking actions and making decisions. The outcome of these actions depend to a large extent on activity webs and systemic behavior. An activity may lead to a result much later in time. Most managers associate activities with short-term results, not results much later. For example, a decision to eliminate features from a product in order to lower its production cost may bring short-term profits but long-term sales losses. A national decision to improve security by building new weapons causes potential adversaries to build new weapons in response and so in the long-term *lowers* security.

When activity webs have long delays, cause effects in remote places, and have feedback loops, they cause unexpected behavior. They cause consequences of management actions that the managers may not expect.

Avoiding Systems Misbehavior

Understanding systemic behavior and preventing it from having harmful effects is very important in the design of a cybercorp and its interactions with other corporations. It is desirable to map out, or model, systemic behavior and to simulate it in order to understand how it should be changed. When we build interacting cybercorps we computerize long-span webs of activities and change systemic behavior in fundamental ways.

If used well, computer networks can greatly improve long-span behavior. If used badly they can make harmful behavior much more extreme because they amplify it and speed it up.

For example, the use of derivatives has led to some extreme crashes in corporate finances. Global networks can cause sudden worldwide effects that a corporation is not ready for. Discount camera stores, for example, were able to flood the United States with foreign models of cameras that the stores could not service. Worldwide sales may grow so explosively that a corporation cannot handle them, and then its competition steps in.

The interactions that cause the most serious systemic problems usually span separate functional areas in an enterprise. Many executives understand their own functional area, but not others. Often corporate rules and politics prevent them from interfering with other areas. The separate fiefdoms for research, marketing, manufacturing, and distribution tend to prevent managers from thinking about the patterns of systemic behavior that need to be redesigned. Stovepipe IT systems hide the true cause of a problem rather than solving the problem.

As downsizing became popular in IT in the early 1990s, much money was spent to create departmental systems. These were built with an understanding of how one department worked and often no understanding of the problems caused by long-span webs of activities. Such systems often cast in concrete procedures that were causing problems. If a procedure or a value stream is redesigned without an understanding of long-span activity webs and their behavior, it will cause harmful side effects.

References

1. "How Hill's Reengineered Its Logistics Network," *Traffic Management,* November 1992.
2. J. M. Tenenbaum, R. Smith, A. M. Schiffman, A. Cavelli, and M. Fox, *The MCC Enterprise Integration Program* (Austin, TX: MCC, 1991).
3. E.g., ObjectStar from the Antares Corporation.
4. Peter Schwartz, *The Art of the Long View* (New York: Doubleday Currency, 1991).
5. Howard Gardner, *Frames of Mind: The Theory of Multiple Intelligence* (New York: Basic Books, 1983).
6. Marvin Minsky, *Society of Mind* (New York: Touchstone, 1985).
7. Ibid.
8. Peter M. Senge, *The Fifth Discipline* (New York: Doubleday Currency, 1990).

12

Counterintuitive Behavior

The cybercorp, a global human-electronic creature with conditioned reflexes and a nervous system, has certain types of behavior inherent in its rules and mechanisms. It may under certain circumstances behave in ways that we do not anticipate or do not understand. It may have surprises in store.

Big Surprises

The surprises can be pleasant or unpleasant. Nokia's sudden astonishing growth in worldwide sales of digital cellular phones in 1992 and 1993 was great for Nokia and bad news for the telephone companies that thought they owned that business.[1] In 1985, when the cost of microelectronics should have been steadily dropping, the prices of memory chips doubled, tripled, and quadrupled.[2] Semiconductor prices have suffered wild swings as they pursued their downward journey, sometimes crippling semiconductor companies.

On Black Monday, October 19, 1987, Wall Street—with almost no warning—crashed. The Dow Jones Industrial Average fell 508 points. It was a collapse that almost all investors at the time thought was impossible. The crash was made large and precipitous by the electronic systems in use. Chaos spread rapidly to every stock exchange on the planet.

Portfolio insurance, a method of hedging a stock portfolio by selling future contracts on stock indices when the market falls, was used aggressively throughout Black Monday. Computers were programmed to sell in an attempt to limit possible losses and dragged the market down with each computer-aided trade. Specialists, the buyers of last resort, were so overwhelmed by sell orders that they lacked the capital to support prices. The *Wall Street Journal* commented that such factors "fed upon one another in a furious chain reaction that was fueled by the cataclysmic power of the new global market. Linked by computers and communications networks investors big and small, from Tokyo to London and New York, leaped into the selling frenzy."[3]

Market Meltdown

The investing public remembers Black Monday as the day the markets crashed, but what happened on the next day was potentially far more dangerous. The U.S. stock market and, by extension, the world's financial markets faced a desperate crisis. In the words of the *Wall Street Journal,* "The New York Stock Exchange died."[4] Precarious but concerted intervention managed to raise it from the dead but only narrowly averted a collapse of the entire system.

On the morning of Tuesday, October 20, 1987, one after another of the major stocks broke down and could not be traded. Sears stopped trading at 11:12 A.M., Eastman Kodak at 11:28, IBM and Philip Morris at 11:30, 3M at 11:31, Dow Chemical at 11:43. The Chicago Board Options Exchange had closed. At 12:15 P.M. the New York Merchantile Exchange ordered a halt in trading of Standard & Poor's 500 futures contracts. New York Stock Exchange officials feared that selling would cascade as investors hit margin calls and big mutual funds dumped stock in the face of huge shareholder redemptions. Many large security firms called the SEC asking that the exchange be closed. An emergency meeting was held to consider closing it, but Big Board Chairman John J. Phelan commented bluntly, "If we close it, we could never open it"—reopening hundreds of stocks at once could prove impossible.[5] But by 12:30 the closing of the Big Board seemed imminent. Specialist firms, which make markets in stocks, borrow large sums from banks. These market makers, normally the last bastion of liquidity, enable investors to buy or sell stocks when no other investors are in the market. On that Tuesday morning they were shocked to find that banks refused to lend them the necessary cash. Bank credit is the lifeblood of Wall Street, and on that Tuesday morning Wall Street securities firms, as well as specialist firms, found that it had dried up. Federal Reserve Chairman Alan Greenspan and the president of the New York Federal Reserve Bank suddenly realized that this credit squeeze could cause something far worse than a stock market panic. Securities firms and specialists could start to collapse, much as banks had suddenly collapsed in the 1929 crash.

At 12:38 P.M., virtually all futures and options trading was halted; closure of the New York Stock Exchange seemed inevitable; the U.S. financial system was on the brink of total meltdown.

Then something happened that was later described as a miracle. In six minutes the Major Market Index of futures contracts, the only major index still trading, staged the most powerful rally in its history. Its sudden rally was the equivalent of a 360-point rise in the Dow Jones Industrial Average. The *Wall Street Journal* speculated that it must have been manipulated.

At the same time the Fed issued an extraordinary statement saying that it would "serve as a source of liquidity to support the economic and financial system." The Fed flooded the banking system with dollars by buying government securities. Major investment banks called the chief executives of major clients urging them to buy back their own stock. First Boston alone called about 200 clients.

It was like jump-starting a patient when his heart has stopped in an operating theater. At 1:00 P.M. buy orders started flowing into securities firms. With pressure and dollars from the Fed, the ten largest New York banks doubled their lending to securities firms that week. In the nick of time collapse was averted, but key participants said that they were "deeply shaken by how close to catastrophe the system came."[6] Perhaps the most extraordinary fact about these events is that they occurred in the middle of an economic boom in absence of any calamity. The events represented *the behavior of the system,* not some external crisis.

Counterintuitive Consequences

Much of the skill of managers is based on what experience has taught them. They observe the results of their actions and learn from them. However, there are certain results that they cannot observe because these results take place far away or far in the future. Intuition is trained by experience, but that experience has a black hole in it: it cannot directly observe cause and effect when the effect is distant in time or space.

In the cybercorp world we increasingly build systems that span long distances, span separate organizations, and span time; hence cause and effect are separated. Managers then do not learn correctly from observable experience. Such systems can give counterintuitive results. A manager does what seems obvious, but it does not produce an obvious outcome.

Local autonomy often results in decisions that are disastrous for the organization as a whole. Sometimes corporations find themselves in downward spirals where vigorous corrective actions only seem to make things worse. The managers are trapped in a pattern of systemic behavior and do not comprehend the mechanisms at work. To get out of the downward spiral they need to change the system. The incremental improvement process of TQM does not work; a fundamental change in the systemic behavior is needed. Sometimes this can be achieved with relatively straightforward redesign of procedures using information technology to eliminate time delays or the effects of distance.

System Dynamics

Counterintuitive behavior was demonstrated by Jay Forrester in his seminal book *Industrial Dynamics.*[7] He modeled webs of activity with a computer and demonstrated how they can cause various forms of counterintuitive results in corporations. Decision makers intuitively expect their actions to have a certain effect, but in reality they cause a different effect. Decision makers are often pleased with the good short-term effects of their decisions and unaware of the harmful long-term effects. Often a corporation has policies that are well-intended but cause a web of activities that behaves in harmful ways. If managers had understood the systemic behavior, they would have acted differently. Decision makers often focus on symptoms and take actions that give benefit in the short term, but cause problems in the long term.

Forrester's work is referred to as *system dynamics.* He has helped apply system dynamics modeling to many corporations, some of which refuse to talk about it because they believe it gives them a major competitive advantage. Forrester expanded his system dynamics work from corporations to government issues and illustrated how many issues such as urban decay, unemployment, and ecological problems are characteristics of systems that are counterintuitive to decision makers. The problems are often made worse by well-intentioned policies that cause a complex system to behave in ways that are not understood.[8]

Peter Senge and his colleagues at MIT have studied and simulated *systemic behavior* in corporations. Senge refers to the understanding of systemic behavior as "the fifth discipline."[9] He believes that most managers and corporate decision makers do not understand corporate systemic behavior. The widespread development of such understanding will change the way we engineer our enterprises.

Senge shows that controls that managers put into place to deal with problems often have a limited effect on corporate behavior. He comments that the system perspective tells us we must look beyond individual mistakes or bad luck to understand important problems. We must look beyond personalities and events. We must look into the underlying *structures* that shape individual actions and create the conditions where certain types of events become likely.

The system causes it own behavior. Placed in the same system different people tend to produce similar results. When we plug into the Internet we may dramatically change systemic behavior.

Oscillations in a Distribution System

Senge has run an extraordinary demonstration (based on Jay Forrester's work on Industrial Dynamics, reference 7) of how management can take what appear to be rational actions but the counterintuitive nature of a system defeats their good intentions. For over twenty years, at MIT's Sloan School of Management, a classroom simulation has been conducted of a retailer-wholesaler distribution system referred to as "the beer game." [10]

In the beer game, retailers respond to customer orders for a specialty beer by placing orders with a wholesaler. Wholesalers respond to this order by placing orders with the factory that makes the beer. Classes are divided into three groups playing the roles of retailer managers, wholesaler managers, and factory warehouse managers, respectively. Each group is told that it will be judged on how well it runs its business and is instructed to manage its inventory in an optimal manner, placing appropriate orders so as to maximize profits. What happens astonishes the participants. They think they are making clever decisions but the results, far from maximizing profits, are disastrous.

The beer game has been played innumerable times with people trying to run their simulated business as well as possible, but all generate similarly catastrophic results; they all build up excessive inventories of beer they cannot unload, and there are wild oscillations. The fault lies not in the intelligence of the decision makers, but in the structure of the system. The simulation starts with a situation in which the order rate from retailers' customers has been constant for a long time—4 cases of beer per week. Suddenly, the order rate doubles to 8 cases per week and remains constant at this new level. One might expect the retailer and wholesaler to adjust their orders in an equally regular fashion. What actually happens is that the simple change in customer behavior triggers wild overreactions in the system.

In a typical session the retailer reacts to the increase in sales and doubles the weekly order it places with the wholesaler, from 4 to 8. There is normally a delay of four weeks between the retailer's placing an order and the wholesaler's truck delivering it. The truck comes once a week, and each week the retailer gives the truck driver a new order. The retailer usually maintains an inventory of 12 cases, which gives a comfortable 8-case surplus in the store. In week 2, the inventory falls to 8; in week 3, it falls to 4. Alarmed, the retailer orders 12 cases in week 3 and telephones the wholesaler instead of merely filling in the truck driver's weekly order form. Responding to this, the truck delivers 5 cases in week 4, so the inventory falls to 1. The retailer reacts by ordering 16 cases in week 5 but completely runs out of stock.

The retailer has loyal customers and many of them leave their phone numbers saying they will buy beer when it comes in. Its entire inventory of beer has gone, so it places large orders to try and replenish it.

The wholesaler serves a big city and its surrounding area. It places orders for beer with the brewery. It serves many retailers all of whom have increased their orders in a broadly similar way. The wholesaler places orders by the gross each week when the brewery truck arrives, and again, it is four weeks before the truck delivers the order. Before the rise in customer orders the wholesaler ordered 4 gross, week after week after week. That was enough to maintain an inventory of 12 gross.

In week 4, the wholesaler starts to receive higher orders from the retailers. These continue in the following weeks, and by week 6 the wholesaler's inventory has also dropped to zero. The wholesaler telephones the brewery, and in week 6, the brewery manages to make extra shipments from its warehouse. In week 7, it makes larger shipments but exhausts its limited warehouse stock. In week 8, the wholesaler is expecting to receive still larger shipments but the brewery delivers only 4 gross.

The brewery can ramp up production only slowly, and meanwhile the wholesaler's backlog is rising alarmingly, so the wholesaler jacks up the weekly order rate. Soon the wholesaler has over 100 gross in unfilled orders from retailers and makes the order rate even higher.

The brewery eventually catches up. It delivers large shipments in weeks 14 and 15. The wholesaler ships all this beer to retailers to make up past orders. The retailers are then suddenly overstocked, so they reduce their orders to zero. In weeks 16, 17, and 18, the wholesaler receives large deliveries in fulfillment of earlier orders. Inventory suddenly grows massively, and the wholesaler is alarmed that the retailers are ordering nothing. Because of this situation the wholesaler also stops ordering.

This sudden build-up of inventory is expensive for the wholesaler, but it is catastrophic for the brewery. The brewery spent money to prepare for the increase in production. New people were hired, and a second shift was established. By week 14, the brewery was still well behind its order rate. By the time it had caught up, to its total surprise, the orders dropped to zero. The beer-drinking customers continued to buy this beer at double the old rate for several weeks and then drifted back to the old level. Retailers stop ordering as they slowly sell their excess stock.

In many runs of the beer game the brewery becomes so overstocked with unsalable beer that production has to be stopped. The surge in sales that should have been good news for the brewery caused it be closed.

Lessons From the Story

Senge describes how this beer distribution simulation has been played out thousands of times in classes and management seminars on five continents, with young people, old people, people of all different cultures, often with seasoned managers, and sometimes with executives with years of experience in production-distribution systems. Every time the simulation is played out, the same crises ensue. Almost all players end up with large inventories that they cannot unload. The effect on the factory is catastrophic.

Many real-life examples of crises in production-distribution systems exist, where a small change in customer demand has caused excessive overstocking, wild oscillations, and severe losses. In the semiconductor industry, it has happened multiple times. There are many different examples of webs of activities with built-in delays that behave in a similarly counterintuitive way.

Erratic or suboptimal behavior is usually caused by decision makers' not having the right information. Long-span webs of activities tend to have bad information because of time delays and long distances. Information is often channeled in an organization and not given to a decision maker who needs it. The flow of information needs to be changed.

Senge describes three lessons from the beer distribution simulation.

First, *systems cause their own crises.* Different people trying to maximize profits produce similar results. The cause of the problem is not external forces, such as customer behavior, and not mistakes by individuals; the cause is the system. The systemic mechanisms need to be redesigned.

Second, *human decision making is part of the system, and the effects of this are subtle.* We translate perceptions, goals, rules, and cultural behavior into action, and this often has counterintuitive effects.

Third, *leverage comes from new ways of thinking.* The cause of a system's bad behavior is often not understood. If it were understood, we could redesign the system so as to avoid bad behavior. We fail to understand that it is the design of the process that is causing instability.

Redesign With Cybercorp Thinking

Perhaps the most extraordinary aspect of Senge's beer game is that *an almost trivial use of computers would have completely prevented the problem* (and Senge, after ten years of beer gaming, does not mention it in his book). This reflects real life.

In many corporate situations seriously harmful behavior could have been prevented by relatively simple IT systems, but managers thought of computers only in terms of e-mail and spreadsheets.

The problem, like the problem in the Beer Game, is caused by the players' not having the right information. If the wholesaler knew the *real* customer orders it would not have overstocked; if the factory knew the real customer orders it would have modified its production rate by a realistic amount. It would be easy to build a computer system that makes the customer orders visible to the wholesalers and the factory.

We are now rushing into the cybercorp era. Cybercorps often have long-span webs because computer-linked events are separated by great distances. Computer power, cyberspace, and virtual operations are *amplifiers of systemic behavior.* They make possible sudden growth like Netscape, extreme success stories like Nokia cellular phones, and sudden crashes like Barings Bank. To lessen the danger of beer game oscillations, computer systems are needed that get full information to decision makers. To survive, a jungle creature needs alert senses; the cybercorp needs networks that give it immediate knowledge of events.

Once we realize that the problems are caused by the *structure* of the system, we can change the structure. Often a major change in behavior can be brought about by a relatively simple change. *Major leverage can result from an inexpensive change.*

Delayed Knowledge

Delays are a major cause of systemic problems. The overstocking of beer in the above example is made worse by long delays. If the wholesaler delivered the retailer's orders in one week, not four, and the factory responded to the wholesaler in one week, then much less overstocking would take place. In the cybercorp world, the wholesaler and factory should have immediate knowledge of customer orders.

In general, the shorter the delays in a system, the less prone it is to extreme overshoots or oscillations of high amplitude. Delays and expense are caused by having three levels of inventory holding—factory, wholesaler, and retailer. Some organizations have simplified distribution by changing to two levels. Knowledge of sales ought to pass directly from the customer outlet to the factory production planner. In worldwide organizations like Benetton, information about customers' buying patterns should go immediately from retail stores to the central computers that plan production and distribution.

A Canadian firm invented snowmobiles and sea scooters. It found itself in trouble, losing world market share rapidly to Japanese machines that it regarded as copies of its products. The firm had organized its factory to make snowmobiles in the summer for sale next winter and sea scooters in the winter for sale next summer. However, it did not have good information about worldwide customer demand. Sometimes its inventory of sea scooters ran out early in the season. The Japanese then moved aggressively to fill the gaps.

What the firm needed was cybercorp senses. All dealers worldwide should have transmitted immediate details of customer orders to the factory. They should also have transmitted detailed sales forecasts. The factory should have been designed to respond quickly to changes in sales by making a varying mix of snowmobiles and sea scooters, to help ensure that orders were not lost. The change was needed with extreme urgency because of the rate of market loss, but the IT management, thinking in terms of traditional mainframe networks, thought that such a system was too difficult to build, and the top management did not know that such a system was possible. *Today it would be trivial to implement—every dealer's PC could be linked via the Internet.*

A factory needs the best information possible to plan its production schedules. In traditional retailer-wholesaler-factory networks, production planning is based on old information badly distorted by retailers and wholesalers trying to protect themselves. The best solution would be to have point-of-sale data transmitted electronically to the factory.

> **Throughout corporations today, one finds numerous examples of not getting the right information to the right people at the right time. For every decision and planning process the cybercorp designer should ask, "What is the best possible information? What system is needed to produce it fast enough?"**

Feedback

Control engineers are familiar with the concept of *feedback.* In electronics, for example, a fraction of the output signal from one stage of a circuit is returned to the input of that stage or to a preceding stage. The signal that is fed back is used to regulate the behavior of the circuit. Similarly, in business, knowledge about the output of a process is fed to whoever controls that process or a related process.

Nature is full of feedback systems. A lake has a few fish in it. In April, they produce hundreds of babies. Next year, the pond is teeming with fish, and they produce thousands of babies. Next year, there are tens of thousands. Not all of these babies can grow into adults because there is not enough food, so the older fish start eating the babies and the only ones that survive are those with a place to hide. The pond develops a cycle of population growth and dieback.

Recent management theory has become concerned with such systemic behavior. We all work as part of a system in which there are feedback loops. *The effects of this are often not clear to us because we are part of the system. The fish in the pond do not know why their population grows and dies back.*

Cybercorp mechanisms change the feedback loops in business. They often make events happen much faster. They link together events over large distances and in separate corporations. An event in one corporation can trigger an event in a different corporation at electronic speed. Such linkages need to be put to use with conscious design rather than being allowed to cause unexpected interactions.

Positive and Negative Feedback

Feedback is a chain of cause-and-effect relationships in the form of a loop. The result of a process is monitored and fed back to whatever is controlling the process. There are two types of feedback, positive and negative. With *negative feedback,* when an output variable changes in one direction the process reacts so as to change it in the *opposite* direction. With *positive feedback,* when an output variable changes in one direction the process reacts so as to change it in the *same* direction.

Negative feedback is a very widespread phenomenon. Information about the results of a process are fed back to whatever is controlling that process. If the temperature is too high, the process acts to lower the temperature. Negative feedback is used to continually adjust a variable to a desired value. A person driving a car is exercising feedback control over it. A missile homing in on a target is steered using negative feedback.

Positive feedback can cause accelerating growth. When a variable grows this triggers action that makes it grow more; when it grows more this triggers action to make it grow yet more; and so on. Compound interest is a form of positive feedback. The longer your money grows at a fixed interest rate the more money there is to grow. If Henry VIII had left his money in a fixed-interest account it would have been a large amount by today.

Positive Feedback

With positive feedback an increase in A may cause an increase in B, which causes an increase in A. For example:

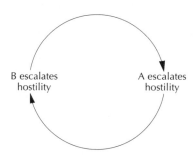

Exhibit 12-1. Positive feedback driving ongoing growth of the cellular phone business

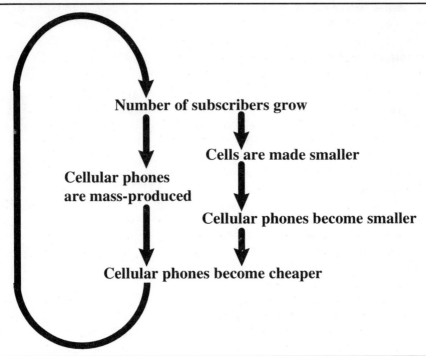

Number of subscribers grow

Cellular phones
are mass-produced

Cells are made smaller

Cellular phones become smaller

Cellular phones become cheaper

Positive feedback can have good effects or bad. For example, Exhibit 12-1 shows positive feedback causing ongoing growth of the cellular phone industry. Companies (or individuals, like Craig McCaw) that understood the interactions in Exhibit 12-1 and made it their business in the 1980s experienced spectacular growth.

Positive feedback often causes *exponential* growth. The growing item doubles in a certain time period and continues doubling. The more it grows, the more it is capable of growing. It continues to grow exponentially until other forces limit the growth. The capability of microchips grew exponentially for three decades, for example, enabling ongoing growth in the power of computers.

When exponential growth encounters an unmovable limit, that limit can be approached very rapidly. For example, a patch of weed on a pond doubles in size every day. As more weed grows, that weed also doubles. It will choke the entire pond in 100 days. By the start of day 97, nobody takes much notice; it still occupies only 6.25 percent of the surface, a narrow band around the perimeter. In four more days, it will destroy the pond.

Negative Feedback

We often do not think of negative feedback as having harmful effects. It is generally used to keep something on target. However, when long delays occur, negative feedback causes oscillations. The thermostat maintains the room at almost constant temperature, whereas the man permits large swings in temperature to occur because he does not act quickly or often enough. He waits until he feels cold and then loads logs on the fire, but it takes some time to bring the temperature back to 70 degrees. It is characteristic of a human controller that, when he realizes that the *error* has become large, he overcompensates; he loads too many logs on the fire in an attempt to correct the error quickly and so causes the temperature to swing too high.

In this way, *oscillations* occur around the desired state. They may be small and of no significance, or they may be large, wasteful, and damaging. At worst, oscillations can increase in magnitude until the system becomes unstable, as with the beer game.

Multiple Interactions

In business there are many feedback loops. Some of them are subtle and many take months or years to play out their effects. Often, there is not one feedback loop but multiple causality paths that interact with one another. The patterns of interactions tend to have a behavior of their own that may be counterintuitive to decision makers.

- A highly successful real-estate developer makes large profits and borrows to the hilt for aggressive expansion. The area becomes overbuilt, and the market turns bad. The developer is stuck with high costs on long-term projects and massive loans that it cannot repay. The developer goes bankrupt.

- A company making educational products persuaded its customers to sign long-term contracts so that they would receive new products at a discount. When they had many customers with long-term contracts, financial executives decided that they could improve the profits by trimming back the production of new products. For a time, this improved the financial picture, and the company was very profitable. The business was managed so as to maximize the profits. However, the customers perceived the cutback and did not renew their contracts. A collapse in expected contract renewals caused disastrous cash-flow problems and wrecked the company.

- Department A adjusts its budget numbers in an unrealistic way, trying to obtain a larger slice of the pie. Other departments react to this by similarly adjusting their budgets. Department A, determined to increase its share, further adjusts its budget. The other departments follow suit. Higher-level management is led to believe in a totally unrealistic set of numbers.

- A car manufacturer planning a new model goes to many potential suppliers, and aggressively tries to drive the price down. Suppliers deliberately bid low in order to win a contract that will provide business for many years, knowing that they will have to raise the price later. This causes many cost increases for the car manufacturer, which may make it difficult to make the new model a success. The suppliers keep their true costs secret, and hence there is much less detailed communication between the supplier and manufacturer than there should be about mutually beneficial design changes.

Electronic Speed

Because cybercorp linkages give *fast* feedback they have two effects. *Negative feedback can be made more efficient,* and harmful oscillations like those in the beer game can be removed. *Positive feedback can become more extreme,* causing very rapid growth or unexpected collapse.

A control mechanism needs its feedback to be sufficiently rapid. James Watt's invention of the flying-ball governor was essential to the design of the steam engine. If the steam engine went too fast, the governor released steam and the engine slowed down. This needed to happen reasonably quickly otherwise the boiler might blow up. (It did on early steam engines!) The craziness demonstrated by the beer game is rather like the behavior of a steam engine without a fast-acting governor. Cybercorp mechanisms must be designed to make negative feedback suitably fast.

Fast positive feedback can cause an avalanche effect. This is highly desirable in marketing if products can be delivered fast enough to keep up with it. Feedback mechanisms should detect when a product is capable of high growth and every possible action taken to cause an avalanche. Positive feedback can also cause arms races, market panics, or competitive fights that no one can win.

I was lambasted by one corporate president who expressed the view that events are happening too fast. Computers, he said, cause financial crashes and wild currency swings. That chief executive should understand that *with negative feedback* speed is desirable, otherwise the steam-engine boiler might blow up, and *with positive feedback* speed can cause an avalanche effect that can be great if it is like Nokia's conquest of the cellular phone market but disastrous if it is like Black Monday on Wall Street.

The effects of electronic feedback mechanisms need to be understood by executives, harnessed where helpful, and controlled where harmful.

Leverage

The term *leverage* is used to imply that a small change in a process produces a large effect. It is desirable to search for high leverage. High leverage can often be achieved by building systems that move information to decision makers with electronic speed. These systems may need to span functional areas or electronically link separate corporations. Computerized systems can eliminate the delays that cause systemic oscillations.

High-leverage changes are usually not obvious to the corporate players because the systemic behavior is not understood. It is desirable to map out the systemic behavior, and possibly simulate it, in order to understand how it can be changed.

Cybercorp World

> **Corporations of the cybercorp world will be increasingly intertwined in complex interdependencies, like the ecology of a rain forest, except that cybercorp relationships span global distances.**

Cybercorp design demands a nonparochial viewpoint. We need to redesign old procedures with an understanding of long-span webs of interactions. The speed of electronic linkages makes it possible to simplify interactions and eliminate many of the delays that cause overswings. At the same time, new complexities are being invented with virtual relationships through computer-to-computer links. However, most enterprises are building parochial systems today. The pressure for downsizing encouraged the building of localized systems. Old mainframe systems often make it difficult to optimize long-span interactions. Instead of reengineering their obsolete code, IT organizations should be designing new systems with an understanding of cybercorp interactions.

> **Very often we tend to focus on the symptoms of problems rather than the underlying systemic structure. We can repair or improve the symptoms, but this has only a short-term effect. Failure to deal with, or even understand, the underlying cause usually makes matters worse in the long run.**

There are many examples in business of managers giving aspirin when the patient has cancer.

Actions That Are Needed

There are important actions that should be taken to limit the harmful effects of long-span interactions:

1. *Eliminate delays where possible.* Delays in systems cause counterintuitive behavior, as in the beer game. We should use cybercorp techniques to reduce the delays by just-in-time techniques, continuous-flow manufacturing, point-of-sale information transmitted to distributors, worldwide sales information transmitted to production planners, travel-department computers online to airline computers, and so on.

2. *Link causes and geographically distant effects.* Dangerous feedback occurs when cause and effect are far apart so that decision makers do not associate them. A decision that looks good locally may have distant effects that are harmful. We can build Internet or intranet systems that enable decision makers to observe cause-and-remote-effect relationships.

3. *Link causes and time-distant effects.* When an action has effects that occur at a different time, the effects are often not visible. We must make such effects *visible* to the decision makers by gathering the relevant information and creating appropriate reports or displays.

4. *Combine responsibility for cause and effect.* In hierarchical organizations, an action taken in one part of the organization is often entirely separate from the consequences of that action that take place in a different part of the organization. The cybercorp should be designed around value streams, with each value-stream team responsible for actions and associated results. If the results occur far away, the team should be linked electronically to those results.

5. *Stop feedback before it becomes dangerous.* Positive feedback that can cause escalation of problems, or growth and collapse, should be stopped before it does harm. Negative feedback should be prevented from causing large oscillations. Processes should be designed to prevent harmful escalation or overswings.

6. *Simulate the system dynamics.* Managers or staff can learn with computer models of reality rather than reality itself. The models shrink time and space and permit endless experimentation.

7. *Facilitate learning about system behavior.* Managers and decision makers need to be taught about systemic behavior. We can create examples of typical systemic patterns and train managers to look for them, recognize them, and understand the behavior. While rarely done today, this is likely to become a valuable form of training for management and decision makers. Senge describes ten common archetypes of systemic behavior that are counterintuitive unless an executive's intuition is trained to recognize them.[11]

8. *Build closer interactions among trading partners.* Close computerized relationships should be built between trading partners to prevent overswings, delays, and harmful feedback. A vendor may have on-line access to a customer's inventory file. Information from bar-code readers in retailers may be transmitted directly to manufacturers. Ecosystem members may agree to exchange computerized information.

9. *Simplify systems and their human interactions.* Thrashing and suboptimal behavior is often made worse by systems or webs of activities that are unnecessarily complex. IT makes it possible to eliminate intermediate stages in processes. Hierarchies and middlemen can often be eliminated. Multistage processes can often be replaced with one team with computerized information. We need ruthless simplification of complexity.

10. *Stop building stovepipe systems.* In the beer game situation, if the retailer, distributor, and factory each had its own computer systems optimized to its own needs, this would not stop the harmful overswings. Many systems built today have a narrowly focused viewpoint that makes overswings worse. Systems should be designed with cybercorp principles.

References

1. William Echikson, "How Nokia Wins in Cellular Phones," *Fortune International,* March 21, 1994.
2. Steven Burkey and Ken Siegmann, "Memory Board Prices Surging in the Wake of Chip Shortage," *PC Week,* March 1, 1988.
3. "Black Monday, What Really Ignited the Market's Collapse after Its Long Climb," *Wall Street Journal,* December 16, 1987, p. 1.
4. James B. Stewart and Daniel Hertzberg, "Terrible Tuesday, How the Stock Market Almost Disintegrated a Day after the Crash," *Wall Street Journal,* November 26, 1987, p. 1.
5. *Wall Street Journal,* December 16, 1987, p. 1.
6. Ibid., p. 23.
7. Jay W. Forrester, *Industrial Dynamics,* Portland, OR: Productivity Press, 1961.
8. Jay W. Forrester, *Urban Dynamics,* Portland, OR: Productivity Press, 1969.
9. Jay W. Forrester, *World Dynamics,* Portland, OR: Productivity Press, 1971.
10. Ibid.
11. Ibid.

13

Beyond Darwin

Teenagers blundering their way through "multiuser dungeon" (MUD) games on the Internet might almost be in training for cybercorp adventures in later life. One could design MUD games specifically for such training with virtual venture capitalists instead of dragons.

Intense competition combined with mercurial change will make future business tougher. The slow-changing stability of the past will not come back. *The genie is out of the bottle;* cyberspace cannot be switched off. In the cybercorp world some business operations will work well and some will not; most will need extensive refining. Feeling one's way into the future needs constant trial and error; it is a process of high-speed evolution in which only the fittest will survive.

The central concept of evolutionary theory is that species evolve by a process of undirected variation and natural selection—in Darwin's phrase, "Multiply, vary, let the strongest live and the weakest die."[1] Random genetic mutations occur, and some of these fit their environment better than others. Corporations evolve in a similar way, trying out endless variations. As the environment changes the variations best suited to it tend to survive and those poorly suited to it tend to perish. The genes of the survivors stay in the gene pool, so the species evolves in that direction. Mitsubishi test-markets a variety of camcorders in Tokyo's Akihabara electronics retailing district and quickly withdraws those models that get no customers to bite.

James Collins and Jerry Porras conducted a five-year research project to identify and study corporations that have been exceptionally successful over a long time. This study became the basis for their excellent book *Built to Last.*[2] They concluded that one of the habits that made these long-term survivors successful was that *visionary companies more aggressively* **harness** *the power of evolution*. Great companies succeed, they wrote, "not primarily as the result of brilliant foresight and strategic planning, but largely as consequences of a basic process—namely, try a lot of experiments, seize opportunities, keep those that work well (consistent with the core ideology), and fix or discard those that don't."[3]

The difference in the cybercorp era is that corporate evolution will be much faster and wilder. Records for growth rates in young corporations are being broken constantly. At the same time corporations crash faster. With electronics, new corporate thrusts can spread around the planet at lightning speed but can be overtaken by competitive thrusts equally fast.

Successful corporate processes are likely to be those where there is constant experimentation—systematically trying out new product ideas, marketing approaches, manufacturing techniques, and so on, experimenting with virtual operations, trying new uses of the Net, repeatedly refining ideas that look promising, and quickly dropping the ones that do not.

Electronics should be used to facilitate learning by experimentation. For example, a retail organization can accumulate in a computer details of every transaction and experiment with different sales arrangements in different stores to see which work best. It might display a line of soft toys next to infants' clothes to see whether that increases the sales of soft toys. The Sports Authority, a specialized sporting goods retailer, asked customers to give their postal codes; 98 percent did so. It amassed profiles of about sixty postal codes per store. This enabled it to assess the effectiveness of local advertising. It experimented with advertising, trying different ideas in different postal codes and measuring the results in a set of controlled experiments.

The company with the most new ideas has the best chance of winning if those ideas are constantly tested, refined, linked to good marketing, and the good ideas refined and the poor ones dropped quickly

---

Evolution and Darwinian Profits

Capitalist society is based on competition and survival of the fittest, as in Darwin's world. Even in noncapitalist countries survival of the fittest ultimately prevails because too many unfit corporations can bring down the country's economy. In a world that is increasingly interdependent, there is no hiding place. The evolutionary playing field is global, and as the world changes from smokestack industry to knowledge industry the cycle time of corporate evolution is shortening dramatically.

James Collins and Jerry Porras distill a simple piece of advice from their lengthy study of successful corporations: "Try a lot of stuff and keep what works." They describe the evolutionary process as *branching and pruning:* "If you add enough branches to a tree and intelligently prune the deadwood, then you'll likely evolve into a collection of healthy branches well positioned to prosper in an ever-changing environment."

3M has been a master of evolution. Collins and Porras commented, "If we had to bet our lives on the continued success and adaptability of any single company in our study over the next fifty to one hundred years, we would place that bet on 3M."[4] 3M began life as a failure and had to search desperately for something, indeed anything, that could keep the company going. Many of the products that made 3M successful came into existence more or less by accident. But 3M was a machine designed to encourage such accidents and capitalize on them when they occurred. To stimulate experimentation that might lead to lucky accidents 3M has a long-standing tradition that encourages technical employees to spend 15 percent of their time on projects of their own choosing and initiative. This 15 percent rule has led to many unplanned products and variations on products.

In 1974, for example, an employee, Art Fry, singing in a church choir had difficulty finding the hymns because his bookmarks would flutter out. He dreamed up the idea of sticky bookmarks. A colleague, Spence Silver, had been doodling around with weird adhesives, mixing chemicals "just to see what would happen." Together they managed to make bookmarks with the right degree of stickiness.[5] Initial market surveys said that sticky bookmarks was a cuckoo idea that nobody wanted, but Fry and Silver tinkered with sticky bookmarks that you could write on, and Post-it Notes were born—one of 3M's spectacularly profitable products.

With a somewhat similar story, 3M invented masking tape in the 1920s, and then its immensely profitable Scotch tape. Before that, it had no idea that it would be in the tape business. For seventy years 3M has produced an ongoing stream of unplanned products and mutations of existing products. As in nature's evolution, many were junked but some became successful. An amazing cornucopia resulted: thermo-fax copying, front projection photography, warehouse conveyor systems, airport runway markings, video recording tape, railroad car identification systems, even targets for laser fusion—perhaps not as diverse as on David Attenborough's nature programs, but give it time. 3M management had no idea what they were going to come up with next. By 1990, sales reached $13 billion and averaged about 20 percent return on sales. 3M had forty-two product divisions with many relatively small factories in forty states. Each division was expected to generate 25 percent of its sales from products and services introduced within the previous five years, and in 1993 it heated up that rule to *30 percent of sales from things introduced in the previous four years.*

Evolutionary progress is *unplanned* progress. Many of the innovations that have made corporations great have happened by accident. Silicon Valley is full of accidental empires.[6] The Internet itself was an accident. While the giants were *talking* about information highways the ants *actually built one.* MCI's data services chief commented in 1994, "We thought of the Internet as an interesting model, but not a necessary one," and in 1995, "We're probably investing more money in the Internet than any company in history."[7]

One thing we can say with certainty about the cybercorp world is that it will be chock-a-block full of surprises.

Failure Is Our Most Important Product

R. W. Johnson, Jr., of Johnson & Johnson (J&J) became famous for his statement "Failure is our most important product." He meant that an essential part of evolution is to recognize failures and terminate them. J&J has had some expensive failures, including ventures in heart valves, kidney dialysis equipment, and Ibuprofen pain relievers, but in spite of these J&J has never posted a loss in its 108-year history.[8] Growing many branches and pruning the failures has been an essential part of growing J&J's spectacular growth. Collins and Porras comment that it looks to outsiders as though the tree has been mapped out by a strategic genius when in fact it grew by trial and error with periodic failures and favorable accidents.[9]

Playing God

Darwinian evolution appears to have directed the growth of species on earth for several billion years (probably in the neo-Darwinian form described by modern biologists, some of whom provide highly entertaining reading).[10] But it is a very crude form of evolution. The cybercorp needs something much better.

The first problem with Darwinian (or neo-Darwinian) evolution is that it is very slow. Mutations occur infrequently, and natural selection chooses those that are well suited to their environment, but at a glacial pace. It works if you have a billion years. Second, there is no intelligence at work. Nobody is playing God. Darwin referred to natural selection as "clumsy, wasteful, blundering, slow and horribly cruel."[11] If somebody were playing God they could say quickly: "Yes. I like that. Keep it. No. Scrap that one. OK, of these twenty let's go with number 17."

The Pompidou modern art museum in Paris once had an extraordinary exhibit showing art being created by a process of evolution. A Connection Machine 5 supercomputer, a black cube covered with dancing red lights worthy of an art museum, was connected to twenty large monitors each displaying a spectacular image.

Karl Sims had programmed the machine to "breed" pictures. The machine identifies patterns of pixels, creates an image, and can create endless mutations of that image. It displays twenty variations of an image and asks a person to choose which he likes best. It takes the image he chooses, creates twenty variations on that, and repeats this process over and over again. The machine generates each new set of images faster than the person can point out his favorite. The result was an ever-evolving collection of astonishingly beautiful images.[12]

The results are truly astonishing. One can start with an image of a flower arrangement, a Mondrian, a space station, the Mona Lisa, a centipede, a gothic cathedral, or even a telephone bill and after twenty or thirty iterations have images of rich and bizarre complexity that no human artist would have created. The individual plays God, directing a very fast process of aesthetic evolution. Sims's evolution is very different from Darwinian evolution because instead of *natural selection* there is *intelligent selection.*

The mathematical logic of breeding pictures is essentially the same as that of breeding horses, but the mutations occur in milliseconds not years and have infinite variability, whereas a horse is a horse. Mutations of cybercorps will come fast and often be surprising.

Second-Order Evolution

Karl Sims's breeding of pictures evolves a *product.* It is fascinating because the evolution is so fast. A deeper form of evolution is that which evolves a *process for creating a product.*

We will refer to evolving a product or service as *first-order evolution* and evolving processes and the rules governing processes as *second-order evolution.* Business process redesign should be an ongoing evolutionary activity. The rapid evolution of lean manufacturing processes in Japanese car factories was second-order evolution. So is the reinvention of value streams and steady improvement of value-stream processes.

First-order evolution evolves goods or services; second-order evolution evolves the clockwork by which the goods and services are created.

If we consider the movie industry, first-order evolution would apply judgment to movies. Good movies would become well known and accessible; bad movies would be forgotten. Second-order evolution would apply judgment to the process of making movies. Good processes would be increasingly accepted and enhanced; bad processes would die. Similarly in software: first-order evolution would select the good products at the expense of the poor ones; second-order evolution would select and enhance the methodologies for making good products.

First-order evolution is directly visible to customers; second-order evolution is not. In the 1980s, for example, a customer might have judged that a Toyota car was better than a General Motors car; she would not have known that Toyota factory processes were better than the GM factory processes.

The successful cybercorp needs fast second-order intelligent evolution. It applies intelligence to evolving its *processes* as rapidly as possible, and to achieve this the processes must be *designed* for rapid evolution.

Third-Order Evolution

A third type of evolution takes place outside of the corporation. We have stressed that cybercorps of different types interlink to form an ecosystem. Cybercorp ecosystems evolve rapidly. A leadership corporation should understand the ecosystems it plays in and constantly reevaluate its role in shaping and benefiting from these ecosystems.

As the hardwired clockwork of the industrial era gives way to the electronic caprice of the cybercorp era, the rules of the game will not stay constant like soccer rules but will change in an increasingly mercurial way. There will be no fixed goalposts. First- and second-order evolution are about playing the game well; third-order evolution is about changing the rules of the game.

In 1992 Intel was confronted with competitors cloning its highly profitable processor chips. Intel could only stay ahead of them by introducing a succession of faster chips. However, if customers only used PCs for spreadsheets and word processing, they did not really need faster processors. So Intel demonstrated to the computer community the potential value of multimedia computing, graphical user interfaces, and video. It helped computer makers and software vendors create such products. If customers demanded such applications there would be a market for much faster chips.

Leading corporations strive to rapidly evolve the *ecosystems* in which they play so that those ecosystems need the types of products in which they are dominant.

We can thus distinguish four types of evolution.

Four Types of Evolution

Darwinian. In Darwinian evolution, nobody plays God. The results are eventually selected by "survival of the fittest." This is slow, crude, and sometimes painful, but in society it is necessary because we can't trust anyone to play God for long. Power corrupts.

We contrast Darwinian evolution with three types of *intelligent* evolution in which many variations are tried out as quickly as possible and executives or employees select the most attractive or successful ones.

1. *First order evolution* modifies the *product or service* within a predesigned process and corporate structure. Within that process and structure many evolutionary choices may be tried out simultaneously.

2. *Second order evolution* modifies the *process, methodology, or design of work.* Many variations may be tried out quickly, with intelligent employees selecting the best. The corporate structure may be modified accordingly.

3. *Third order evolution* is concerned with factors outside the corporation, such as its relationships with other companies. The company tries to intelligently evolve the corporate *ecosystems* of which it is a part so that it may benefit.

These three types of evolution are not mutually exclusive. We need all of them. *Darwinian* evolution happens in the marketplace as competition determines the survival of the fittest. Many people in a cybercorp should be involved in *first-order* evolution, constantly trying improvements in products, customer service, or marketing. *Second-order* evolution needs Japanese-style *kaizen,* with suggestions coming from many people, and a careful procedure for introducing and testing changes to operating procedures or corporate structures. *Third-order* evolution needs top-level strategy and a high level of knowledge about the other players in the ecosystem and their strategies.

In 1965 Hewlett-Packard did not want to be a computer company. It built a computer but called it an "instrument controller" because HP wanted to be known as an instrument company.[13] *Darwinian selection* made HP a computer company, selecting certain products that became highly profitable, such as laser printers, and deselecting other products. HP used *first-order intelligent evolution* to experiment with and rapidly improve its products. HP gave its engineers the task of cutting the defect rate in soldered connections; they succeeded in cutting it from 4 in every 1,000 connections to 2 in 1,000. But then HP challenged workers to try any ideas they could dream up for solving the same problem; this evolution resulted in many changes that eventually cut the defect rate a *thousandfold,* to under 2 defects in 1,000,000.[14] When John Young was CEO he stressed cross-functional reinvention of processes to drastically shorten the time to get new products to market. The time from concept to first delivery of new printers was cut from four and a half years to twenty-two months, and Young then set out to drive it down to ten months. On many products HP *halved* the time from concept of a new product to profitability of that product. This *second-order evolution* helped HP to move up fairly suddenly to the number two position in the U.S. computer industry. Under CEO Lew Platt, HP set out to define the business ecosystems of which it is part and seek critical roles and leadership positions in these ecosystems, trying to change the playing field for HP's own benefit—*third-order evolution.*

Factory Evolution

In the green hills of Vermont, where there are more cows than people, lies one of the world's most advanced microchip factories, IBM's Essex Junction plant.

The technology for chip fabrication changes at a phenomenal rate, so the production process is being constantly reengineered. Numerous small improvements are made each month, and employees constantly improve their insight about how to make the operations as efficient as possible. The factory is an example of second-order evolution, which in some ways is archetypal of cybercorp operations.

The complex process of chip fabrication has several hundred work steps performed by teams of workers in an environment a thousand times cleaner than a surgical operating theater. The plant has a factory automation system that tracks silicon wafers and monitors their progress through all of the fabrication steps. Employees with computer screens can see the flow of work through the plant. The whole process is monitored and adjusted in real time.

IBM encourages the work teams to invent any improvements they can think of. Some of the workers develop an uncanny intuition for what is causing problems and how to improve yield. The plant manager said their rules of thumb were sometimes more like alchemy than logic, but IBM set out to capture them in an expert system. The expert system worked in conjunction with the factory automation system and became embedded throughout the factory. It advises on the optimum scheduling of work. It attempts to maximize the utilization of expensive machines, prioritize work, minimize rework, reschedule work flow when necessary, and help diagnose and correct problems. The logistics rules and rules of thumb used by the work teams are constantly refined as the work process evolves.

The expert system is a community intelligence for the entire production team. It stores the rules and expertise of all the team members. Any team member can suggest additions to its rules. This expertise represents diverse disciplines and captures know-how from different people doing different types of tasks. Team members can ask it to explain the reasoning behind any of its recommendations if they want to. Each person can think about maximizing the end-to-end results rather than just his or her piece of the process. If one step in the process is backed up, other steps may be adjusted or some of the workload may be moved to other products. The system enables each team member to see the whole picture—a helicopter view of the situation.

A diversity of experience is accumulated in the computer. This enables the team to work as a team, understanding the end-to-end value stream, and collectively inventing how to schedule work better, eliminate delays, deal with problems, and make a rapid succession of evolutionary changes in the process. The expert system has become integral to the rapid evolution. It increases the throughput of the line by 10 to 20 percent, which translates into many millions of dollars increased annual profit.

This is an example of an expert system that is built around a value-stream team. The entire team understands in general what it does. Any member of the team can supply it with rules that he or she, as an individual, understands. As the team processes evolve, the knowledge in the expert system is an integral part of the evolution. Many other value streams should be designed for computer-assisted evolution.

Getting Stuck

Most experimenters with computerized forms of evolution report that evolution is not a smooth, continuous journey; it tends to go in fits and starts.

Many people playing with software for evolving pictures have found that the images change in a fast and fascinating way for a time, and then the process seems to bog down. William Latham, an artist who "bred" pictures by evolution, reported that in some regions tiny changes in "genes" would send him careening through huge alterations in the pictures he generated, whereas at other places progress was glacial and many cycles of mutation would produce no interesting change to the images.[15] During the plateaus of stagnation he knew that there were other peaks to explore but had difficulty getting there. He created a control so that he could vary the mutation rate, sometimes skipping through evolutionary space at high speed and sometimes moving slowly to explore images that were changing fast. Artificial life, evolving in software, has similar plateaus of stagnation and then rapid bursts of roiling change. Evolutionists studying fossils on Earth report the same pattern—long periods of stagnation and sudden short bursts when many new species appear, as at the start of the Cambrian period almost 600 million years ago. This seems to be a characteristic of evolution in complex organisms whether natural or man-made.

Corporations similarly have periods when evolutionary change happens at a breathtaking pace, and other periods when they get stuck. An important management question can be how to get them unstuck. This requires something different from business as usual.

Mutation of a single species can keep it in a plateau of stagnation for a long time. When two species are mixed, however, rapid change happens. Karl Sims found that when his evolution of pictures reached a stagnant plateau, all he had to do was mix pieces of different pictures and fast turbulent evolution came back. Sex was a more important source of variations than mutation. In corporations breakthrough ideas can happen when specialists from different industries that appear to have little in common put their heads together.

Taiichi Ohno was an engineer at Toyota in the 1950s without a college education. He visited the United States and was intrigued to find that in America's new supermarkets shelves were restocked when they needed to be, as good were sold to customers. This was different from the car factories of that time, which stored a large inventory of goods. Ohno persuaded the head of Toyota to build a car factory in which the resupply of goods was triggered by the usage of goods, as in an American supermarket, and just-in-time inventory control was born. This simple idea led to a long succession of evolutionary changes in manufacturing.

The facilities manager at the Convex Computer Corporation wanted to study what his counterpart did at Disney World (which sounded suspiciously like a joyride) because Disney was a master at managing its facilities. The lessons learned at Disney enabled Convex to make many improvements, including slashing electrical breakdowns in its factory by 80 percent.[16]

Xerox appears to have nothing in common with L. L. Bean, the mail-order house, but Xerox studied L. L. Bean's order-filling process. L. L. Bean was "picking" parts for orders three times faster than Xerox. L. L. Bean workers maintained and studied charts of their work flow in an attempt to lessen the motion required or speed up their process. For example, they stocked high-volume items close to packing stations. Using L. L. Bean's techniques, Xerox greatly improved their mailing of copier parts.

Stay Flexible

To facilitate rapid evolution, it is necessary to avoid rigid structures that cannot be changed easily.

Traditional computing is rigid; it takes an age to change mainframe programs written in traditional languages (like COBOL and C). Client-server systems built with power tools can be designed so that they can be changed quickly. Benetton's computer network in the early 1980s was the wrong architecture for the rapid worldwide change of Benetton's high-growth period; with some trauma, a more flexible architecture was put in place. The Internet and intranets offer great flexibility.

Complex new processes have many problems in their early months. They should be designed so that constant improvement can be made very quickly.

Rigid mass-production lines are difficult to change. Japanese cars improved much faster than American cars in the 1980s because flexible Japanese lean manufacturing made changes easier to introduce.

Design of Experiments

Sometimes a problem has many possible causes. We often guess a cause and correct that, but the true cause lies elsewhere. We need to design experiments so that they help us distinguish among the different factors that might cause the problem.

A statistical technique called "design of experiments" (DoE) has been used for decades in fields such as agricultural research to discover what mix of fertilizer, crop rotation, seed varieties, and planting methods gives the best yield. A Japanese engineer, Genichi Taguchi, learned how to apply DoE to improve product quality in manufacturing.[17] Taguchi's method produced a relatively quick way to test a large number of possible causes of defects or variations in quality and statistically rank them in terms of their impact. Instead of seat-of-the-pants experimenting, which we often do, Taguchi's disciples experimented systematically and located the variables that required attention first. Dorian Shainin, an American, developed a simpler and more accurate version of DoE, which is used widely, at Motorola and elsewhere.[18] Simple disciplined DoE can be applied to the continuous improvement of both products and processes in many types of work.

A chef in a good restaurant might want to use only the most expensive ingredients, but a careful set of experiments reveals that, while some ingredients need to be the best; others do not matter. By concentrating on the ingredients that matter, the chef can improve the food and save money. The same is true in many processes.

Corporations often attempt to improve overall quality by tightening *all* specifications. DoE techniques can reveal that only *certain* specifications are critical.

Sometimes a specification that was tightened is found to have very little effect. DoE techniques might reveal that cheaper materials can be used for certain components while other components need the best materials. Cheaper materials may be found to work well if the design is changed. A goal of DoE is to save money as well as to produce a better product. It replaces casual tinkering with planned experiments.

When problems need to be solved, it is often the case that workers and their managers accept plausible conclusions and make changes without any testing. Often a large amount of money is spent on the changes with no experimentation. DoE techniques encourage systematical experimentation to evaluate the effects of different variables and determine which are important. Variables that were thought to be important are often not, whereas others are critical.

We should systematically find out what factors truly make a difference and focus attention and effort on them. *The most effective general concentrates forces on the few significant battles.*

Wild Ducks

Cybercorp evolution needs both rational thinkers who draw analytical diagrams, and wild-duck, brainstorming thinkers known for flashes of inspiration.

Many corporations miss out on uncontrolled unconventional innovation. They encourage and teach techniques for analytical thinking but do not know how to teach wild-duck thinking. Big companies often forget how to innovate because, unwittingly or otherwise, they discourage the thinker who breaks the mold of conventional ideas.

Uncontrolled creative people who produce breakthrough ideas are often loners who do not want to be in teams. Sometimes they fit into a team if the team encourages their flow of wild thoughts. Right-brained inventive thinkers often achieve little working alone. In combination with left-brained analytical thinkers, they can move mountains. Team structures are necessary that link inspiration and perspiration.

Who Will the Winners Be?

How does a company become great in the new world of cyberspace?

Some authorities will advocate grand-scale strategic planning. Boldly go where no corporation has gone before. Plan predator value streams and world-beating projects like VISA's fiber-optic network; shoot for the moon with BHAGs. Think big because technology makes grand schemes possible.

Other authorities will say there is no roadmap for cyberspace, so feel your way. There are too many surprises in store for long-range planning to work. Trial and error is essential. The winners will be the masters of high-speed evolution ready to capitalize quickly on the unexpected. The losers will be those trapped in rigid structures. It is an age of great creativity, so stimulate unplanned experimentation everywhere. **Build a mutation machine.**

In reality, both viewpoints are needed and should not be mutually exclusive. There will surely be 3Ms of cyberspace. But there will also be grand cliff-hanger stories of heroic leaders who bet their companies on great projects, the future equivalents of IBM's 360 or Boeing's 747. A visitor to Boeing, worried about Chairman William Allen's bet-the-company commitment to the 747, asked him, "What would you do if the first airplane crashed on take-off?" After a long pause Allen replied, "I'd rather talk about something pleasant—like a nuclear war." [19]

Projects of Wagnerian grandness used to be appropriate for only a few corporations like Boeing and IBM (whose head office was at Valhalla! New York), but today grand-scale projects can be tackled by connecting together core competences in different corporations. Relatively small corporations may have large ambitions that they fulfill by assembling the right group of partners, as Nokia did when it moved into the cellular phone business.

The building of predator value streams, like those described in Chapter 5, often needs quantum-leap change, not evolutionary change. However, corporate quantum leaps introduce a deluge of new problems, so the troops should be expecting trouble and be prepared to deal with it. All the employees involved with a new value stream, a BHAG, or any revolutionary change should be primed for fast second-order evolution. They should be busy inventing as many improvements as they can think of. Many changes will be tried, and only the best of them accepted. But the more new ideas are tried the greater the probability that some will hit the jackpot, so there should be as many parallel mutation attempts as possible.

Cybercorp success will have both fast evolution and corporate bungee jumps. The two are not mutually exclusive. Grand quantum leaps and intelligent evolution should coexist like the yin and yang of Chinese dualistic philosophy. Technological change will lash about in an ever more frenzied way, and its pace will continue to accelerate, so the search for evolution will be an increasingly intense competitive force.

The winners of the future will be corporations that both thoroughly reinvent their value streams and become masters of all three forms of evolution.

References

1. Charles Darwin, *The Origin of Species* (New York: Penguin, 1985).
2. James C. Collins and Jerry I. Porras, *Built to Last* (New York: Random House, 1994).
3. Ibid., chap. 7.
4. Ibid.
5. P. Ranganth Nayak and John M. Ketteringham, *Break-throughs!* (New York: Rawson Associates, 1986).
6. Robert Cringley called his book about the growth of companies in the computer industry *Accidental Empires* and described how many multimillionaires were surprised at the fortunes they made. They happened more by luck than by planning to be at the right place on an explosively growing curve (but when they found themselves there, they managed the situation well!). Robert Cringley, *Accidental Empires* (New York: Penguin, 1993).
7. "A Survey of the Internet," *Economist,* July 1, 1995.
8. Elyse Tanyoue, "Johnson & Johnson Stays Fit by Shuffling Its Mix of Businesses," *Wall Street Journal,* December 22, 1992, p. A1 (quoted in Collins and Porras).
9. Collins and Porras, *Built to Last,* chap. 7.
10. Richard Dawkins, *The Blind Watchmaker* (New York: Norton, 1986) is a wonder-

fully written book showing that Darwin's views were largely right and anti-Darwin views are largely wrong. See also Stephen J. Gould, *Wonderful Life: The Burgess Shale and the Nature of History* (New York: Norton, 1989), and Stephen J. Gould, *The Panda's Thumb* (New York: Norton, 1980).

11. *Correspondence of Charles Darwin,* Vol. 6 (1990), Letter to J. D. Hooker, July 13, 1856.
12. Kevin Kelly, *Out of Control: The New Biology of Machines* (London: Fourth Estate, 1994).
13. "How Hewlett-Packard Entered the Computer Business," Hewlett-Packard Company Archives document, quoted in Collins and Porras.
14. *Business Week Guide: The Quality Imperative,* (New York: McGraw-Hill, 1994).
15. Described in Kelly, *Out of Control,* chap. 14.
16. *Business Week Guide: The Quality Imperative.*
17. "Case Study: Taguchi's Design of Experiments," *Productivity,* 10, no. 2 (February 1989).
18. Keki R. Bhote, "DoE: The High Road to Quality," *Management Review,* January 1988.
19. Robert J. Sterling, *Legend and Legacy: The Story of Boeing and Its People* (New York: St. Martin's, 1992).

14

Experiment!

Fast change confronts all corporations today. Technology snakes in new directions fast, and David corporations are attacking the Goliaths. The cybercorp must be constantly alert to unpredictable changes. Many of its people need to be involved in experimentation and research.

Research Cemeteries

In traditional corporations, research has often take place in a research laboratory far away in the countryside. The laboratory inmates never talk to anyone in manufacturing or to customers, and certainly not (God forbid) to anyone in marketing. Gordon Forward, the appropriately named CEO of Chaparral Steel, describes the large corporate research centers as being like the Forest Lawn Cemetery, "After you spend some time there you realize that you are in Forest Lawn not because there are no good ideas there, but because the good ideas are *dying* there all the time." [1]

The legendary Xerox PARC (Palo Alto Research Center) invented the mouse, the dialog style of the Macintosh, LANs, Ethernet, object-oriented programming, Smalltalk, client-server systems, laser printers, and the first continent-wide satellite network, XTEN. Any of these could have made a fortune, but Xerox failed to turn any of them into profit-making products. IBM's Thomas J. Watson Laboratory at Yorktown has produced an amazing series of breakthroughs (at enormous expense), but they rarely reached customers. Videotape recording was invented and developed in the United States, but today not one videotape machine or camcorder is made in the United States. I reflect how much Philips, in Holland, has improved my own quality of life. Philips invented optical disks for music, data, and video. But as I shop for such products in the United States, I find the stores full of Japanese products, not Philips products. Over and over again, Western research laboratories invented things but the Japanese improved them and cashed in.

To help reverse this situation, research and development (R&D) must not be confined to the laboratory; it must pervade the entire corporation. The cybercorp should be thought of as a laboratory environment that constantly invents, improves, records its know-how, and puts new ideas to work. The extent to which it does this will determine its success. In many cybercorps, there will be no laboratory as such; the whole corporation will be a laboratory.

Chaparral Steel

One might think that the steel industry, denigrated as being part of the old "smokestack" world, would be an unlikely place to find such an enterprise. Dorothy Leonard-Barton studied Chaparral Steel in Midlothian, Texas, and describes it as a spectacular example of a learning-laboratory corporation.[2] Chaparral Steel was founded in 1975 and from its inception set out to operate with research being done throughout the entire organization instead of having a separate R&D laboratory. Gordon Forward comments, "Every employee is in R&D."

Japan and Germany had reputations for being the world's most efficient steel producers. However, by 1990, *Chaparral's productivity was 1.5 worker-hours per rolled ton of steel, whereas the Japanese average was 5.6 and the German average 5.7.* This difference in productivity between Chaparral and traditional steel companies is so great that one must ask how long old-style steel companies can survive. In addition, Chaparral was recognized for quality. It was the first U.S. company to be awarded the right to use the Japanese Industrial Standard certification on its structural steel products. It was the only U.S. steel company certified by the American Institute of Mining, Metallurgical and Petroleum Engineers (AIME) for nuclear applications and one of two companies (out of fifteen) whose steel is certified by the American Builders of Ships.

If a learning-laboratory corporation makes such a difference in steel, it is likely to make far more difference when the products or services change rapidly as with cameras, electronics, training, clothing, entertainment, computers, or information products. As intensifying global competition brings too many copycat products, the art of innovation will be the key to survival.

Experiments in Steelmaking

Chaparral set out to make large structural I-beams for about half what they cost at big steel mills. This required a drastic reduction of energy costs, and casting of steel into a shape that was close to the shape of the final product. The closer the steel could be cast to the final shape, the lower the amount of expensive rolling required. No steel mill had ever cast steel into the shape of large I-beams, except with a very expensive process.

To achieve this near-net shape, the white-hot steel had to be cast through a copper alloy mold cooled with high-speed water flow. The vendors of molds thought it impossible to make such a mold. Chaparral wanted to cast the steel horizontally (not vertically as is usually the case) in almost its final shape so that it could race directly into the rolling mill. Computerized equipment would cut it to length for specific customer orders. The steel would pass through the rolling equipment once, stop, reverse, and go through again. This needs split-second timing. While the rolling is occurring, the flow of white-hot steel is diverted. The goal is to divert as little of it as possible because every second of diversion costs money; the diverted steel has to be reheated before being rolled.

Endless experimentation went on at Chaparral to make processes such as this ever more efficient. The workers joined in the experimentation, constantly fixing problems. Chaparral often did experiments on the production line itself. Most factories never do such experiments on a live production line, but Chaparral wanted the experimental environment to be as close as possible to the production environment, and wanted all production workers to participate in the experiments, learn from them, solve problems, and produce ideas.

In one set of experiments with the near-net-shape casting, the workers had a crazy idea: built prototype splashboards for the molten metal out of plywood. By continuously soaking the plywood with water, they could prevent its being burnt for just long enough to test its function. Many plywood splashboards were built until the shape was perfected. Similarly, they experimented with copper molds, as opposed to the more heat-resistant expensive alloy molds. With the soft copper molds, they could experiment with many variations of the shape, even though the mold was quickly destroyed by the steel.

As well as experimenting on the actual steel-casting equipment, the employees built a one-sixth scale model that used water to approximate the flow of steel. This model stood alongside the actual steel caster. Employees could compare its operation with that of the actual caster and do many experiments with it quickly, some of which led to improvements in the actual caster. Many such experiments were done by shop-floor employees without authorization from a higher level of management. This gave employees a feeling of "ownership" of the research activities and enabled them to make many innovations in the steelmaking process. They had great fun doing it.

> **When encouraged to do so most people love to experiment and try out new ideas. In an era of unpredictable change everybody should participate in brainstorming. Experimentation should be encouraged at all levels to explore ways of improving work processes. Techniques for efficient design of experiments should be taught.**

An Integrated R&D Culture

A learning-laboratory enterprise needs a culture with four characteristics integrated into its management practices and underlying values.[3]

1. *A value-stream organization with a* kaizen *culture.* Although most corporations are far from it today, a *kaizen*-style value-stream structure (value-stream teams that never stop searching for improvements) should be regarded as a bread-and-butter necessity for the cybercorp.

There must be constant striving to solve problems, increase productivity, and successively "raise the bar" of performance. This is best accomplished with value-stream teams focused on delighting their customers and motivated to achieve aggressive goals.

2. *A knowledge infrastructure.* An infrastructure is needed to capture knowledge, improve it, store it, disseminate it, and put it to use (Chapter 16). The corporate intranet should make the knowledge easily accessible to everybody. There should be no "ownership" of ideas and no boundaries that prevent data sharing.

The knowledge infrastructure, value-stream organization, and *kaizen* culture are the foundation on which the learning-laboratory enterprise is built.

3. *Constant experimentation; enterprise-wide striving for innovation.* The learning-laboratory corporation constantly experiments and searches for new ideas. There is a culture of constantly reaching beyond what is done today. Innovation is targeted to selected goals, core competences, or strategic value streams. Some new ideas do not work out, so failure is never punished. There is constant risk associated with innovation. Management, like R&D management, must strike the right balance between risk and potential reward.

In R&D laboratories, several hundred ideas are often generated before one innovation comes to fruition. When the entire corporation becomes a learning laboratory, it should be accepted that many ideas are needed but only the best will be implemented. If the corporation has few ideas, it tends to implement them even if they are not very good; it can spend much money on something that was a bad idea to begin with.

Good R&D executives are skilled at encouraging many ideas and shelving the less good ones before much is spent on them. Cybercorp managers need to do the same, guided by a strong vision of where the corporation is going.

---

4. *Virtual R&D.* The cybercorp should have a virtual research organization. More valuable ideas are likely to come from outside the corporation

than inside it. The search should be systematic. Some corporations have become highly organized at picking brains elsewhere. A virtual R&D organization can tap a much larger variety of knowledge sources than an isolated laboratory.

Cybercorp employees should be scanning the world for relevant ideas. It is much less expensive to beg, borrow, or steal new research results than to do the research yourself. In a planned way, employees should be going to conferences and visiting other companies. Often there is much to learn from companies not in quite the same business. The enterprise should benchmark the performance of processes in other companies. It should examine in detail products from which ideas can be gleaned.

When employees find ideas or obtain studies from visits or affiliates, they should be expected to make presentations and create reports and videotapes that communicate this information. They should spread the knowledge and educate their colleagues.

A learning-laboratory enterprise needs an enterprise-wide environment designed to maximize how quickly the enterprise can innovate.

Three Attitudes to Change

It is appropriate to categorize corporations on the basis of three cultures of corporate change: stagnant, TQM, and learning laboratory.

1. *Stagnant.* In a stagnant culture employees accept the current way of doing things. To criticize it is to ask for trouble, so keep your mouth shut.

2. *TQM.* A TQM culture is one in which all employees identify problems and systematically try to solve them. Everybody searches for refinements to existing processes. Some American corporations have succeeded spectacularly in establishing a TQM culture, but many have failed.[4] Europe established ISO 9000 standards and guidelines that many corporations followed, but sometimes created a bureaucratic culture rather than the fever for excellence.

3. *Learning laboratory.* A learning-laboratory culture goes far beyond TQM. The goal is to find breakthroughs quite different from current procedures that change the competitive position. Experiments are necessary to validate and evolve new approaches. The breakthroughs often extend far beyond one person's department into territories where he or she has no jurisdiction; they need to integrate knowledge from across the enterprise. Every employee is challenged to participate in experimentation, research, and the garnering of new ideas.

These three cultures can be observed in software development, a field that changes constantly because of new tools, techniques, and templates:

1. *Stagnant.* Programmers continue to write code in the time-honored way, thinking that everything should be written in their favorite language.

2. *TQM.* The principles of TQM are used to establish processes that are well documented and well managed, catch defects as early as possible, and improve quality. ISO 9000 certification may be sought. Radical breakthroughs are generally resisted.

3. *Learning laboratory.* Software is built by small high-performance teams using the most powerful tools with the goal of completing their piece of a project quickly (say, in three months). Between projects, a team consolidates what it has learned and searches for better tools, methods, and building blocks. A central group constantly surveys the vendors of tools, templates, objects, and methodologies, examining new ideas, experimenting with them, going to conferences, visiting leading-edge developers, and generally researching the field.

> **When a team achieves consistently better results than other teams, the control group finds out why and tries to spread the improvement to the other teams.**

General Electric consists of many companies in diverse businesses, all of them striving to improve their IT applications. A small control group at the GE head office works with the software development groups in the different GE corporations, measures their productivity, and introduces new tools, ideas, and application packages. It does constant research on new tools and techniques. When one team does better than the rest, that team's methods are studied and, if possible, transferred to the other teams. Software productivity is measured by the central group with a common metric.[5] GE's measurements show that its best teams achieve both productivity and reliability way ahead of the industry average. In most corporations, few projects of a million lines of code are ever completed successfully; GE has completed projects far exceeding this size in a relatively short time and with high software reliability.[6]

Which Value Streams Need R&D?

> **Not every value stream needs aggressive innovation. It is essential to map a cybercorp into value streams and ask which should be a learning laboratory.**

Often the strategic predator value streams described in Chapter 5 are the ones that need the fast learning rate. The bread-and-butter value streams might be outsourced (e.g., do the accounting in India). The learning-laboratory value streams will be totally controlled in-house but should often have links to specialist partners who can help with research or experimentation, as in the case of Chaparral's near-net-shape steel casting.

Processes that pass work from department to department in a hierarchical organization are difficult to change rapidly. Value-stream teams, on the other hand, can quickly adjust their overall behavior. The value-stream team is a particularly effective unit for experimenting. It should have clear tough goals and high motivation and should be constantly searching for ways to achieve its goals better. The results of this learning should be communicated to other teams of the same type.

A Multicorporate Learning Laboratory

A particularly important type of learning (which barely happens in some corporations) is joint learning with suppliers, customers, agents, and companies that cooperate to share competences.

As a manufacturer drives to improve its manufacturing process it often needs components from its suppliers that are fundamentally redesigned so that the assembly process can be more automated. The manufacturer and the supplier both learn how to improve their processes. They can help each other. It makes sense to climb a joint learning curve. This may need very close cooperation.

A learning-laboratory corporation needs suppliers who can learn also. It should select suppliers who are willing to cooperate in climbing a joint learning curve, and who are willing to be pushed beyond their current capability. When a corporation invents new tools or equipment, its customers need to change their methodologies. As customers change, they discover new requirements in the tools. Improved tools push the frontier of methodologies; improved methodologies push the frontier of tools. Joint learning is needed.

Chaparral identified two mold fabricators who might provide a special mold for near-net-shape casting, one in Italy and one in Germany. The forces on this mold are brutal. It needs to be made of an alloy that is tough and that dissipates heat rapidly. The hot steel shrinks as it goes through the cooled mold, so the mold is shaped to compensate for the shrinkage. The shape must be just right so that the metal will not bind. The metal must emerge with a smooth skin not crinkled by the mold. A mold like this had never been used before for casting large beams in a shape close to their final shape. Much experimentation was needed.

Chaparral employees visited the Italian and German companies frequently, telling them how their experiments were progressing. Sometimes, the rate of innovation was so fast that the German mold developers were told not to bother shipping a mold they had built; it already needed redesign. The $37,000 for the unshipped mold was part of the cost of experimentation.

At Chaparral every employee is in R&D, even machine operators. Nobody understands the practical problems of machinery better than its operator. Operators see everything that goes wrong and try to prevent it. Of the three-person team from Texas that repeatedly visited Germany trying to perfect the new casting mold, one was an operator. The German mold makers were so skeptical of Chaparral's ideas that at first they were unwilling to make molds with such a radical design.[7] Eventually, the German mold-making expertise combined with constant experiments in Texas resulted in a new type of mold that the companies patented. Neither company could have produced it alone.

Molding the hot steel into its near-net shape resulted in less rolling of the I-beams. Rolling affects the metallurgical properties of steel, and it was not certain at first whether high-quality beams could be made. Experimentation was needed to learn how to test and adjust the process. Chaparral found a steel-production laboratory in Mexico with equipment sufficiently flexible to do such experiments and simulate future mill design; it succeeded in producing samples with superior metallurgical qualities.

Risks

There are severe risks in pushing the frontiers. Risky experiments such as those at Chaparral would be meticulously avoided in most production environments. However, Chaparral views risks as part of the process of R&D. If there are no risks, no breakthroughs occur. Failures are expected in R&D and are not penalized. Risk has to be accepted and managed.

When everyone experiments, any employee might do something that doesn't work. Employees must not be blamed if their experiments fail; on the contrary, they must be commended for trying. If failed experiments were penalized, nobody would experiment.

One mill superintendent championed the installation of an arc saw for cutting finished beams. It cost $1.5 million and always had problems. For a year, the employees tried to solve its problems, but it never became satisfactory. The superintendent eventually eliminated his own brainchild. He was later promoted to vice president. Even very expensive failures are regarded as part of the cost of research.

Gordon Forward's view is that to do nothing may be a greater risk. If the company does not push the frontiers, its competition will, and the company might lose its market.

Holistic Interplay

A vital characteristic of a learning-laboratory cybercorp is that it cannot be constructed piecemeal; all the components relate to one another. Just as the parts of our body only make sense in the context of the entire body, so the learning-laboratory corporation needs to be perceived as an organic whole. This whole is in a state of constant flux, continuously evolving at a speed never seen before the cybercorp era. Management has to pay constant attention to holistic integration. A knowledge infrastructure communicates the innovations across the enterprise. There is no "throw it over the wall now it's his problem" separation of activities. Computers and networks are used to help choreograph the complex interplay of activities.

Leonard-Barton comments that Chaparral can only be understood in a holistic manner. She comments that the most important characteristic of a learning-laboratory factory is that it is a totally integrated system. If competitors copy a part of such a system, they achieve little because it is the interrelatedness that provides the value.[8] Leaders must be able to see and manage the interconnectedness, and that relates to deeply held values and widely observed management practices.

Selecting and Keeping Employees

A learning-laboratory corporation needs to select employees who will be effective in the R&D process. Cybercorp success relates strongly to its selection of employees. At Chaparral only about one out of ten applicants who are interviewed for jobs are actually hired. The final decision whether to hire a person belongs to the foreman with direct responsibility.

A learning-laboratory corporation depends on selecting employees who are willing to learn, who can innovate and constantly challenge the way things are done. They need to enjoy on-the-job experiments, learning by doing, learning by talking to people, learning by tinkering. Making innovative contributions should be what makes them happy. A person who learns to be a great photographer constantly experiments. He searches for different camera angles, tries new lighting, shoots into the sun to see if it works, tries different lenses, films, portrait settings, experiments with short depth of focus and very fast shutter speeds. It might be thought that bright college graduates would be the most capable of learning, but many graduates want an ivory tower environment rather than the rough-and-tumble of a factory. The person who learns from books is usually quite different from the person who learns by tinkering. The brilliant hacker who learns at her computer screen is quite different from the manager who learns by interrogating people. *Corporate learning takes many forms and must employ diverse types of people.*

Probably most people could be capable of lifelong learning, but somewhere along the way they lose the ability to learn. Deadly jobs make them afraid to speak up, nonconfident, bureaucratic, or paranoid. Just as bad schools can stamp out creativity in children, so most companies stamp out creativity in employees. If a person stops learning for five years, it is extremely difficult to start learning again. It seems that the learning circuits of the brain go dead just as a muscle would go dead if not used for five years.

A would-be cybercorp should look for people who can learn new jobs with enthusiasm, who are articulate and communicate well. Spreading knowledge is as important as creating it. It should hire people who will be excited about the creativity and will consequently work hard. After hiring, employees need intensive training with daily evaluations to make sure that they will fit into the cybercorp culture.

Many corporations have a "boot camp" for new employees with a substantial pay increase for those who survive it. Much ongoing training, including external education, is needed in a learning-laboratory corporation. The employees that succeed in the culture are valuable, and the corporation needs to do everything it can to retain them. The pay structure needs to reflect the growth of individuals and reward their learning of greater skills. Most employees in a learning cybercorp should have profit-related bonuses. Sometimes bonuses relate to specific goals, such as completing projects on time, increasing productivity measures, or closing large orders.

Careful attention to each individual is needed to make sure that he finds his job satisfying. Employees should be made proud of their accomplishments.

Although the cybercorp world is one of constant change, the core competences remain for many years and need to be constantly improved by experimentation and learning. The individuals in whom these competences reside are uniquely valuable resources, and management should do its best to ensure that they do not leave.

References

1. Interview by A. M. Kantrow (1986), quoted by Dorothy Leonard-Barton, "The Factory as a Learning Laboratory," Sloan Management Review, Fall 1992.
2. Leonard-Barton, "The Factory as a Learning Laboratory."
3. These four characteristics are described in Leonard-Barton's excellent paper. They have been adjusted here to link to the themes of this book.
4. James Martin, *The Great Transition* (New York: AMACOM, 1995), pt. 3.
5. GE's software metric was one that is widely accepted in commercial IT: *function points per person-month* (FPPM). Function points are a measure of the complexity of transaction-processing software. Guidelines for calculating function points are

kept up to date by the International Function Point Users Group (IFPUG). The industry average around the world is less than 10 FPPM; GE's best teams achieve 50 to 100 FPPM.

6. Figures about GE's software development productivity are from Don McNamara, GE Head Office, Fairfield, CT. McNamara was the driving force behind GE's dramatic improvements in application development capability.

7. This experience is put under the microscope in Leonard-Barton, "The Factory as a Learning Laboratory."

8. Ibid.

Part III

People and Management

15

An Exciting Place to Work

> **In the cybercorp just about every aspect of employment is likely to be different from traditional corporations—compensation, appraisal, rewards, measurements, motivation, education, teams, management, unions.**

Traditional mass-production companies were designed so that most employees did not think. The cybercorp is an organization where everyone thinks. It competes on the basis of customer enrichment with products that incorporate knowledge and services, and so it increasingly depends for its profits on the knowledge and creativity of employees. Dumb jobs with no skill are disappearing. Chrysler CEO Robert Eaton comments, "The only way we can beat the competition is with people." If that is true in car manufacturing, it is even more so in the service and knowledge industries. The knowledge and skill of people is the key resource, not plant, technology, or equipment.

Energy

> **A vitally important but subtle question in building a corporation is, "How do we maximize the energy and creativity that employees give to the corporation?" No drawing of organizational charts or adjustment of work flow diagrams will answer that question.**

Richard Branson, the colorful British billionaire who built Virgin Records and Virgin Atlantic Airways, has excelled at devising ways to make his companies fun to work for. He preaches that if you put your staff first and make them happy and satisfied, then they make the customers happy and satisfied. Federal Express stresses a "people-service-profit" (PSP) philosophy that says that if you focus on developing people, you can achieve higher levels of service and hence higher profits.

Human energy comes from excitement and enthusiasm. The enthusiasm of employees can be one of the most valuable assets of a corporation. In too many situations, employees suffer their jobs solely to earn money. They can hardly wait for the clock to say it's quitting time. Far from being a source of excitement, work for many people has been a sad waste of much of life. In the old economy employees achieved fulfillment through leisure time; in the new economy fulfillment will increasingly be achieved through exciting creative work.

Top management should create a corporate vision that thrills employees and is worth striving for. Value streams or projects should have an exciting vision or goal. Employees can take a pride in their work, create something original, or fight to make their team win. In some cases the goal that generates enthusiasm is that of delighting the customer in any way possible. We should design organizations that tend to maximize the energy their members contribute.

> **In the past what was thought to be good for the corporation was often bad for the individual. We created soul-destroying jobs on mass-production lines and in mass typing pools. In the cybercorp most boring jobs can be abolished or outsourced. What is good for the corporation can usually be exciting for the individual.**

The twentieth century is a journey from Kafka to cybercorp. It started with Frederick Taylor timing workers with a stopwatch. Employees were cogs in the machinery like Charlie Chaplin in *Modern Times*. Employment then evolved to respect for professionalism and education, and later to TQM programs that challenged all employees to improve quality. It changed from monolithic procedure manuals to constant volatile reinvention; from Kremlinesque authoritarianism to the creative anarchy of the Internet. It ends with the cybercorp challenge of climbing the fastest possible learning curves and sometimes regarding the entire corporation as a learning laboratory—the culmination of a journey from treating employees as dumb slaves to challenging them to use their wits.

> **We are moving into an era of great creativity. Creative people have powerful tools; they can explore and debate ideas worldwide on the Internet and intranets. As drudgery is automated, the work that is left will demand uniquely human skills.**

One of the great joys of life is to be creative. New corporations are increasingly designed to support creativity, so we are seeing an increase in exciting, enjoyable work.

The Downsizing Disaster

Many corporations, especially in the United States, have gone through a period of massive downsizing. As business processes were redesigned the business could operate with far fewer people. Often, highly capable people were laid off.

Downsizing should not be regarded as a way of life; it is part of the painful transition from the old world to the new. The cybercorp should be designed for continuous change, not periodic Hiroshimas. Its employees must feel secure, empowered and free to build excellence. But you do not feel empowered if there is an ax over your head. Business is about relationships, and relationships need trust.

If downsizing must occur it should be done with a clear vision of the cybercorp that will emerge from the process. Too much downsizing has been crude slash-and-burn with no vision, done by "turnaround" executives who create short-term profit but destroy long-term viability. Some corporations have been destroyed by downsizing. The corporation is left anorexic and demoralized—the opposite of "an exciting place to work."

There is a danger for society. Most cybercorp employment assumes the ability to read and learn; much of it assumes computer literacy. The revolution now in progress will create a gulf in society between people who would and would not be selected for cybercorp employment.

It is essential that as we reinvent society we do not create an unemployable class.

Who Has Job Security?

Ironclad job security was appropriate to old-world corporations in a static world with routine work. In new-world corporations nothing is static and the employee skills needed are changing fast.

Employees with "tenure" tend to retire on the job. A large New York bank guaranteed that anyone with twenty years' experience would never be laid off. A human resources executive at the bank commented, "We found that people who came for security wouldn't adopt new ways of doing things." [1] Nothing could be further from the fast-mutating world of the cybercorp.

No-layoff policies are a severe restriction in the cybercorp world, but if a corporation changes a long-standing policy of employment security, employees feel betrayed and angry. Some corporations give employees financial inducements to leave or create early-retirement programs. This can be disastrous because the good ones take the money and go, while the turkeys stay. Candidates for layoff are the ones whose skills are not valuable elsewhere.

The cybercorp should encourage constant change and learning but build core competences *for the long term,* designed to give the highest level of excellence. The same evolving competences can be applied to a rapidly changing mix of products and services. A cybercorp needs many employees who have core competences or are members of critical teams. It is necessary to give them a work environment where they constantly improve their skills and invent better ways of doing things. These employees need to feel secure.

Old-world corporations looked after their employees and gave them job security. It is common now to say that security is a thing of the past, but this is harmful for the critical employees. Increasingly, the asset of most value in corporations is skill and knowledge. This asset resides in people who could walk away. The cybercorp must look after and nurture such people. It must give them job security, but not "tenure," because security should be linked to the constant upgrading of critical capabilities.

Different Classes of Employment Package

Sometimes employee deals are talked about as though they are the same for all employees. In reality it makes sense to define different classes of employees who receive very different deals. For example:

Class 1: Core employees who are uniquely valuable. The corporation would be damaged if they left, so every attempt should be made to lock them in. This may be done with stock options, vesting schemes, and long-term benefits, and generally by making them feel like an important part of the corporation.

Class 2: Employees who would be expensive to replace. These include members of high-performance teams, employees with expensive skills, employees who are particularly good with customers. Class 2 employees need to be rewarded for their skills in ways that encourage them to stay.

Class 1 and 2 employees should feel that they will not be laid off when reorganizations occur. When downturns happen and fat must be trimmed, their bonuses will be cut but not their jobs.

Class 3: Employees who do tasks that could be outsourced. Such employees may be paid for results on a contract basis and should understand that they, in effect, compete with external service providers.

Class 4: Employees with no unique skills who are quickly replaceable. These employees can be hired part time as needed. They include laborers, clerks, widget assemblers, and people who can be quickly trained to do simple tasks. These employees are paid for the job, with incentives for good work, but may have no long-term security or long-term benefits. They should know that as they move to more valuable categories they will improve their job security and compensation.

The view that people are interchangeable is not true for class 1 and 2 employees. They often have capabilities that are unique and that are linked to *company-specific* knowledge. They may have a special understanding of the needs of certain customers. As complexity increases, the cost of switching employees increases. Value is added by nurturing high-performance teams who develop deep knowledge of company-specific competences or value streams.

Removing the Ladder

Many traditional employees have spent their lives hoping for promotion. When the hierarchy is largely removed there is little scope for climbing the corporate ladder. Perhaps more alarming to employees, the pay scales associated with the corporate ladder are gone. Compensation schemes in a value-stream enterprise are quite different from those in a hierarchical enterprise. Employees in traditional corporations often expect pay increases at regular intervals even though there is no increase in the value of their contribution. In the new-world corporation, employees cannot expect to automatically climb a hierarchy or automatically climb to higher pay levels. The days of entitlement to automatic salary increases are gone. Instead, pay is related, as far as possible, to the contribution employees make. Employees increase their pay by making themselves more valuable—by increasing their knowledge, capability, or contribution to competitiveness.

> **Instead of aspiring to climb a hierarchy, employees should aspire to increase their value.**

The cybercorp says to employees: *There's good news and bad news. The good news is that this is an exciting place to work and you can earn big money if you add substantial value. The bad news is that promotion prospects are low because the old hierarchy has gone and we cannot guarantee regular salary raises.*

We will challenge you and train you to do interesting jobs and coach you to be members of empowered teams. You will be constantly challenged to find better ways to add value, and we will provide the resources needed for you to pursue that challenge. This is a learning corporation; we expect you to learn and help others to learn. As you learn more, you will become more valuable. If you make yourself valuable you will be employable and compensation will relate to your value. We owe you every opportunity to increase your value.

There is job security for class 1 and 2 employees. But if business turns bad, we have to be free to trim class 3 and 4 employees or people with the wrong skills.

> The new deal says: "You own your own employability. You are responsible."

Changing Compensation Schemes

At Chaparral Steel, 93 percent of the employees are stockholders. In addition to being allocated shares, 62 percent buy additional shares each month through payroll deductions.

> It may become typical of future cybercorps that all employees in classes 1 and 2 are stockholders or have stock options.

Cybercorp pay schemes have characteristics such as the following:

- Substantial bonuses based on individual or team performance
- Substantial bonuses based on achievement of corporate goals
- Sharing in corporate profits
- Stock options, phantom stock, and so forth
- Base pay linked to knowledge, skill, and capability
- No automatic increase in base pay without increase in employee value

All employees should understand that if there is less profit there is less money to go around, but if they reach the Superbowl everybody will benefit. If bonuses are a substantial part of compensation, there is less need to lay off employees when business is bad.

It makes sense to pay bonuses based on results. Bonuses give all employees an incentive to improve the results. Collective bonuses for achievements such as completing projects on time, making a quota, or operating within budget tend to create peer pressure to achieve the target. Nobody wants to let colleagues down and cause the bonus to be lost. Paying bonuses each week has a major effect where that is practical. An employee who took home $970 last week and only $650 this week has some explaining to do!

Nucor, a high-performing steel company, divides its production workers into work groups of twenty-five to thirty-five people and pays work-group members a bonus based on their group's production over a certain predetermined standard. If they produce 50 percent above the standard, they receive a 50 percent bonus; if they produce 100 percent above the standard, they receive a 100 percent bonus—a simple scheme that many companies could adopt. During the 1980s Nucor's sales grew 850 percent and its profits grew 1,250 percent. While most of the U.S. steel industry was laying off workers, Nucor laid off no worker in fifteen years. Nucor does many things well, and its work-group compensation contributes greatly to its performance.

> **It is easier to create effective gain-sharing schemes for employees organized as value-stream teams than for employees organized as traditional departments.**

The value-stream team has a clear customer and goals that are measurable. Appropriate bonuses can encourage value-stream teams to do the best job possible.

To encourage employees to learn skills that make them more useful, employees should be given pay raises when they improve their skills. A pay-for-knowledge scheme ties base pay to knowledge. Instead of aspiring to climb a hierarchy, the employee then aspires to have more knowledge or skill, knowing that as she increases her value she increases her compensation.

Flexible Work Schemes

Peter Drucker has written that work rules and job restrictions, often imposed by unions, are the main cause of the productivity gap between the West and Japan.[2] Old union rules said that an electrician must not saw wood and a carpenter must not change a light bulb. A worker is not allowed to fix a problem on his machine; that's the repairman's job. Workers are forbidden to move from one job to another. A supervisor is forbidden by union rules to fill in for an employee who goes to the bathroom.

Each cybercorp employee needs to be as useful as possible. Teams should be able to perform well even when some of their members are missing. Employees must be able to do multiple tasks so that a small team can be self-sufficient and not have to hand work over to other groups. On an assembly line, workers may be trained to do the jobs upstream and downstream of their own positions to help ensure continuous operation. In general, it is desirable to have flexibility in job assignments.

The U.S. Department of Labor has compiled data on high-performance workplace practices.[3]

Full Explanation

A particularly important aspect of the cybercorp is that management explains to employees what is happening and why. Management should be completely open and honest with employees. The reasons for new compensation schemes are fully described.

> **When companies candidly explain problems to employees and solicit their views they usually find that employees produce valuable ideas, increase their commitment, and work harder.**

Intel holds quarterly business update meetings (BUMs) for all employees. Twice a year it holds meetings describing strategic long-range plans to managers, which help managers understand the shifting demand for skills. It is every manager's job to explain to employees how the demand for skills is changing and to encourage desirable training. Ford and other companies maintain information walls that show details of weekly financial performance, delivery times, and other key measures. TRW's Auburn, New York, plant provides training to help employees understand the balance sheet. This plant makes keyless entry systems for cars and has contracts with carmakers that mandate 12 percent annual price reductions. All employees know this, and it creates a sense of urgency to work with management, designers, and production engineers to increase productivity.

The cybercorp should have better ways to measure value than a traditional corporation. Instead of sitting in a hierarchy slot doing repetitive tasks the value of which is difficult to ascertain, most employees will be members of value-stream teams that produce measurable results. The teams are challenged to constantly improve the results.

When there is pressure for performance and performance effects everyone's pay, employees are impatient with nonperformers. They expect management to do something about the drones.

Emotion

Traditional corporations have ignored human emotion. They have tried to pretend it doesn't exist or, worse, have tried to suppress it. While the chief executive was having violent temper tantrums, the middle managers were supposed to be emotionless "men in gray suits." However, work is an emotional experience. Pride, ambition, anger, jealousy, hate, determination, fear, rage, excitement, and the kicks of accomplishment can seethe in employees, especially when they have their feet hard on the accelerator.

> **The renewed focus on humanity in corporations requires an understanding of human emotions. To energize employees is to harness emotion.**

Negative emotions make employees "tune out," "work to rule," "retire on the job," or actively do harm. Good emotions make employees go all-out to succeed. It is a joy to do excellent work, build something special, and be recognized for it. Employees work late because they are excited about accomplishing their goals. Bad emotions have a bad effect on profit; good emotions are a fuel that drives productivity, quality, and customer satisfaction.

> **The cybercorp architect, rather than trying to suppress emotions because they gum up the works, should create ways to use emotions to release energy, pride, determination, excitement, and the thrill of excellence.**

The enterprise needs a vision and mission that excites people. It needs teams with ambitious goals to accomplish. It needs employees to find the company fun to work for. It should avoid structures that cause energy to be spent on internal politics, empire building, or the size of one's office. It needs challenges and sources of excitement that are directly related to delighting the customer.

Teams and Empowerment

In the early 1990s NASA was in trouble. It had had one failure after another and the press were beginning to suggest that it should close up shop. The Hubble telescope was a multibillion-dollar fiasco. In 1993 NASA planned a mission to rebuild the Hubble telescope in space. To do this on one mission was a *very* tough goal. Seven astronauts were selected. In their training for the mission every astronaut devised every idea they could for helping every other astronaut. So many things could go wrong during the five days of extra-vehicular activity. Every team member was urgently concerned that every other team member should perform flawlessly. This was a stunning example of what a high-performance team should be like. Watched by one of the world's largest television audiences they repaired both the telescope and NASA's reputation.

Corporations around the world are steadily improving their ability to use empowered teams. Instead of obeying detailed orders, these teams create their own way of working. *Empowerment* means delegating the responsibility for results, not tasks. The team may have people from different disciplines so that it combines diverse capabilities. It invents how best to achieve results and constantly learns how to improve.

In sports and in the theater, teams have always been used and honed to the highest levels of effectiveness. Only recently have they come into common use in factories and corporations. It can be very enjoyable to be a member of a great team that functions in an extraordinary way. Many people remember a time in their lives when they were part of such a team and regard it as one of their very satisfying experiences. It may have been in sports, in a task force that learned something intensely and clarified its ideas, in a sales team that battled to close a massive order. It may have been in a theater performance, or in the army where shared dangers intensified human cooperation and camaraderie. Some say that they have spent much of their lives looking for that experience again.

Cyberspace changes the capability of teams. A team can access a vast amount of information. Technology demands new skills from people and in return enables them to achieve more powerful results. The team may be scattered geographically but tightly linked by technology. It can access important specialized talents that do not exist locally, possibly with the Net, possibly with videoconferencing. (The use of teams in corporate redesign is discussed in the author's book *The Great Transition,* Chapter 6 and Part 2.)

Value-Stream Teams

Value streams are a key to building effective cybercorp teams. Each value stream has a clear purpose, and teams are built to achieve that purpose. Teams with a variety of different structures are used. Each team needs designing carefully using technology to make it as effective as possible and to provide it with all the information it needs. Traditional corporate value streams that clumsily pass work from one department to another are hopelessly ineffective compared to ones designed as a cybercorp creature. The creature should have challenging targets and be largely in charge of its own destiny. It may have difficult obstacles to overcome and is challenged to constantly improving the value-stream capability, focusing intensely on how to delight the customer.

Certain value streams, discussed in Chapter 5, are of extreme strategic importance. They represent the core capability of the corporation that enables it to keep ahead of its competition. Unbeatable capability predators need unique technology and dedicated teams. The high-performance corporation of the future is likely to be composed of value-stream teams, each challenged to learn as rapidly as possible how to improve the value-stream processes. One or two value streams will be identified as strategic capabilities, and these will need the most intense focus on building high-performance teams linked to exceptional technology.

The emphasis on tough performance goals makes value-stream teams a very potent asset in coping with rapid change. The successful value-stream team loves new challenges. It can usually make changes quickly, whereas value streams crossing a traditional hierarchy and entangled in its politics can be very difficult to change.

Change demands new learning. Teams tend to integrate learning and performance challenges. They have to learn in order to achieve new goals. Each team member shows the others what to learn, so that they can behave collectively. Value-stream teams translate longer-team purposes into short-term objectives and develop the skills to meet those objectives.

Loners Who Are Different

While today's management literature is full of advocacy for teams, it tends to say little about the loner who is brilliant, and cyberspace is full of loners. It is probably the case that brilliant loners change the world more than teams. Thomas Edison, Gloria Steinem, Edward Teller, Alfred Hitchcock, Henry VIII, Albert Einstein, Abraham Lincoln, Elvis Presley, Saddam Hussein, John le Carré, Robert Oppenheimer—loners do things that are interesting.

There are many loners in corporations, and sometimes they become exceptionally good at a particular activity; they can apply themselves with a fierce intensity. The loner may be impossible as a team member. He does his own thing. Often a support structure grows around the loner to help put his ideas into practice.

Thomas J. Watson, Sr., and then his two sons built IBM, one of history's greatest corporations. They were totally autocratic; their temper was terrifying. They would smash the furniture in meetings if they did not get their own way. Tom Watson, Jr., would suddenly fire the entire crew when he was cruising and sail the boat alone.

Woody Allen plays his clarinet in Michael's Pub in New York every Monday without fail. He refused to go to the Academy Awards. He was a law unto himself. But he made films that were really different. Many people in Europe know the name of only one American film director—Woody Allen.

Sometimes loners are entrepreneurs; sometimes they design startlingly different products; sometimes they create excellence in unique ways. They may be devastating perfectionists; they may use computers to do the most complex analysis, modeling, or synthesis. In a world of intensifying global competition and copycat products, a key resource is the capability to innovate.

People who think differently are valuable; a challenge is to harness and direct their originality. Corporations need the unique capabilities of loners as well as the collective but often conventional capability of teams.

Virtuosos

The best computer hackers can build up a focused intensity that is truly astonishing. One finds them in the morning, having worked all night, bleary-eyed, ashtrays overflowing, surrounded by empty junk-food packets. Some businesspeople with computerized tools have become equally dedicated at pushing computers to the limits—they become total authorities in their particular domains. The screen virtuoso learns everything she can possibly learn about lens design, shop-floor simulation, derivatives, or whatever her subject is, using her computer to do calculations nobody had done before. There are virtuosos worldwide achieving results at their screens that would have been impossible until recently. Kohlberg Kravis Roberts & Co., the firm that drove the leveraged buyout mania in the 1980s, obtained fees of hundreds of millions of dollars with a staff of only twenty. Less publicized are numerous model builders, graphics designers, planners, spreadsheet artists, and so on, who sit at their screens until midnight.

Hackerlike virtuosos exist in many specializations—financial analysts, marketing experts, customer service personnel, production schedulers, quality-control experts, systems architects, decision makers with computerized models. Intensely focused, they develop their skill to the highest level possible. As we race into the knowledge era we will increasingly need intellect workers who are *virtuosos.* Computerized tools of increasing complexity make virtuosos increasingly important.

A large bank may have a senior person who deals with the worldwide needs of a major corporate account. An airline may have a person using a computer to schedule crews for flights around the world. A factory may have a person who uses a computer to optimize production schedules. Such a person may be "line," not "staff," in that he makes events happen. He executes the results of his deeply calculated decisions; but this is not conventional line management because nobody works for him.

Computers, and especially computer networks, hold an uncanny fascination for some people. They work at the screen with an intensity that excludes all else. When aimed at the right target they can be uniquely valuable. A young woman with no degree worked for a company near Chicago that made training products in the early 1980s. She sat up night after night with Lotus 1–2-3. She collected and analyzed data and eventually showed that more than half of her company's products had a net negative return on investment—something that had eluded the company's planners, accountants, and senior management.

David Ogilvy, the legendary advertising executive, commented that great copywriters are ten times as effective as the average copywriter. This applies to virtuosos in general. Genius programmers write ten times as much bugfree code as the average programmer. Today's tools greatly amplify the capability of bright people. The planner has modeling tools; the architect has computerized design tools with libraries of preexisting designs; the programmer has code generators and repositories of objects. The best virtuosos make themselves superbly skilled with the most powerful tools.

The traditional corporation has rarely respected virtuosos and has often failed to put them to work. The world of the "organization man" tended to want interchangeable conformists rather than brilliant hackers and creative thinkers. Even IBM failed to put most of its brilliant people to good use. It put up notices saying that they must wear white shirts and ties in the cafeteria, "to keep the wild ducks flying in formation." Instead of encouraging and growing its virtuosos, it tried to mold them into cogs in the machine. The brightest ones often left.

Cybercorp virtuosos are assets that need to be looked after.

Their decisions or work can sometimes have massive financial effects. The more the planet plunges into cyberspace, the more this will be true. Managers need to know how to hire and develop virtuosos, motivate them, and design work to take advantage of them. Virtuosos are sometimes prima donnas who have to be managed delicately.

Teams and Virtuosos

Some virtuosos can work in teams; others are rugged individuals devoid of people skills and incapable of team interaction. A characteristic of a high-performance team is that its members all help the other members to contribute the most they can. Team members take responsibility for their peers. Most virtuosos will not do that; it is too big a distraction from virtuosoing. However, teams can be designed around virtuosos to provide support for them. A brilliant architect may be a loner but needs a large organization to implement what she draws.

While some virtuosos work completely alone, most need a support structure. The value of the virtuoso and the value of the team can be combined by designing the team as a support structure for the virtuoso. The virtuoso does the unique, creative, intensive, or brilliant work, and the team does the more routine work. The virtuoso may pass work to the team, or the team may pass the interesting cases to the virtuoso. Much creative work needs a small amount of inspiration and a large amount of perspiration. The virtuoso may provide the former, and the support structure provides the latter.

Teams need not be antithetical to virtuoso performance. On the contrary, high-performance teams may demand it. The team finds ways to make use of what each individual is good at. There are different types of team design involving virtuosos. It is important to adopt the right team structure. Inappropriately designed teams fail to deliver the needed results.

The Cybercorp HR System

The cybercorp should use its intranet to help manage human resources. Employees ought to be able to use their own computers to help manage their own career, and find out about vacancies and opportunities, training courses, benefit options, and so on. Employees should maintain their own electronic résumés.

Electronic résumés have many advantages over paper résumés. An electronic résumé gives guidance to the person who fills it in on a computer screen. It can collect information in a well-structured database that you can search when looking for people with specific skills. An electronic résumé can have photographs and spoken interviews. Employees seeking opportunities within their corporation should have résumés available over the internal network. A cybercorp should have its own internal database of employees, with the ability to match employees to jobs. There are a variety of electronic résumé systems on the Internet but the use of electronic résumés has not yet become widespread practice.

Federal Express built a cybercorp human resources (HR) system; in effect it reinvented its corporate personnel function. A corporation-wide computer system called PRISM was built to help grow the capability of employees. It enables employees and managers to carry out personnel functions that in most other companies are done by an HR department. PRISM gives employees access to a worldwide database from their own PCs. All employees can examine their own personnel data and are securely locked out of data that they should not see about other employees. Employees maintain their own personal details in the system, and supervisors maintain management data about employees who report to them.

Federal Express puts great emphasis on its PSP philosophy, which says, "Focus on developing *people* because that leads to higher levels of *service* and hence to higher *profits.*" PRISM's main purpose is to ensure that employees are well trained and have advancement opportunities open to them. Employees can see what jobs are vacant anywhere in Federal Express, and they can bid for those positions. Every employee is free to seek the most satisfying job opportunities anywhere in the company. Detailed job descriptions are maintained on the system, and any employee can apply for any position. The computer verifies the employee's qualifications.

Surveys show that PRISM has substantially increased employee commitment and morale.[4] It helps to make employees feel that they are treated fairly and given the best opportunities for advancement. The system helps to ensure that their skills are constantly upgraded. An employee might aspire to a job that he is not yet qualified for, and PRISM tells him what training he needs. Much training and testing is on-line. The company has over 4,000 different courses available through interactive video. Employees' managers receive test reports and discuss improvement plans with their employees. Employees can advance their pay levels. Points are assigned for courses or projects finished, or objectives met, and the computer forwards earned points to the payroll system.

A variety of other HR functions are carried out by the system, including enhancing compliance with government guidelines on equal employment opportunity and affirmative action. All job applications are entered into PRISM, and PRISM contains details of all job vacancies. The system tells a hiring manager if an applicant applied before and what happened. PRISM facilitates internal promotion where possible. It conducts periodic surveys of employee perceptions and produces trend charts for management.

In the future, cybercorp HR systems like PRISM are likely to run on corporate "intranets" and link to the public Internet. Both internal and external résumé databases will be accessible. Many of the training courses will be purchasable on the Internet.

Skills Inventory

In spite of the growing value of expertise a surprising number of companies have no systematic inventory of their expertise. Some search for expertise from outside without realizing that they have it in-house. The cybercorp should have a constantly updated inventory of its own skills. Before tackling key projects or moving into new markets it should be able to systematically access the skills it needs and then examine any skills shortfall that requires new training, temporary personnel, or new partnerships. This capability is an important feature of HR systems like PRISM and should link to the ongoing training program.

Critical Success Factor: Automated Training

So much training is needed in today's corporations that it cannot all be done by stand-up teachers. Computer-based training, CD-ROMs, and videotapes are essential components of a training program. Classroom training has a role to play, but most classroom training is slow, inefficient, and inadequate

Exhibit 15-1. Advantages of automated training over classroom training

- The world's best teachers can be used, making available the highest level of knowledge.
- Interviews with top experts and practitioners can be used.
- Key managers can (privately) bring themselves up to date.
- Students can quickly and efficiently select what they need.
- Students can fast-forward or follow computerized links to knowledge they need.
- Students often repeat segments of the training to reinforce their understanding.
- Students can study at home or in the evening.
- Just-in-time training is used.
- Students can link training directly to the tasks they have to perform.
- Training is always available.
- Training is accessible on-demand via the Internet (or private intranets).
- No travel is needed.
- The cost is usually lower.

by itself. Automated training is needed. Exhibit 15-1 lists the benefits of automated training.

Some executives who would never sit in a classroom (and show their ignorance) desperately need to be brought up to date. For them, a library of educational CD-ROMs that they can use on their notebook computer (or tapes to play at home) is a valuable asset.[5]

The IT profession contains many lessons about the need for training. For the last ten years new tools and techniques have flooded into the world of IT. For each new wave of powerful tools, some corporations have succeeded spectacularly in putting them to work, and others have completely failed. There have been more failures than successes, and the failures try to avoid having egg on their faces by saying, "The tool doesn't work," when in realty some of their competition have put it to work very effectively. Failures to succeed with powerful new techniques almost always relate to inadequate training and motivation. This pattern of failure and success will increasingly apply not just to IT but to the cybercorp as a whole because the skills needed are changing so fast.

The faster technology changes, the greater the investment needed in education and training.

Fun

In a detailed study of corporate teams, good and bad, Katzenbach and Smith comment that a characteristic of high-performance teams always seems to be that the members are having fun. They comment: "There may be some humorless high-performance teams out there. But we doubt it."[6]

The abnormal personal bonds and commitment that characterize high-performance teams only develop when the goals are tough and exciting. They arise not from exercises or training but when the right group of people finds itself with a very tough challenge and knows that it must bond together to confront that challenge. Members of such teams describe their experience as participating in something bigger and better than oneself.

Happy employees do better work and give better customer service. The cybercorp should be designed and managed, as far as possible, so that employees are having fun.

References

1. Brian O'Reilly, "The New Deal," *Fortune,* June 13, 1994.
2. Peter Drucker, "Worker's Hands Bound by Tradition," *Wall Street Journal,* August 2, 1988.
3. Available (in digital form) from the Agility Manufacturing Enterprise Forum, Bethlehem, PA 18015–1582, fax: (610) 694–0542.
4. Prashant C. Palvia, James A. Perkins, and Steven M. Zeltmann, "The PRISM System: A Key to Organizational Effectiveness at Federal Express Corporation," *MIS Quarterly,* September 1992.
5. E.g., with the Knowledge Navigator from Computer Channel Inc., Syosset, NY, E-mail: jrizzo@ix.netcom.com.
6. Jon R. Katzenback and Douglas K. Smith, *The Wisdom of Teams* (Boston: Harvard Business School Press, 1993), chap. 4.

16

The Steepest
Possible Learning
Curves

In cyberspace there are few secrets. Information passes around the world at electronic speed.

When one corporation produces a good idea others can copy it quickly, and increasingly those others are in distant countries. While many organizations ignore anything "not invented here," the Japanese systematically troll the world for ideas they can adopt and gurus whose brains they can pick. Most headlines about a technology giving a corporation a strategic advantage turn sour because, unless the innovation is an exceptional BHAG effort, other corporations soon do the same. Success in business can be short-lived.

> **Arie de Geus when he was head of planning for Shell expressed the view that the only *sustainable* competitive advantage will become *the ability to learn faster than one's competition*.[1] The cybercorp must learn fast at all levels and implement the results of its learning.**

Competition can quickly replicate a new thrust, and the time for replication is getting shorter. It is often easy for cheap-labor countries to copy products and find alternatives to patents. This is happening more and more as business know-how spreads around the planet. As information highways turn into superhighways the flow of knowledge will become a flood.

Knowledge Infrastructure

> **A key characteristic of the cybercorp is a *knowledge infrastructure* that uses the Internet and an intranet to help acquire knowledge, enhance it, store it in an organized way, and make it accessible to everyone who needs it in the enterprise.**

Today larger and larger organizations need to learn faster and faster in a globally dynamic environment. It is essential to use technology to facilitate learning and experimentation and to disseminate the knowledge acquired and ensure that it is put to good use. Internet and intranet software provides "open" connectivity and makes it technically easy to create a knowledge infrastructure designed to accelerate this process. To use the infrastructure effectively all employees should use the same tools. They might all use Microsoft Office, for example, and communicate ideas and presentations with Powerpoint. They should all use the same groupware. For more specialized communication a corporation needs to standardize on software such as CAD, software development tools, data warehousing, and so forth.

Process repeatability is critical. Without repeatability, every situation is unique, and nothing can be learned that has value for the future. Many local, individual learning experiences occur; a knowledge infrastructure should help communicate them so that people throughout the enterprise benefit. Without some structure for knowledge, it is extremely difficult to communicate learning experiences from group to group. An efficient knowledge infrastructure becomes more important as an organization grows large.

> **A small organization can "muddle through," but as it grows it needs to invest in its knowledge infrastructure.**

Learning Curves

In the cyberspace era many corporations find that their external environment is changing faster than the corporation's efforts to keep up.

> **A key operation should be designed with two characteristics: First, it has a learning curve that is *as steep as possible* (i.e., can be climbed as rapidly as possible), and second, the new learning curve goes to *the highest level possible.***

A common experience when operations are reengineered or new techniques are introduced is that at first productivity *drops*. Managers are often disappointed because the new approach has more problems than expected; rapid learning is needed. Exhibit 16-1 shows two learning curves. An old

Exhibit 16-1. A new process replaces the old process and establishes a new learning curve. The new learning curve should be designed to be as steep as possible and go to the highest level practical before it plateaus.

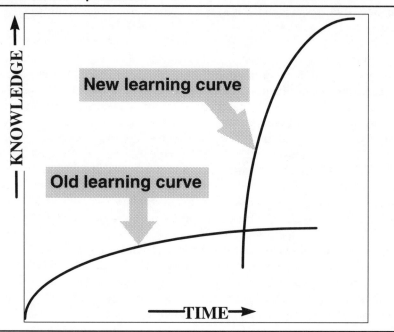

operation with a learning curve that has almost plateaued is reengineered and has a new learning curve. The new operation gives lower performance at first but is designed so that people learn quickly.

Often a succession of techniques are needed, each building on the previous one. Exhibit 16-2 shows a succession of learning curves. The journey may be planned a milestone at a time.

Learning How to Learn

There are many different ways in which an enterprise can learn. Most articles and books describe one form of enterprise learning and ignore the others. A cybercorp should be designed to learn in every way, not just one, and to record the results of its learning.

Learning needs to take place at every level, from the chief executive to the janitor. All employees must be challenged to learn constantly to respond to the ever-quickening pace of change. They contribute little if they hang

Exhibit 16-2. A planned succession of learning curves.

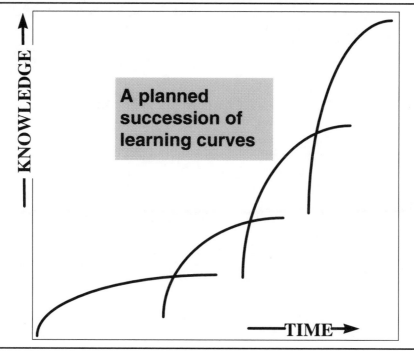

A planned succession of learning curves

their brains up with their overcoats when they enter the workplace. Planners at all levels should plan for learning of all types.

Corporations, like people, have learning disabilities. An enterprise has many types of learning disabilities, some more dangerous than others. Peter Senge comments, "Learning disabilities are tragic in children, but they are fatal in organizations."[2] The cybercorp should be designed to remove the many forms of learning disability. Many enterprises grow senile faster than their executives. The life expectancy of new corporations today is shorter than my dog's.

The enterprise that knows *how* to learn better than its competitors has a significant edge. Learning in organizations goes on continuously, but most of it is not put to use as it should be. Sales and service people are always learning—customers are constantly giving feedback about products and how the enterprise satisfies their needs—but this information doesn't reach the product designers. Engineers encounter interesting things in their work but don't use them to help the organization. Employees learn to solve problems but often solve the same problem over and over without reflecting on and fixing its source.

> **The cybercorp should be designed to be a learning-efficient organization. It should use networks and computers to capture, enhance, store, and disseminate knowledge from both internal and external sources.**

Exhibit 16-3 summarizes the many different types of enterprise learning.

A Perpetual Mutation Machine

The cybercorp should be a perpetual mutation machine. Management should encourage employees to do the following:

1. Generate a large number of new ideas (until a plateau of creativity is reached).
2. Use maximum parallelism—have all employees brainstorming new ideas.
3. Test the ideas and quickly cull the poor ones.
4. Minimize the cycle time to get new products to market.
5. Identify virtual operations and relationships that can minimize cycle time and accelerate growth.
6. Use cybermarketing techniques to enhance and understand market reaction to products.
7. Have employees and Net contacts brainstorm ideas about how to respond to market reaction.
8. Respond quickly to market reaction with a fast cycle of refinement and reinvention.
9. Have all employees improving the processes (Japanese *kaizen*-style).
10. Eliminate poorly performing products quickly.
11. Based on market reaction, establish core competences and components that can be in diverse products.
12. Establish the best possible skills and relationships in the chosen competences.
13. Build a knowledge infrastructure that communicates new ideas and makes relevant knowledge accessible.

Capturing the Results of Learning

A particularly important aspect of learning, if corporations are to improve, is the recording of what has been learned so that it can be revised and others can benefit from it.

The same type of work may be done in many locations. There needs to be an organized mechanism for transferring learning that results in improved

Exhibit 16-3. Types of enterprise learning

A cybercorp must learn in many different ways; it must record and communicate the results of its learning.

Kaizen

The Japanese culture of *kaizen,* meaning "everybody improves everything all the time," should pervade the enterprise. It should employ techniques such as:

- Quantitative analysis of problems
- In-depth analysis of the causes of problems
- Statistical quality control
- Systematic suggestion schemes
- Awards for suggestions and improvements
- *Kaizen* targets for managers, foremen, and supervisors
- Focusing on delighting the customer
- Quality circles
- Self-motivated teams
- Top management driving *kaizen* culture

TQM is a Western variant of kaizen, *often much less effective.*[3]

Learning by Reinvention

The reinvention of value streams is a dramatic form of learning experience in which many new ideas need to be explored. The challenge of quantum-leap reinvention puts the learning processes into high gear for a time. When the new value-stream teams go to work they should be trained to search for constant improvements with the techniques of *kaizen*-style learning.

Learning Teams

Teams, either permanent or short term, should be designed for fast learning. They can be at any level—at the workplace, designing the process, designing the infrastructure, or at top management. Team members learn from each other and stimulate each other. They are often people with different knowledge who need one another in order to act, so that the sum is greater than the parts. No one individual embodies all the learning of the team as a whole. They should consciously employ both debate and dialog.[4] In debate, different arguments are presented and defended, with an attempt to choose the best. In dialog, there are explanations and exploration of ideas with deep listening and suspension of one's own views so that one can learn.

(*continued*)

Exhibit 16-3. (*continued*)

Team Problem Solving
Learning often occurs rapidly when there are urgent and tough problems to be solved. High-performance teams tend to gel when jointly confronted with tough problems. Value-stream teams have explicit goals and motivation, and their learning process can be actively managed for maximum effectiveness.

Simulation and Prototypes
When a complex process is to be performed, it makes sense to simulate it in order to train the participants. In a new factory, for example, with fundamentally new methods, factory workers may be trained with simulated operations before they work on the factory floor. Simulations range from the use of Lego blocks to elaborate computerized models. When preparing for a reinvented value stream to become operational, a value-stream "laboratory" should be set up so that team members can learn their new roles and at the same time help to debug the processes. The laboratory simulations and prototypes usually cause substantial modifications to be made to the processes. The laboratory should be an ongoing resource for training new recruits and trying out new ideas.

Experimentation
Experimentation, described in Chapter 14, should be encouraged at all levels to explore ways of improving the work processes. Techniques for efficient design of experiments should be taught. Some value streams should be operated like laboratories, with management encouraging continuous experimentation and research to acquire new learning.

Customer Observation
Often the only way to learn about improvements needed is to observe the customer in action. Milliken uses "first-delivery teams" to accompany the first shipment of products.[5] The team follows the product through the customer's processes, records any difficulties, observes how the product is used, and develops ideas for improving the product. Some companies employ "usability labs" to videotape users learning to use the product and record their difficulties and human-factoring problems. Customer difficulties often surprise the designers of the product, and many iterations of improvement are possible.

Benchmarking
Benchmarking involves a systematic study of procsses in other corporations to identify which corporations are doing a process in a better way or achieving better results. Where possible, a systematic comparison should measure the results achieved. There is usually a large difference between the best and the average in an industry. Benchmarking should be an ongoing investigation to uncover the best practices and to analyze, adopt, improve, and implement them. ("Benchmarking" is often too narrowly defined.)

(*continued*)

Exhibit 16-3. (*continued*)

Facilitated Workshops

Workshops with diverse participants are conducted under the guidance of a "facilitator" to achieve specified results such as redesigning a work process, creating specifications for a system, or validating enterprise models. Well-run workshops can generate many new ideas, solve communication problems, and engender excitement about new directions.

Workout Sessions

The term "workout session" was used at GE for thousands of facilitated workshops in which collective learning resulted in major changes:

- A psychological "workout" with management
- Collectively "working out" how processes can be improved
- Taking the work out of processes

Quality Circles

A quality circle is a chosen group of people who set out to find a solution to a problem, or something that needs improvement. In some organizations *any* employee can convene a quality circle and can ask for *any* person to be involved.

Brainstorming

Brainstorming may be a component of workshops, in which for a period everyone is encouraged to voice wild ideas without criticism and to refine the ideas if possible into something workable. Various scenarios may be used to encourage the voicing of new ideas.

Enterprise Modeling

Models of the enterprise are created in a computer and steadily refined. The models may reflect the work flow, policies, and rules for running the business. They enable alternative work flows, rules, and procedures to be simulated. Management or designers can experiment with the models and use them to learn more about how the enterprise functions.

Demonstration Projects

Demonstration projects are sometimes established for major changes. They range from relatively inexpensive demonstrations, such as the introduction of a self-managing team, to massive demonstrations, such as a new type of factory. Demonstration projects are usually the first to adopt principles and approaches that the corporation hopes to adopt later on a larger scale. Mistakes, backtracking, and evolution of ideas are expected on demonstration projects.

Study of Successes and Failures

Failure can be a great teacher. It is desirable to analyze the reasons for failure in

(*continued*)

Exhibit 16-3. (*continued*)

detail and to record them in such a way that they can be applied to future projects. Similarly, success stories should be examined, and an analysis of the reasons for success disseminated. Too often failures are hushed up rather than milked for their insight.

Scenario Exploration
A useful technique to assist top management visioning is to create a variety of possible future scenarios. Management then works out what it would do if such scenarios become reality. Shell was much better prepared than the other oil companies for the OPEC crisis of the 1970s because it had used this technique and had thoroughly explored what it would do if such a situation occurred.[6] Scenario exploration helps a corporation avoid being caught by surprise. It learns ahead of time what actions may be needed if its market or external forces change, or crises occur. It can then make preparatory plans and establish readiness in its management.

Counterintuitive Learning
Intuitive human learning takes place where cause and effect are close so that humans can associate them. However, cybercorp mechanisms may separate cause and effect in complex ways. Because of this, enterprises have systemic behavior that can be counterintuitive. Unless management learns to understand the systemic behavior, it may repeatedly take actions that cause problems. When complex systems behave in counterintuitive ways, it is necessary to lessen the counterintuitive behavior where possible and to educate management's intuition.

Cross-Communication of Learning
When a group in one location learns and hence improves their work processes, the improvements need to be transmitted to groups in other locations who can benefit. Deliberate procedures need to be put into place and managed in order to achieve this cross-communication of learning.

Conferences to Exchange Experience
When people discuss their experiences at conferences, they learn from each other in informal ways. Conferences should occur for groups doing similar work, and groups doing dissimilar work can often gain creative insight from listening to each other's experiences and examining each other's methods.

Industry Seminars
There is much to be learned at external seminars. Some of the better industry "gurus" have much to communicate. Some gurus give internal seminars that help an enterprise to learn and change.

Computerized Representation of Procedures
Operating procedures and methodologies should be represented in computers in

(*continued*)

Exhibit 16-3. (*continued*)

such a way that they can continually evolve to reflect the continuous learning in the company. Details of problems and how to avoid them should be recorded.

Expert Systems
Expert systems can be built to capture specialized know-how and make it available to other people. The knowledge in expert systems should be continuously added to as more is learned. Some expert systems contain the knowledge of multiple people and in such a way that the system can solve problems too difficult for any one person. The best expert systems often have the effect of making a person who is already skilled more skilled.

A Knowledge Infrastructure
Computers should act as accumulators of information or know-how. An intranet can accumulate much of the learning of an enterprise, making it available at any location.

processes from one location to another. When one location learns from mistakes, this learning should be transferred to other locations; otherwise the same mistakes are made over and over. The results of learning may be recorded in *standard operating procedures.* These procedures should steadily evolve as more is learned.

Lenscrafters, for example, a shop that makes custom eyeglasses, expanded rapidly to 500 outlets because it learned how to test customers' eyes and produce prescription eyeglasses in less than an hour. The workers at the outlets were empowered to invent their own techniques, find solutions to problems, and improve the work process. Because these empowered activities took place at all outlets, it was necessary to capture what was learned in each outlet and transfer the valuable ideas to the other outlets quickly; otherwise the same problem would be solved many times in different ways. Lenscrafters developed a formal process for capturing and disseminating new techniques. It grew faster than its competition because it learned faster.

In a consulting company, consultants learn to solve complex problems and create methodologies for tackling those problems. New techniques are learned at a rapid rate. To spread this know-how requires some consultants' time and some overhead expenses. Left to their own devices, consultants all tend to invent their own techniques rather than optimize a shared pool of know-how. Intranet applications should be designed for storing know-how and steadily adding to it as more is learned. The intranet can act as an accumulator for human learning and help employees to apply expertise.

Northrop Aircraft manufactures jet fighters that contain many different parts, each of which requires a detailed plan spelling out steps in the manu-

facturing process. The parts must fit together, and their assembly also requires detailed plans. For a jet fighter, there can be more than 20,000 plans.
The process of drawing up the plans is lengthy and error prone, and the errors
can be very expensive. Northrop built an expert system to gradually capture
know-how and assemble a living library of planning expertise. This system
made it possible for relatively inexperienced planners working on the more
routine tasks to behave like planners with years of experience. The experienced planners were then freed for more exceptional tasks where new learning was needed. Northrop greatly speeded up its learning process.[7]

Spreading the Know-How

The task of learning how to improve the work process is very different from
the task of spreading this know-how. Usually, the learning is done by the
people who perform the work, or by quality circles who tackle particular
issues. The job of spreading the improved know-how is a task to which somebody must be assigned. It does not happen on its own; it requires management. In many organizations, this transfer of learning is unmanaged, so many
improvements are not applied where they should be. Most computer programmers, for example, are creating things that have been created thousands
of times before, when they could employ reusable designs and code, but reus-
ability is a management act that is missing.

The cybercorp needs a mechanism for capturing and spreading what has
been learned. As people become more and more "information literate," they
will demand more and faster access to knowledge and a more active role in
knowledge development. Knowledge workers will judge the companies they
work for by the knowledge leverage they have access to.

Maximizing Experiential Learning

Much effective learning is learning from experience. People reflect on their
experience and learn from it. The efficient learner experiments and broadens
his experience. Teams can sometimes learn better than individuals because
the team consists of people with different talents who discuss their collective
experience from different points of view.

Boeing top management established a high-level employee team to study
the development processes of the Boeing 707, 727, 737, and 747 aircraft.
Boeing had many difficulties with the 737 and 747, whereas the 707 and 727
programs had fewer problems. The study, called Project Homework, established many "lessons learned" and produced hundreds of recommendations
for future projects. Several members of the team were transferred to Boeing's

Exhibit 16-4.

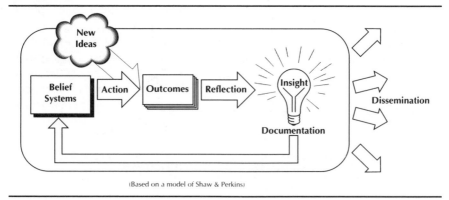

(Based on a model of Shaw & Perkins)

757 and 767 projects. This carefully managed learning from experience resulted in the 757 and 767's being the most successful, error-free aircraft launched in Boeing's history.[8]

Exhibit 16-4 illustrates experience-based corporate learning.

An enterprise has certain beliefs that influence behavior. The vision and mission translate into action; new ideas produce action; groups of employees reflect on the outcomes of their actions, and reflection leads to certain insights or improvements in know-how. If one group learns and improves its procedures, the learning should be documented so that others can benefit from it. The results of learning need to be disseminated to other groups in the enterprise. The dissemination of new insights does not happen without a deliberate management effort. The reflection process is critical to learning. A group needs to examine its experiences, discuss why things happened as they did, and determine how to make improvements. Dissemination of what has been learned helps the reflection process. It brings different perspectives into play in examining experience. If a group has to disseminate what it has learned, it is forced to think clearly about it and articulate it well. The group gains new information and insight from others, which helps to interpret the experience.

Barriers to Experiential Learning

Robert Shaw and Dennis Perkins use a model of enterprise learning like one in Exhibit 16-4 and observe that experiential learning is deficient when the components of the model are performed inadequately. Exhibit 16-5 shows barriers that exist to such learning.

Exhibit 16-5. Barriers to organizational learning

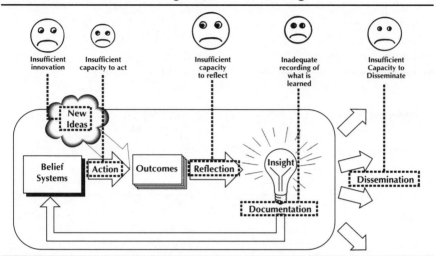

Insufficient innovation. Many organizations subtly discourage innovation. There must be a strong urge to learn by innovation and to test ideas by acting on them.

Insufficient capacity to act. Many corporations have subtle disincentives to act on innovative ideas. Many employees are risk averse, and managers reluctant to stick their necks out. Sometimes the work pressures are too great to try out new methods even though they would help. A well-known cartoon shows a machine-gun salesman approaching a general whose army is fighting only with spears. The general says, "Don't bother me. Can't you see we are in the middle of fighting a war!"

Insufficient capacity to reflect. Much learning comes from reflecting about the outcomes of the approaches tried. Often the work pressures seem too great to spend time on reflection. There is frenzied action; everybody keeps busy, and some work late at night. But action is a substitute for thought. Reflection requires a lack of action for certain periods. Often reflection is biased toward the bible of current practices; employees are prisoners of what they understand the best. Reflection is done better if it involves outsiders, who bring different perspectives and ignore current taboos.

Inadequate recording of what is learned. When insights are gained, they should be recorded; otherwise they will be lost. There is often no budget for doing this, or no time, or no talent or inclination. If the literacy needed to record insight is absent in working groups, an external facilitator may record it.

Insufficient capacity to disseminate. When one group learns and improves its work process, the learning should be transmitted to other groups in the enterprise; otherwise much of the potential value of the learning is lost. The dissemination will not occur unless it is deliberately planned and appropriate motivations established. There should be rewards associated with disseminating know-how and applying the insight of others.

When Learning From Experience Is a Delusion

A subtle and dangerous form of learning disability occurs when learning from experience breaks down. It breaks down when we cannot see the consequences of our actions.

Corporate learning, like learning in life, is to a large extent based on experience. We take action, observe its effect, and learn from that how to improve performance. This describes how we learn to drive a car, conduct a meeting, or run a factory shop floor. It describes how a child grows to adulthood and how the adult obtains "street smarts." However, it only works when we can clearly associate an action with the results of that action. It depends on our observing *cause and effect,* and we can do that only when the effect is close in time and space to the cause. In complex systems, *the cause and effect are often not close together in time and space.* In that case, we do not easily associate them or learn by observing their interaction.

As computerization spreads, executives increasingly make decisions for which they cannot directly experience the consequences. A person can click on a screen and a smart bomb is launched, or 500 people are laid off. The results occur in a distant place or after a long time delay. Long-span webs of activities like those discussed in Chapter 12 may result in counterintuitive behavior because there is no observable link between cause and effect.

Experiential learning requires the feedback of results to the person learning. The feedback loop may be faulty for the following reasons:

- Time delay is too great for feedback.
- The consequence is too distant to be visible.
- There is no human emotional contact with the effects.
- The cause-and-effect relationship is different from that expected.
- The decision has unperceived side effects.

Many of the most critical decisions that executives make have consequences years later. Some affect many different areas in the enterprise. Where cause and effects are separated electronically, the way we think about effects may be fundamentally different from reality. Often the most important deci-

Exhibit 16-6. Causes of the learning barriers

Barrier to Learning (See Exhibit 16-5)	Potential Causes
Insufficient innovation	▪ Taking of risks discouraged ▪ No time to experiment ▪ Attitude of "Things have always been done this way." ▪ Mistakes punished ▪ Arrogance: "We know what is best." ▪ Standard operating procedures regarded as a "bible" ▪ Lack of experimentation
Insufficient capacity to act	▪ Employees powerless to try new things ▪ Individuals or teams overcontrolled; "wild ducks" discouraged ▪ Stress from too many priorities ▪ Unclear objectives ▪ Inadequate funding ▪ Poor implementation of new ideas ▪ Excessive delays ▪ Blind eye turned to problems ▪ Complacency ▪ Discomfort with new approaches ▪ Incremental improvements permitted but not fundamental redesign
Insufficient capacity to reflect	▪ Time not taken to examine results ▪ Employees unable to criticize ▪ Problems denied ▪ Successes of the past precluding valid reflection on new approaches ▪ Reflection biased toward the "bible" of current practices ▪ Incorrent analysis ▪ Incomplete analysis ▪ Short-term pressures precluding adequate reflection ▪ Inadequate set of knowledge brought to focus on the outcomes ▪ Frenzied action; no reflection ▪ Excessive performance demands ▪ Focus only on what can be measured ▪ Decision makers using spreadsheets: "If it's not in the spreadsheet, it doesn't exist." ▪ No discussion with people outside the group

(continued)

Exhibit 16-6. (*continued*)

Barrier to Learning (See Exhibit 16-5)	Potential Causes
	▪ Employees prisoners of what they understand the best ▪ Absence of learning forums ▪ Interpretations blocked if at odds with current philosophy ▪ Challenging core assumptions forbidden ▪ Cause and effect not linked in obvious ways ▪ Embarrassing conclusions avoided
Inadequate recording of what is learned	▪ No budget for recording insight ▪ No management directive to record insight ▪ No talent for recording insight ▪ No established mechanism
Inadequate capacity to disseminate	▪ No budget for dissemination ▪ No management directive to disseminate ▪ No communication between separate groups ▪ Parochial attitude ▪ Competitive attitude ▪ Uncooperativeness: "We want to be the best. Why should we help competing departments to be the best?" ▪ Higher management ignorant of the need for, and value of, dissemination of insight ▪ The group reluctant to discuss its failures ▪ Strong intergroup boundaries ▪ Internal rivalries and politics ▪ Distortion of facts to increase group funding ▪ The myth of uniqueness: "We are different from them." ▪ Geographic distances not bridged

sions are those for which there is the least opportunity for trial-and-error learning.

Learning based on the *observable* results of our actions is limited in what it can teach us. Managers, policymakers, and system designers need to understand the long-span webs of activities discussed in Chapter 12, the types of *counterintuitive* behavior they cause, and the techniques for lessening problems with them. Often counterintuitive behavior is of large magnitude. In many cases, it has caused severe corporate decline. Management wrestles with a situation that refuses to behave as expected.

Many cybercorp mechanisms give long-span interactions, and we need to control these by taking the actions listed at the end of Chapter 12.

References

1. Arie de Geus, "Planning as Learning," *Harvard Business Review,* March/April 1988.
2. Peter M. Senge, *The Fifth Discipline* (New York: Doubleday Currency, 1990).
3. James Martin, *The Great Transition* (New York: AMACOM, 1995), chaps. 17 and 18.
4. Senge, *The Fifth Discipline,* chap. 12.
5. David A. Garvin, "Building a Learning Organization," *Harvard Business Review,* July/August 1993.
6. de Geus, "Planning as Learning," 70–74.
7. The Northrop expert system is discussed in Edward Feigenbaum, Pamela McCorduck, and H. Penny Nii, *The Rise of the Expert Company* (New York: Times Books, 1988).
8. Garvin, "Building a Learning Organization."

17

The Outrageous Cost of Obsolete Thinking

In October 1992, a report from General Motors' financial staff warned the board of GM that GM was in danger of going bankrupt. A year before that GM had announced that it was closing twenty-three more plants and laying off 75,000 workers.

GM had been the world's largest and grandest corporation. It had magnificent research laboratories, very advanced technology, and massive expenditure on computers; it had built its own telecommunications system larger than many national telephone companies. It was a spectacular illustration that great technology does not compensate for obsolete management thinking.

Few executives calculate the cost of obsolete thinking; in fact, few even admit to it. But we are surrounded by it everywhere, and its costs are enormous. The danger of obsolete thinking is rapidly becoming more severe as we race into the cybercorp vortex.

The Wreck of Barings Bank

After Barings, Britain's oldest merchant bank, crashed in flames so suddenly the Bank of England produced a post mortem.[1] When systems professionals discussed this report they shook their heads in disbelief and described Barings's management as "utterly cretinous."[2] The most elementary and standard computer controls would have prevented what went wrong.

Violating the most basic principle of security, Barings's management allowed the fox to guard the chicken coop. Nick Leeson, a twenty-five-year-old with no college education, who had been refused a trading license in London, was made a key trader in Singapore, although he had almost no experience with the extremely complex type of investment he was to handle. Leeson was given the job of operating the back office as well as being a trader. He had the job of policing his own trading.

Leeson declared a profit of $15 million in 1993 and $50 million the next year, so he became a star with a legendary reputation and was given huge customer accounts to invest. Leeson, however, as back office manager, had set up an "error account" of the type used by brokers as a record of incomplete or questionable transactions. Usually error accounts are cleared within twenty-four hours, but Leeson used his Error Account 88888 to hide his vast long-term losses. In 1993 when Leeson reported a *profit* of $15 million the Error Account held a deficit of $30 million, so there was really a *loss* of $15 million. Similarly, in 1994 when Leeson reported a *profit* of $50 million the Error Account held a deficit of $80 million so Leeson had in effect *lost* $30 million. Leeson discovered that instead of being fired for such losses, he could be idolized as a genius trader if he hid the losses. Barings awarded him a $208,000 bonus in 1993 and planned to increase that to $720,000 in 1994 to reward him for his fictitious profits. A Barings director described Leeson as "the Michael Jordan of trading," and enormous customer investments were handed over to him to trade.[3] On the day in 1995 when Nick Leeson fled Singapore the Error Account held a deficit of $386 million.[4]

Six weeks before the collapse of Barings Bank, officials from SIMEX, the Singapore market, warned the finance director of Barings of a shortfall of $74 million. Leeson told his management that his massive trades were being made on behalf of a client, Felipe Bonnefoy, so the huge losses did not put the bank at risk. In reality, Bonnefoy did not have an account with Barings; he only used Leeson as an agent. Leeson was gambling with the bank's money.[5] Leeson tried to cover his gigantic losses by desperately betting even more of the bank's money. In the weeks before the collapse, the bank's treasury in London transferred over $1.2 billion dollars to Singapore to cover margin calls. This exceeded Barings's entire capital base.

Leeson was not a skilled criminal; he was a young, out-of-his-depth, happy-go-lucky, blundering gambler, a kid in a candy store with no one watching over him. If the information systems had been sensibly designed, Nick Leeson's activities would have been *visible* to management. Any "error account" should have obeyed simple computerized rules to ensure that it was used as intended. It should have been clear what was customers' money and what was the bank's money. It is outrageous that Barings management thought that Leeson had made "Michael Jordan" profits at a time when he had in fact made a loss of $45 million.

The Wrong Systems

When Marconi invented radio he thought of it only as a point-to-point wireless telegraph. He did not initially recognize its potential for broadcasting. Thomas Edison once said that the value of his newly invented phonograph was to allow "dying gentlemen" to record their last wishes. Using computer networks to automate processes that were invented before computer networks misses their potential in a similar way.

By the start of the 1990s a shocking realization began to spread among top executives that they had spent a vast amount of money on computers but most of the time they were the wrong systems. *Worse, most of the systems being built today are the wrong systems.* Managers should have been thinking in terms of cybercorp opportunities and value added by value-stream design, but most were thinking about computer applications for existing departments.

> **The more the mechanisms of an efficient cybercorp became understood, the clearer it became that computers were being used incorrectly and that most IT organizations were unaware of this.**

The service industries of the United States spent a mind-blowing $800 billion on automation during the 1980s, but during that period white-collar productivity went *down* by 3 percent.[6]

Many corporations installed large mainframe systems that consumed much money in computer staff, analysts, programmers, and software, but that in some cases gave a net negative return on investment. PCs spread to everybody's desk but turned out to be much more expensive than anyone originally imagined. Many corporations have not calculated the true cost. Executives worried that the benefits seemed to be less than the costs. Japanese companies, which had far fewer computers, grew faster.

General Motors spent vast sums on automating its factories in the 1980s with expensive computers and mass-production lines with robots that looked spectacular on television, but it failed to achieve the cost levels or the quality and reliability of Toyota and Honda. The Japanese had drastically changed the nature of the car factory; there is little resemblance between a Toyota lean-manufacturing plant and a Detroit mass-production plant. When at last the giant began to react, it built startlingly different plants, like the Saturn plant or the Opel plant in East Germany, which demonstrated dramatic new capability.

The moral of these stories is that as chips and information superhighways become more capable at an astonishing rate, corporate structures need to be totally reinvented. The most important role of the IT organization is to play a leadership role in designing the cybercorp and the stage-by-stage transition needed to implement it. In various Ford Motor companies around the world the head of IT has the title *vice president of process leadership.* This title emphasizes the importance of the role of IT in fundamentally reinventing Ford's cross-functional operations, including those with computerized links to suppliers and dealers.

The Wrong Focus

The computer industry captivates its professionals with a mind-gripping fascination unlike any other profession. Computer professionals acquire deep sophisticated knowledge about how to make software work, but few think about how the *business* should be reinvented. They may think about how to automate a procedure that already exists, but that approach negates the value of the technology. The true value lies in fundamentally rethinking how the enterprise works. The more complex the technology becomes, the more IT professionals tend to focus on the technology rather than the big opportunities it presents.

Many computer professionals focus intensely on making the electronics and software work, but not on how to create business value with IT; *they build the wrong applications.*

The financial implications of this are staggering. In most corporations the computing budget is the largest capital budget. The true cost of computing goes well beyond the computing budget. It includes the time businesspeople spend in IT-related meetings and tinkering with PCs. The costs across society as a whole are enormous, and the financial impact of lost opportunities are much greater than the cost of computing.

Social commentators and unions worry about employees' being laid off because of computers. In reality, many employees are being laid off because foreign corporations are more efficient. Britain used to have a vigorous car industry, admired worldwide. Today there is no British-owned mass-market car factory. The industry has been taken over by the United States, Japan, and Germany. The same has happened with many other factories in Britain. Countries described as "Third World," like South Korea, far outperformed Britain. Obsolete thinking will time and again exact massive penalties.

It was often assumed in the West that the Japanese competed better because of cheap labor or because they moved like armies of insects (the French Prime Minister called them "ants"). Neither of these assumptions was true. They are intelligent businesspeople who reinvented their business processes. They reinvented every aspect of how car manufacturers should design cars, relate to their suppliers, assemble cars, and interact with customers. What happened in the car industry then happened in other industries.

Paving the Cow Path

Many managers fail to understand the potentials of technology because they think of it in terms of solving the problems they have today. They ask, "How can we automate what already exists?" The great potential of technology is to *replace what exists* with something different and fundamentally better. Tibetans invented the turbine mechanism but used it only for the rotation of prayer wheels.

In the 1980s engineers at IBM often cursed the paperwork they had to fill in. Procedures contained multiple references to other procedures. Special cases raised complicated questions about which procedures applied and which did not. The procedures were often geared to the worst case, or included every contingency, and so created unnecessary difficulties for the majority of people who had relatively simple cases. Because the number and complexity of forms had become overwhelming IBM built an expert system called CASES designed to tell employees what forms must be filled out and how, what signatures are required, where to send the forms, what other departments to notify, and so on. The system used leading-edge "artificial intelligence." The system worked well and produced a noticeable reduction in noncompliance with procedures. However, most of the forms related to procedures that should have been reengineered or scrapped long ago.

One might ask why *paper* forms are needed at all in the age of computer networks (at IBM!). Ed Feigenbaum, the pioneer of expert systems, comments that it "has to do with people who 'own' various forms, who've fallen in love with them, and can't bear to give them up."[7] The bureaucratic procedures that took so much time away from doing valuable work were ridiculous. They should have been scrapped, not enshrined. Like a garden overgrown with jungle, the right thing would have been to plow it under and replant. This happened when Louis Gerstner, an outsider, became CEO.

Much computer software has been designed to capture old procedures that ought to be replaced. "Knowledge engineers" are taught how to interview people and represent what they do in rules that can be computerized. This can be like identifying a cow path and setting it in concrete, when the whole activity should have been reinvented.

Organizations have sacred cows: You can change anything but not the sacred cows. The sacred cows almost always date back to an era long ago before cybercorp technology. The first thing that should be done when reinventing value streams is to identify the sacred cows and question their existence. If a system is built without doing this, the sacred cows become part of the computerized procedures.

We not only concrete the cow path, we cast the sacred cows into concrete.

Do Not Automate Yesterday's Processes

In its early days, office automation became discredited because the costs exceeded the benefits. Users did not want to give up "hard copy" when mail or documents became electronic. An *IBM Systems Journal* article expressed the popular wisdom: "The customer is anxious to avoid disruption of their established organization by introduction of office communications. As a matter of philosophy, the system must fit the users and not the reverse."[8] This is the wrong philosophy. The users must be carefully trained in new ways or most of the advantages of automation are lost.

Enterprises sometimes seem unable to take seriously the change needed in their organization until they have spent significant money on automation first. Despite the advice, "Think before you automate," many executives seem to have to automate first in order to understand it, then rethink the process. They spend in order to focus; then think; then redo. This is expensive and slow. But if you have to "spend, think, then redo," be sure that the steps done before thinking are easily changeable.

Automation Without Reinvention

On television in the 1980s we repeatedly saw images of robots welding or spray-painting cars. One would expect there to be a correlation between automation and productivity. Perhaps something like that in Exhibit 17-1.

Unfortunately, such was not the case. MIT carried out a detailed study of the world's car factories—their IMVP survey.[9] Exhibit 17-2 plots productivity and automation for European and U.S. car assembly plants. There is almost no correlation between automation and productivity!

Exhibit 17-3 shows the same information for Japanese car factories.[10] With one exception, the Japanese factories in 1989 achieved higher productivity than car factories in the rest of the world. Japanese car factories, starting with Toyota, invented lean manufacturing and changed every aspect of how a car should be designed and assembled. The MIT survey form asked how many days of inventory were in the plant. A manager at Toyota politely asked whether the form had an error: "It says *days* of inventory. Shouldn't it say *minutes* of inventory?"[11]

When automation is applied to the fundamentally reinvented car factor-

Exhibit 17-1. One might expect that higher levels of automation bring higher levels of productivity as here. Exhibits 17-2 and 17-3 indicate that this is not the case unless the processes are reinvented.

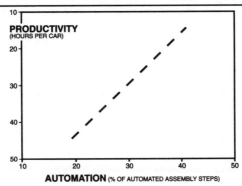

Exhibit 17-2. A comprehensive study of the world's car factories done by MIT reveals almost no correlation between automation and productivity in the United States and Europe.[13] This is in sharp contrast with Japan as shown in Exhibit 17-3.

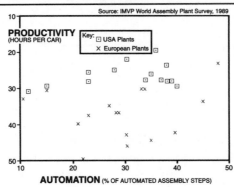

ies, in Japan and now elsewhere in the world, startling productivity improvements are achieved. A car with 10,000 parts is built in less than fifteen person-hours.

One might expect quality to suffer if cars are built fast. Exhibit 17-4 shows the opposite.[12] The Japanese plants exhibit higher quality (in terms of assembly defects), as well as higher speed of manufacturing. If automation is used in the right way, both speed and quality can be greatly improved.

Exhibit 17-3. In Japan the car factory was totally reinvented, using lean manufacturing and then applying automation. With one exception higher productivity was achieved than in the West. Lean manufacturing is now spreading to some Western car plants.[14] The factory of the future needs thorough reinvention of its processes to take advantage of new technology.

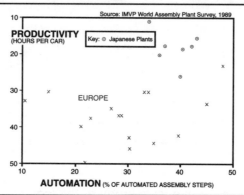

Automation can prevent many of the defects that humans make. To do so, both the product and the manufacturing process need to be redesigned jointly to take advantage of automation.

The lesson is "Never apply automation without totally redesigning the end-to-end process."

Clumsy White-Collar Processes

The lessons learned in lean manufacturing apply even more to administrative procedures. We have applied expensive computer systems to outrageously old-fashioned processes. The clumsy nature of the process itself prevents the computers from making much difference. We can make a big difference if we scrap the entire end-to-end process, fundamentally rethink its goals, and invent something that meets those goals as directly and simply as possible using modern technology and new teams of motivated people.

Dealing with a customer who says she has found an error in her credit card bill may involve multiple letters and perhaps forty process steps. It sometimes takes weeks to resolve the problem. With cybercorp design the customer dials an 800 number and is routed to a person who has a screen image of the credit card slip. The problem can be corrected during one telephone call. Many administrative procedures have been reinvented to achieve dra-

Exhibit 17-4. Productivity must not be increased at the expense of increased defects. Reinvention of processes must seek out those techniques that both increase productivity and reduce defects. The Japanese reinvention of car factories did this successfully.[15]

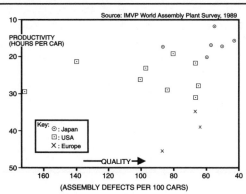

matic reductions in the time and work required and major improvements in the ability to please the customer.

Most administrative processes are even more in need of reinvention than manufacturing processes. Immense reinvention is needed in service industries. Enterprise reinvention is in the air everywhere, and corporations that do not do it will go the way of the dinosaur car factories.

In most corporations traditional hierarchies have taken on lives of their own. Divisions and departments carry out specialized functions as though we were still in the age of punched cards not cyberspace. Each department performs its own part of the process. It has little awareness of what other departments do and jealously guards its own data. Many departments want their own computer systems. Their latest idea is to have a client-server system in which PCs are connected to a departmental server. Many enterprises are furiously building departmental client-server systems, but these systems automate the type of work structure that made sense before the cybercorp revolution.

New Media

New media are a challenge to the publishing industry, but many publishers will be devastated because of obsolete thinking.

One publisher had a detailed study done that showed that its *paper* publishing would have difficulty making a profit but estimated that publishing similar information *electronically* could achieve a 40 percent return. The top management ignored the study because they were comfortable only with paper publishing.

In early 1995 a magazine of the Dutch publishing industry had a lead article headed "Say No to the Internet." The Anglo-Dutch publisher Reed-Elsevier publishes many expensive and obscure journals and volumes of scientific papers. It charges a high price for these and also charges scientists for the privilege of being published. The scientists took matters into their own hands and started publishing on the Internet. They submit articles by e-mail, editors e-mail them to referees, and the final revised versions are published in an electronic journal. By the end of 1995 there were 306 electronic academic journals.[16] *Forbes* magazine commented that Reed-Elsevier could become "the Internet's first victim."[17] There will be many more.

The BBC makes many programs that deserve an audience around the planet. Only a tiny fraction of them are marketed on videos. The BBC's gems are hidden in a mass of mediocrity, often broadcast only once; viewers stumble across them by accident. The talented program makers work like ancient monks illuminating manuscripts that most people will never see. The Internet or a CD-ROM could index decades of past programs and could be an effective marketing vehicle for such programs because of its natural reach to special-interest communities. Many people would like to be able to buy tapes of BBC gems that are not available. The obsolete thinking of the BBC loses it hundreds of millions of dollars per year. (It does not matter because it's taxpayers' money.)

Reinventing Government?

The twentieth century is a journey from Kafka to cybercorp. An alarming scenario is that survival of the fittest will make the transition happen vigorously in competitive corporations, but not in government. Government could be Kafka while everything else is cybercorp.

A few government agencies have achieved dramatic cybercorp-style value-stream reinvention. The U.S. Agency for International Development recognized that it sometimes took so long to get needed items to developing nations that they were of little use by the time they arrived. It set out to replace its cumbersome bureaucratic processes with streamlined value-stream teams. It cut costs dramatically and produced results much more satisfactory to its "customers."[18]

There is generally more scope to achieve dramatic reinvention in government then in corporations that have lived under competitive pressures. When there is no competition, all manner of inefficiencies grow like weeds choking a garden.

It is estimated that an average of twenty-three signatures are needed when the U.S. federal government guys goods or services. There are ten pages of specifications for ashtrays (which are called "ash receivers, tobacco, desk type"). The General Services Administration approval process for ordering a computer takes as long as three years; computers become out-of-date in one year. At the Ochoco National Forest in Oregon the five district rangers spend most of their time with paper, not trees; there were 53 separate budgets, 577 management codes, and 1,769 accounting lines.[19] A study of Washington's low-interest rehab loan program found that each civil servant processed an average of only one loan application every three months. Each $20,000 loan had $11,000 of administrative expenses.[20]

In 1993, U.S. Vice President Al Gore started a vigorous initiative for "reinventing government." In some pockets of U.S. government changes occurred, but many government bodies had the attitude: "Keep your head down. This problem will go away after the next election."

Peter Drucker, in his book *Post-Capitalist Society,* lists reasons why the techniques of business reengineering are unlikely to work in government. Because of this he states that any activity of government that *could* be outsourced to competitive corporations *should* be.[21] It is the forces of competition that drive the reinvention of corporations; these forces say, "Reinvent or die." Most (but not all) of the activities now being done in government could be done by competitive enterprise.

References

1. Bank of England Report on the Collapse of Barings Bank, July 18, 1995.
2. Frank Kane and Mark Franchetti, "Leeson money-making legend exposed as sham," *Sunday Times,* July 9, 1995, sec. 1.
3. "The Final Chapter," Insight report on the collapse of Barings Bank, *Sunday Times,* July 9, 1995, Business section.
4. Kane and Franchetti, "Leeson money-making legend."
5. "The Final Chapter," p. 4.
6. Stephen Roach, chief economist of Morgan Stanley, *CIO Forum: The Re-Engineering Challenge* (videotape from CCI, Syosset, NY, 1993).
7. Edward Feigenbaum, Pamela McCorduck, and H. Penny Nii, *The Rise of the Expert Company* (New York: Times Books, 1988), chap. 5. This book is an excellent description of the creation of many leading-edge expert systems.
8. A. H. Engel, J. Groppuso, R. A. Lowenstein, and W. G. Taub, "An Office Communications System," *IBM Systems Journal* 18, no. 3 (1979).
9. The International Motor Vehicle Program (IMVP) at MIT publishes a list of its working papers.
10. James P. Womack, Daniel T. Jones, and Daniel Roos, *The Machine That Changed the World: The Story of Lean Manufacturing* (New York: Harper Perennial, 1991).
11. The IMVP at MIT has produced many publications. A list of IMVP working papers is available from MIT, Cambridge, MA.

12. Ibid.
13. Ibid.
14. Ibid.
15. Ibid.
16. "Paperless Papers," *Economist,* December 16, 1995.
17. *Forbes,* December 2, 1995.
18. Example from James Martin Government & Co., Fairfax, VA.
19. "Godzilla Zaps the System," *Time,* September 19, 1993.
20. J. D. Davidson and Lord Rees-Mogg, *The Great Reckoning* (New York: Simon and Schuster, 1993).
21. Peter Drucker, *Post-Capitalist Society* (New York: Harper Business, 1993).

18

How to Drive a Corporation Nuts

It is extremely difficult to convert a sow's ear into a silk purse, but that is what many efforts at business reengineering have been attempting to do. Not surprisingly, most of them fail. If you were made the chief executive of a sow's-ear company, how would you proceed?

Most older corporations have a structure and modus operandi derived from the past. They are completely out of line with today's agile value-stream thinking and cybercorp mechanisms. The tragedy about many failed attempts at reengineering is that what they sought to achieve was in fact the right thing to do. The failure condemned them to obsolete operations.

If reengineering attempts too great a cultural change, it will probably fail. It is easier to grow new units and then wind down the old ones. Rather than attempting to convert the sow's ear, it is better to build new silk purses.

When Corporations Go Crazy

Nurit Cohen, a clinical psychologist, became what she describes as an "organizational shrink." She and William Cohen wrote an entertaining book called *The Paranoid Corporation*.[1] Asking readers whether they have ever thought an organization's behavior was crazy, they conclude, "You may have been closer to the truth than you realized."

A corporation has a personality separate from the individual personalities of its employees. An organization, the Cohens say, can become psychologically sick even when it is composed of individuals who are psychologically well. A lynch mob may carry out a gruesome task that any of the members of the mob would recoil from as an individual. The mob becomes its own creature with its own psychology. The German philosopher

Friedrich Nietzsche wrote, "In individuals insanity is rare, but in groups, parties, nations and epochs it is the rule."[2]

Organizational sicknesses can be given the same names as those of human sicknesses and to some extent can be treated with similar methods:

- Psychoses
- Paranoia
- Manic behavior
- Schizophrenia
- Neurotic behavior
- Intoxication
- Obsessive compulsion
- Posttrauma syndrome

The Cohens give examples of these corporate sicknesses and discuss their treatment.

They're Out to Get Us

A paranoid corporation is one in which fear has become pervasive. Employees find the work environment hostile; few people are to be trusted. In such a corporation performance goes to pieces.

The Cohens describe how paranoia spread at General Motors when Americans became enamored with small foreign cars. The leaders of the various GM divisions wanted to develop their own small cars, but the head office had other ideas. The divisional managers' proposals were viewed as revolt. Head office executives became convinced that divisional managers wanted to dismantle the company, and so they tightened central controls. This behavior was the opposite of the classical strategy of Alfred E. Sloan, who built GM with centralized strategy but decentralized control. The more divisional managers fought the change, the more central management tightened its grip. Paranoia spread throughout the company. Suspicion and rivalry grew, with finance and accounting conspiring against engineering and marketing, and vice versa.[3] The paranoia soon affected the product. Between 1978 and 1982, GM recalled 70 percent of its cars.

This change in GM was much slower and less traumatic to employees than the recent drive toward corporate reengineering.

The Cohens conduct a game at their seminars to demonstrate corporate paranoia. They divide the participants into teams and give them a task to perform. The team that does it in the shortest time wins. Each team member is given a sealed envelope that they open and hand back. They are told that if the slip in the envelope contains an X the person who receives it is designated a spy. No one else knows who the spy is. The spy's duty is to impede the team's chances of winning without doing anything so obvious that she gets caught. A team can fire a person they think is a spy only if there is unanimous agreement among the team members.

In almost all games the teams identify spies and fire them. After the game is over the participants are told that *there were no spies*—no X's on the slips. All the spies caught and fired were innocent, and usually they were team members who could have been highly productive.

When a traditional hierarchy is reengineered, employees know that after the transition there will be fewer managers, some departments will be dissolved, probably a substantial number of employees will be let go. Some employees may have an inside relationship that will ensure their survival. Most will be asked to do new and perhaps more difficult jobs instead of continuing to do what they are comfortable with. There may be a traumatic break with a deeply rooted culture. Bruce Rupport, senior vice president at Agway, commented: "You can survive the old way. You can survive the new way. It's the goddamn transition that'll kill you."[4]

Management Terrorism

Mike Hammer has one of the century's most quotable PR lines: "When my children ask me what I do for a living I say I'm reversing the Industrial Revolution." He talks like a revolutionary using terrorist methods—using language that could hardly be more likely to cause paranoia: "On this journey . . . we shoot the dissenters." "What you do with the existing structure is *nuke it*." "Reengineering must be initiated by someone who has the status to break legs." "We will take care of the wounded but shoot the stragglers." "A lot of people have to be clouted." "I think there are a lot of people who will never find a job again."[5]

Dysfunctional behavior in employees is caused by uncertainty and lack of understanding, the loss of a role they were comfortable with, or terror at the prospect of a corporate bunjee jump accompanied by language about "shooting the stragglers." Employee emotions should be anticipated and dealt with in a caring manner, with good communications, education, and explanation of reasons. "Downsizing" causes fear and panic, and anger at the breaking of the perceived employee compact that traded employee loyalty for job security. To deal with such feelings, sensitive human attention is needed.

Dysfunctional Behavior

Management needs to spell out in detail and with clarity why change must happen and how the results will be better. They need champions of the change who will spread their enthusiasm. The key to transition is relentless and clear communication.

Cynical employees have been confronted with threats of change before and may believe that "this too shall pass" or "If I ignore it, it will go away." Some employees or managers may be active, rather than passive, in their resistance. They believe they can stop the reengineering and set about doing so in either an overt or underground way. It may be necessary for management to demonstrate that they will root out the dissidents. The dissidents often say, "The whole thing is crazy. They don't know what they're doing. It's unnecessary. The process works well today and this will wreck it."

When value streams are reinvented it is desirable to implement them *fast*. The excitement of change is short lived. If the change process takes too long, resistance to change usually prevents it from happening.

Management needs to carefully address fears and dysfunctional behavior. It is often said that we do our best work under pressure, but many studies have shown that people have an optimal level of stress. Up to that level, pressure stimulates results, but beyond that level, stress causes mistakes, poor performance, and cognitive dysfunction, and people are too tense to develop creative ideas. The very qualities that managers need in new corporations—empowerment, creativity, flexibility—are destroyed by the stress of downsizing.

Change agents must design work environments that are exciting, fun, and financially rewarding: "Your job will be more interesting. You will be empowered and constantly challenged to use your creativity." Particularly important, management must design an employment deal that is good in the long term for the key players and demonstrate how these players participate financially when they make major improvements.

Paranoid Dogs

When Pavlov did his famous experiments with dogs he showed that a dog can be conditioned with either rewards or punishments, *but the results are not the same.* The experiments indicated that behavior learned through punishment is more stable than behavior learned through reward. This finding has been put to use in some unpleasant organizations in the past, many of them in the USSR.

If you always ring a bell before you feed a dog, the dog learns to associate the bell with the reward. If then the food stops coming when the bell is rung, the dog *unlearns* the association fairly quickly. On the other hand, if you put a dog in a green room and when a bell rings give it a painful electric shock, it will quickly learn to avoid green rooms. When the shocks are turned off the dog will *not* unlearn the behavior; it still avoids green rooms. If the experiment were done repeatedly, the dog would acquire a severe phobia about green rooms. It would be difficult to remove this phobia. People who have been conditioned with punishment limit their behavior to what they think is safe. They avoid trial-and-error learning. When the cause of the phobia has gone, they do not lose the phobia.

> **We can motivate employees with carrots or sticks. In times of rapid change carrots work well but sticks do not. If we establish behavior with sticks, when we need to change that behavior we cannot easily remove the phobia caused by sticks.**

Organizations that have emphasized punishment over reward are extremely difficult to change. People continue to use behavior patterns that avoided punishment in the past. Communist enterprises, Kafkaesque bureaucracies, the Chinese Cultural Revolution, or their corporate equivalent leave long-lasting phobias. Executives building learning enterprises have found it easier to start from scratch than to convert organizations in which people were strongly conditioned by punishment.

The most difficult organization to change is one in which conditioning by punishment is combined with upgrades by seniority. A dreaded form of punishment is delay of a seniority upgrade. Employees avoid any unsafe behavior. They keep their heads down, incur no risks, and wait for promotion. They think: "If you do everything by the book, you are safe. Any deviation from the book is risky and could incur wrath if there are complaints." This stultifying attitude is reinforced by the view that if you do everything by the book you will eventually get a seniority upgrade or promotion; if you attract wrath you might not. So don't take risks.

Such organizations ought to be regarded as part of the obsolete past. They may have worked in static situations, but few situations are static today. Successful corporations are those that change faster than their competitors because competitors will always copy what works well. But conditioning by punishment inhibits change. The dog who got electric shocks cowers in areas that are safe.

Edgar Schein, a professor of management at the Sloan School, compares learned emotional behavior in enterprises to Pavlov's dog experiments and suggests that "the 'green room' is any form of corporate reorganization."[6] People remember previous reorganizations as being traumatic, with everyone worrying about whether they would be fired, "downsized," or put through other forms of pain. As soon as a new reorganization is announced, or a new leader takes over, the phobias from previous reorganizations are activated. The employees are being forced into Pavlov's green room again.

A leader who wants to bring about changes must create a vision of an exciting future. The problem is that for many people the vision represents a green room. Paranoia spreads because the vision does not overcome the green-room anxieties. Schein comments, "Our complex human mind is able to defend itself against messages which make it anxious." There are three common defenses:

- Employees do not hear the message.
- Employees deny that the message applies to them.
- Employees rationalize that their leaders do not understand the situation.

Some managers think that fear of change must be countered with a greater fear of not changing. Employees are told, "The company is in trouble. Your jobs are in jeopardy if we do not reorganize for action."

Pavlov set up experiments in which the only alternative to the green room was a red room. If the dog fleeing the green room is given shocks in the red room also, and then all shocks are turned off, the dog rushes back and forth between the green room and red room until totally exhausted. It does not learn that the shocks have been turned off. To counter one anxiety by emphasizing a different anxiety needs to be done with caution. Both anxieties become phobias, and in the general agitation morale goes to pieces.

The change agent should not create alarm in order to "get their attention." A transition needs clear guidelines, careful training, coaching, praise, and rewards for moving ahead. If the road ahead is clear, the vision of the future is exciting, and people know that they will be well trained and not punished for mistakes, employees can become exhilarated and will work hard not to let their team down.

The Exciting Enterprise

At Chaparral Steel radical change is always in the air, but the absentee rate is about a quarter of that reported by the U.S. National Association of Manufacturers.[7]

> **The cybercorp must be designed so that employees expect rapid change and are very excited about it. Change occurs constantly within an environment of job security.**

The problem is not the nature of the cybercorp but the difficulty of transition from old-world corporations to new-world.

The cybercorp should be designed to be both an exciting and psychologically nurturing place to work. Psychological comfort in an environment of rapid change needs the following:

- Full explanation from management of the direction of the business and the reasons for actions
- Constant demonstration from management that innovation and experimentation is important and exciting
- Constant demonstration that management nurtures employees or teams with critical capabilities
- Rewards for innovation
- Careful coaching with attention to employees' feelings
- Good education and training
- High-performance teams where all members help fellow members
- Clear team goals
- Opportunities for practice; a fully supportive environment
- Most employees with stock options or "a piece of the action"
- Encouragement to overcome worry about making errors
- No punishment
- Hollywood-like ceremonies in which "Oscars" and substantial rewards are given to innovative employees

In general, when major changes are made, sensitive attention is needed to the fears and emotions of employees. A sledgehammer approach to reengineering can cause vitally needed changes to fail.

Establishing a Learning-Laboratory Cybercorp

Just as lean-manufacturing plants have caused some mass-production plants to close their doors, so learning-laboratory corporations will cause some static corporations to close. In some industries, the only long-term survivors will be learning-laboratory cybercorps.

> **A conventional operation will not grow into a learning-laboratory operation by a process of evolution. Learning-laboratory operations come into existence only by a strong, deliberate, well-thought-out act of top management.**

In many corporations, top management works in pristine surroundings designed by expensive architects. At Chaparral the workers' locker room is in the one-story head office building. Sweaty steel workers interact with high executives. Many ideas originate from meetings in the corridors. There is no executive dining room; everybody queues and eats in the same cafeteria. All employees can make their views known to top management. This intermin-

gling of top management and employees is essential in many high-tech companies—Microsoft, for example.

To maintain this interchange, Chaparral deliberately held its size to under a thousand employees. A thousand people is the size of a village, where
everybody knows what everybody else is doing. With a thousand people,
meetings that unify the entire corporation are possible. (A conductor of
Mahler's Eighth unifies a thousand players.) The plant layout and electronics
should be designed to facilitate constant interaction among employees and
management. When a cybercorp grows to more than a thousand people it
should probably be split into separate villages, each a learning laboratory in
its own right.

Top executives who create such corporations need to be consistent in
their vision for many years. They must put into place a culture with a strong
sense of values that pervades the entire corporation. It must be seen that
innovation is supported and rewarded. Employees must feel that it is their
job to make improvements constantly and feel free to openly discuss ideas
with management. Management talks to them anywhere they may be and
asks them what they are excited about. The mechanisms must be in place for
constant learning, research, and discovery, for the search for knowledge and
transfer of knowledge. There must be continuous management effort in communicating this sense of values and checking the smallest details to ensure
that employees' behavior grows to support the learning-laboratory culture.
Like creating a garden, management's caring attention must be constant or
the weeds take over.

To achieve the learning-laboratory interchange with top management,
management must be seen to be excited by the constant experimentation and
to understand it. At KnowledgeWare, a software company that had created
breakthrough tools, Fran Tarkenton, the great football quarterback, became
its CEO after a merger. Tarkenton was an authority on human motivation
and had written a book on the subject. He mixed with the creative troops
exuding charisma, but it was blatantly clear to them that he did not understand the products. Instead of the products' evolving as they should, many
wrong management decisions were made. Top management did not learn
from the bright employees, and the company went to the dogs.

Starting Afresh

A friend who can imitate a strong Irish accent likes to tell a story about
asking a person the way to Dublin. The person replies, "Now, if I was going
to Dublin I wouldn't start from here!"

If long-term survival requires a boundaryless, value-stream, learning-
laboratory corporation (or whatever other characteristics describe the survi-

vor), a critical question is, "Can you get there if you start from here?" It is impossible to turn a bureaucracy into a learning laboratory. It is painful to transform a 1980s-style enterprise into a cybercorp. Brute force will not do it.

It would be just about impossible to turn a traditional big-steel corporation into a learning-laboratory corporation like Chaparral, but if big steel is in competition with many Chaparrals, big steel will die. It is interesting to note that in staffing Chaparral, its management avoided hiring workers with steel industry experience. They hired, and continue to hire, farmers and ranchers from the local area with mechanical experience. They look for "a twinkle in the eye, a zest for life, basically conscientious people who can put in a strong day's work and enjoy what they're doing . . . people who have not been exposed to other companies' bad habits."[8] As commented earlier, Chaparral has a productivity more than three times the industry average:

Productivity	Worker-Hours per Rolled Ton of Steel
U.S. average	5.3
Japanese average	5.6
German average	5.7
Chaparral	1.5

Many other corporations that are harbingers of the twenty-first century are new corporations, not born-again old corporations. Often the best strategy for the existing traditional corporation is to start green-field subsidiaries designed to follow cybercorp principles.

We have stressed that fast corporate *evolution* is essential, but a woodchuck is not likely to evolve into a cheetah. New corporations should be designed to be cheetahs from the beginning. They should be learning-laboratory cybercorps, uncontaminated by old-style hierarchies, bureaucrats, bean counters, unions, lawyers, or guardians of past methodology.

The MIT IMVP showed that there are no examples in which mass-production car factories, or European craft-style car factories, have converted successfully to lean manufacturing. The lean factories with high productivity and high quality were new start-from-scratch operations. Pygmalion stories are for the theater. At General Motors the most interesting steps toward the future car factory—the NUMMI plant, the Saturn plant, and the East German Opel plant—were all green-field factories, fundamentally rethinking what a car factory ought to be like.

George Gilder, describing how revolutionary change occurred in the microelectronics industry, comments: "No matter how persuasive the advocates of change, it is very rare that an entrenched establishment will reform its ways. Establishments die or retire themselves, or fall in revolutions; they only rarely transform themselves."[9] He describes how some microelectronics companies did succeed in transforming themselves by starting new units. Today, equally fast changes are needed in many companies because of the intensifying pressures of microelectronics, superhighways, cybercorp agility, globalism, and customer demand for quality and service. Even the greatest companies (like IBM and Apple) get in deep trouble if they do not change.

One reason why German and Japanese corporations became so successful in the decades after World War II was that their factories had been bombed until the rubble bounced. They *had* to rethink and begin again.

Healthy Paranoia

Andy Grove, CEO of Intel, has a dictum, "To succeed you have to be paranoid." The enemy is everywhere; they're out to beat you in surprising ways; they're cleverer than you think. No matter how successful its latest processor chip, Intel is racing at enormous expense to create its replacement. This is an appropriate message for the cybercorp era. All markets are now subject to rapid and uncertain change. Jim Clark, CEO of Netscape, says that his job is "creating paranoia among the troops."[10] Netscape's programmers work astonishingly long hours, driven by the feeling that Netscape is under intense attack from Microsoft and hundreds of Internet entrepreneurs.

> **Paranoia where the enemy is the competition can be healthy; the whole company can unify with intense dedication. Paranoia where the enemy is internal is a disaster; the company tears itself apart.**

When a sledgehammer approach is taken to changing an embedded culture it almost always fails. In contrast, it is easy to generate excitement and energy in cybercorp start-ups that are beginning an adventurous journey into a new world. Creating thrilling new units is more successful than endlessly patching the old corpse.

Green-Field Business Units

Many corporations are now beginning to build small business units. Hitachi Ltd. has 600 companies (27 publicly traded). Johnson & Johnson has 106. Some large corporations in the future may have thousands of small business units. The autonomous units may obtain services from their large parent, such as financing, advertising, and global distribution, but they should be built with value-stream teams and cybercorp principles. This may become the primary form of transition to the new world.

There can be problems when operating a fundamentally reinvented value stream in an otherwise traditional enterprise. It creates a group of employees who play by different rules, have different type of compensation and rewards, and have a different relationship with management. Unless carefully managed it can be an alien body within a strong culture, which causes cultural antibodies to attack it.

To make sure that it has its own new-world culture, a new business unit needs to be autonomous. It should be separate from its parent company; otherwise the old culture will drag it down. It must be free to hire its own people and build its own culture. It may be guided at arm's length by the "chief organizational architect" of the parent company, who should determine what services of the parent it can use without inhibiting the new culture.

When the new growth is healthy, the deadwood can be removed, like pruning an apple tree. To do this humanely, the deadwood employees are retrained, indoctrinated, and made part of the new-growth organization, where their success with new-style work will be appraised along with everyone else's. The learning that occurs in new units should be documented, and as the subsidiaries succeed they are multiplied rapidly. An intranet knowledge infrastructure is important for spreading what is learned.

Global Rebuilding

Corporate rebuilding has massive social and national implications. Whereas America used to be the "melting pot," the whole planet is now the melting pot. Nations thought of as "Third World" are industrializing spectacularly. Countries with reengineered enterprises will pull ahead of those stuck with traditional enterprises. Parts of the world that have vigorous new growth like Southeast Asia will build new-style corporations capable of competing better than non-reengineered Western corporations.

The United States has a tradition of entrepreneurs. Its venture capital structure, bankruptcy laws, and absence of layoff inhibitions encourage fast growth of new corporations that re-create the rules. The United States may reinvent itself faster than Europe.

Europe has a much higher unemployment rate than the United States, but most of its large enterprises could be run with far fewer people. Probably the reason why the United States has lower unemployment is that it creates new corporations faster. New corporations provide new employment, whereas old corporations are shrinking their staff. U.S. business start-ups nearly tripled from 270,000 in 1978 to some 750,000 in 1988, creating 15 million new jobs.

Its *kaizen* culture causes Japan to constantly improve what it does until it achieves excellence. Its traits like discipline, conformity, and uniformity help greatly with TQM. But Japan generally avoids traumatic human upheaval. Value-stream reinvention involves traumatic change. To scrap and rebuild is often better than continuous improvement in an era when business paradigms are shifting fast.

The American dream is to have a piece of the action. America's fast growth of new corporations, driven by entrepreneurs who reinvent everything, gives power to the U.S. economy. Japan discourages nonconformists; America thrives on them. Diversity, nonconformity, autonomy, inventiveness, originality, and entrepreneurialism are strengths that the West must tap.

The danger in the West is its large number of old self-satisfied enterprises with overpaid executives protecting their power structures. While China, India, and the Pacific Rim are vigorously building new corporations with new principles, the Western country-club set is complacently unaware of the revolution. The West has allowed its schools to go to pieces at a time when reading, communication skills, and basic mathematics are badly needed. Many skilled employees in countries like Indonesia and the Philippines earn one-tenth of equivalent people in Europe and America. This differential obviously cannot last. The country-club set of the West is destined to be swept away.

> **The West has a challenge: Can it build new corporations fast enough using the principles summarized in this book?**

References

1. William A. Cohen and Nurit Cohen, *The Paranoid Corporation, and Eight Other Ways Your Corporation Can Be Crazy* (New York: AMACOM, 1993).
2. Friedrich Nietzsche, *Beyond Good and Evil*, "Maxims and Interludes," no. 156 (1886).
3. Cohen and Cohen, *The Paranoid Corporation*, chap. 5.
4. "Reengineering: The Hot New Management Tool," *Fortune*, August 23, 1993.
5. *Forbes ASAP*, Summer 1993; "Mike Hammer: The High Priest," *Site Selection*, February 1993; R. M. Randall, "The Reengineer," *Planning Review*, May/June 1993; Mike Hammer's lectures (1994); J. Champy and M. Hammer, *Reengineering the Corporation* (New York: Harper Business, 1993); "Managers Beware: You're Not Ready For Tomorrow's Jobs," *Wall Street Journal*, January 24, 1995.
6. Edgar H. Schein, "How Can Organizations Learn Faster? The Challenge of Entering the Green Room," *Sloan Management Review*, Winter 1993.
7. Dorothy Leonard-Barton, "The Factory as a Learning Laboratory," *Sloan Management Review*, Fall 1992.
8. Chaparral's Administrative Vice President Dennis Beach, quoted in ibid.
9. George Gilder, *Microcosm* (Englewood Cliffs, NJ: Simon and Schuster, 1988).
10. *Fast Company* 1, no. 1 (1995).

19

Power and Propellerheads

To old-style executives in chandeliered dining rooms the world of cyberspace might as well be a different planet. It is populated by weird aliens who have as much disdain for the "suits" as the suits have for the aliens. But as business increasingly enters the cybercorp world, the suits and the aliens are in the same boat.

In one corporation in Canada the top management refer to their computer people as *Martians:* "They talk a strange language; they live in a world of their own. Do you know, they have the nerve to call us 'end users' and talk as though *we* were the aliens. They ask questions with an astonishing lack of knowledge about our business; they might as well ask, 'Does this end user have three fingers or seven?'" In the same corporation the computer people told stories about how if you give top management a computer they try to use the mouse as a foot pedal.

The Two Cultures

C. P. Snow in the 1960s chronicled the problems of having two cultures in society: the arts and science.[1] He observed that this gulf of mutual incomprehension was particularly strong in Britain and predicted (correctly) that it would damage the British economy. Today again, we have two cultures, often butted up against each other in the same corporation, technophiles and technophobes.

Left to their own devices, technophiles, commonly referred to as "techies," often do not think like businesspeople. They should not be expected to decide, on their own, what is best for the business. Similarly, left to their own devices, businesspeople usually do not dream up the technological inventions that cause business to be done differently. They will often be antagonistic to the idea that technology should change the corporate structure and be highly antagonistic to suggestions that their *own* jobs need reengineering.

The technophobe is always suspicious of the technophile. The technophobe executive suspects that a technophile left in charge of something will soon switch emotions to some new techie game rather than what is best for business. The savvy technophile, on the other hand, suspects that the technophobe executive will always miss the best opportunities because they depend upon subtle thinking about technology. Yet to implement the cybercorp mechanisms and opportunities that are necessary across all of our institutions today, a high level of technical know-how is needed; a chief executive needs to be fully in control of how technology is used.

Often at board meetings in big corporations, when an issue comes up related to essential computer systems, nobody wants to deal with it. The buck is passed rapidly from one board member to another. It is vitally important for top management to understand the dangers of bad system building. Top management may regard the long-haired hackers as lunatics, but the lunatics can put the business in a straitjacket.

I'm Too Old for This Stuff

Information technology is the primary enabler of the cybercorp revolution. Even in traditional corporations of any size the largest capital budget today is usually the IT budget. IT is usually the only *line* (as opposed to *staff*) organization that bridges all other functional areas. Amazingly, in spite of its importance, many chief executives have had little involvement in the management of IT. Leo Heile, vice president and CIO of ITT Corporation, states: "The most important reason for the ineffectiveness of IT is the absence of active management of this resource from the top of the organization. As an increasing number of recent business failures show, IT can only be left alone at the peril of top management."[2] Heile lists reasons why the chief executive has abdicated responsibility for IT:

- I'm too old for this stuff.
- It's too complicated.
- I have a CIO.
- I don't hear many complaints about what they're doing.
- The people asking for new technologies should know what they need without my involvement.

Lack of top-level business guidance of IT has sometimes resulted in systems that are largely a waste of money, systems that are expensively over-engineered, maintenance expenditures with a negative return on investment, unnecessary upgrading to the latest gadgets, but more serious, failure to focus on cybercorp mechanisms that would give a major competitive advantage. Chief executive judgment about IT decisions would be important even if the only concern was IT's financial magnitude. However, now cybercorp capability is critical to competitiveness, profitability, and, in the long run, corporate survival.

> **Technology has become too important to be left to the techies.**

Now many management gurus are warning that the chief executive must take a businessperson's grip on the use of IT. Charles Wang, for example, states, "If CEOs stay at their average level of ignorance about information technology, they are doomed to failure."[3]

The Language Gap

Part of the culture gap is a language gap. To most businesspeople, IT professionals talk a foreign language. Many IT terms are unnecessarily obscure. IT is a profession that uses acronyms like a secret society. But computing is full of complex ideas that must be expressed with precise words. Philosophers describe how the thoughts we are capable of thinking relate to the language we use. The evolution of any discipline depends on the creation of well-defined terms. Cybercorp thinking needs some terms of its own—value stream, virtual operation, cyberspace, firewall, *kaizen,* and so on. Terms with imprecise meanings, like "process," and terms that are vaguely understood lead to miscommunication. The future corporation cannot work well unless the top IT professionals and managers talk the language of the businesspeople (as well as their own technical language).

I wrote a book about rebuilding corporate IT organizations, and Prentice-Hall sent it to one of their usual reviewers. He suggested removing all the chapters that had to do with business. The Prentice-Hall editor agreed. On the other hand, when the American Management Association published my book on enterprise engineering, *The Great Transition,* the chapters on IT bit the dust. Publishers, knowing their markets, say that techies don't want to read business stuff and businesspeople don't want to read techie stuff. They are alien cultures. In many corporations the computer people seem to be retreating further into a shell of technology, isolated from business thinking, as technology becomes more complex. They would say that they are becoming more professional. At the same time the businesspeople tend to think of computing in terms of what their PCs can do, which is far from the big-money opportunities.

To build the cybercorp, top management desperately needs help from top-quality professionals who understand cybermarketing, archetypal forms of value-stream reinvention, virtualness, the control of long-span webs of activities, software design for fast evolution, rule-based modeling, cyberspace security, and so on. Unfortunately, in many enterprises the chief executive is barely on speaking terms with the IT organization. The IT organization has allowed itself to become largely irrelevant to business, often nursing obsolete mainframes, struggling with software reengineering not business reengineering, and building systems that, though they might use the currently fashionable buzzwords, are the wrong systems because value streams were not reinvented as they should have been.

Before Barings Bank vanished in a puff of smoke it was thought to be indestructable. The blue-blooded management in London had no adequate communication either with IT professionals or with the working-class trader Nick Leeson, who could hide his errors because there was no adequate IT system. Leeson ultimately lost $1.24 billion, substantially more than the net worth of the bank.[4] *Newsweek* wrote, "Barings's biggest problem was a desire to hold onto the antiquated tradition of its founders."[5] It was a blundering, blinded semicybercorp. In its last hours, trying to negotiate a rescue at the Bank of England, the top management expressed no mea culpa, no humility; with spectacular arrogance they blamed it all on a rogue trader as though it was not their fault and demanded that any rescue package must include over $160 million in bonuses to top management.[6] Systems people described the same management's failure to establish elementary computerized controls as "cretinous."

We are in the early stages of a total revolution in the nature of the enterprise; corporations slow in making the change will be swept away, and IT is used not merely to automate existing procedures, as it was in the past, but to rip out old structures and replace them with the most effective cybercorp mechanisms. This requires the highest level of *trust* and communication between the top computer professionals and the business leaders.

Different Personalities

The personality of the typical corporate president could not be more different from the personality of the typical computer hacker. The corporate president usually does not want to understand computers; he or she is concerned with people, profits, and business intuition.

The hacker lives in a world of intellectual games, endless mnemonics, sometimes a bizarre science-fantasy world with its own weird language and logic. One president referred to the programmers as "vampire stenographers," but they are becoming increasingly critical in the cybercorp jungle. The hacker sits at a screen for hours on end, sometimes late into the night, often eating junk food. Hackers commune with other hackers, talking a language unintelligible to outsiders, full of strange jargon, and are largely uninterested in business. Bewildered users of computers often become dependent on hackers, and the Byzantine tools of their profession, to make their systems work.

It is ironic that many computer people were attracted to the IT profession because they were happier communicating with machines than with people. Now they are being told that the main skill of the IT professional is intimate communication with businesspeople. Machines are predictable; people are not. If you tell a computer to do something it does exactly what you say; if you tell a human to do something he may be snarled up in all manner of emotional miscommunications and rarely does exactly what you say. Computers obey orders with absolute precision. Sitting in front of a computer screen until the small hours of the night, a programmer can invent and polish code, unimpeded by the difficulties that humans create. Communication with people, especially businesspeople, is more difficult, illogical, and embarrassing. Now his manager is saying that code should be generated, not hand-crafted, and that he should invent business procedures, not COBOL or C procedures, and that the skill he must develop is the ability to work with businesspeople.

For some young people the computer and the Internet is the one thing with which they seem able to truly communicate. The executive has just the opposite view. She loves probing and manipulating the complex uncertainties of people and hates computers because they insult her with brusque error messages and make her feel a fool.

Hackers are often avid fans of science fantasy and have a rich sense of humor that fails to amuse the "suits." One software genius, Jack Good, became a great expert on palindromes: phrases or sentences in which the words are the same whether read forward or backward. He programmed his computer to scan vast amounts of text, searching for near-palindromes that could be converted into true ones. He wrote to the Queen of England suggesting that he should be in the House of Lords because he had the world's largest collection of palindromes. When a long-suffering royal secretary sent snail mail asking why this was relevant, he explained that people would be able to say, "Good Lord, here's Lord Good." Rebelling against the suits, hackers will work barefoot if allowed to, and have strange messages on their T-shirts. One grossly overweight programmer had a picture of a whale on his T-shirt and the caption "Save the Humans," while his female colleague's T-shirt carried a message from an Australian beer company saying, "Won't Make Your Dingo Limp."

However, the culture gap is much deeper than the differences in language, clothes, and code of behavior. Indeed the technophiles who want to get ahead take care to dress, talk, and behave like the businesspeople. Lou

Gerstner, the CEO brought in to head up IBM after its train wreck, commented, "Most of this industry is run by propellerheads."[7] His point was that much more attention was needed about how to make IBM customers successful. He commented that he was probably the only IT customer to run a major IT company. He had great respect for IT's ability to transform industries, but it needed much more than just technology. Gerstner was using the term "propellerheads" to refer not to hackers who dressed like Rasputin but to IBM technophile executives in suits.

Fundamental Changes in IT

IT organizations (referred to in the past as IS or MIS organizations) need to support the rapid rate of change and evolution that we have described. Ironically, the biggest inhibitor to change in many enterprises is the difficult of changing the software. The IT organization has built a straitjacket.

In the fast-changing, knowledge-intensive cybercorp environment, adaptability is the key survival issue. Adaptability can be helped or hindered by computer systems. Open access to information with powerful tools for manipulating information helps adaptability. So does software that enables applications to be built so that they can be constantly changed. On the other hand, large systems hand-programmed in COBOL or C, and systems with ill-structured data, are so difficult to change that they prevent adaptability.

The cybercorp has vital characteristics that require IT operations different from traditional IT:

1. The IT leadership must be constantly concerned with creating business value. The best way to do this is to constantly improve the most important value streams.

2. IT designers need to understand value streams and the many ways in which new technology can be used to reinvent value streams. Many computer systems in corporations are stovepipe systems designed to support functional silos rather than cross-functional value streams. Often systems have been created that support one functional area, with a database for that functional area rather than data designed to be shared across the enterprise. The value stream, crossing multiple functional areas, requires information systems and transaction processing completely different from the stovepipe systems.

3. The IT organization needs to support the corporation's use of the Internet and build an internal intranet. The internal network should be designed to be an in-house version of the Internet using much the same software so that it is easily connectable to the Internet and can take advantage of the Internet's rapid evolution of new facilities. Some different internal net-

works may be needed, for example, for high-volume transactions or video-conferencing.

4. Computer security needs to be designed and administered in a professional, not an amateur, way.

5. A webmaster should help people throughout the enterprise use and find the resources they need on the networks.

6. It is essential to build certain systems *very* fast. The process of building systems rapidly is referred to as rapid application development (RAD).[8] A variety of techniques exist for building systems rapidly, using powerful development tools along with templates, packages, or libraries of components.[9] Coding complex systems by hand, as in the past, is slow and error prone.

7. Speed of change is essential for the cybercorp. Systems must be designed so that they can be changed very quickly—changed *overnight* in certain ways. This can only be done if they are built with tools that facilitate very rapid change. Some tools generate code from rules that businesspeople can modify.

8. IT should provide guidance in modeling complex streams of processes so that they can be redesigned as efficiently as possible. It should clarify the feedback loops of long-span interactions, discussed in Chapter 12, and design mechanisms that avoid potentially harmful effects.

9. IT should provide guidance in putting information resources, including the Internet, to good use. It must be able to build information warehouses, where techniques such as data mining can extract value from the mass of corporate data.

10. A knowledge infrastructure is needed that enables the corporation to capture, disseminate, and multiply the effects of knowledge across the corporation. The essence of organizational adaptability is enabling every employee to accelerate the process of corporate learning.

11. IT needs a broad-based professional understanding of all the potential mechanisms of the cybercorp.

Reengineering the IT Organization

Most IT organizations need reengineering in order to support cybercorp capabilities. The deeper we go into the cybercorp revolution, the more business procedures will be encoded in software, but at the same time the faster those procedures are likely to change. It is increasingly important to build systems *fast* and change them *fast.* The cybercorp is dependent on skilled IT capability to establish its software, build its nervous system, and help put cyberspace facilities to work. The capabilities of traditional IT organizations fall far short of what is needed.

Rebuilding the IT organization needs to be thoroughly discussed at the top management level.[10] The transition of IT and the transition of the corporation should be planned together. Both require time, toughness, determination, and technical understanding. A road map is needed that sets realistic targets and timetables. The chief executive should understand the reasons for transition, the road map, and its milestones.

The head of IT needs to plan the human resources needed, the hiring targets, and the training. Everyone in IT should understand and be excited by the cybercorp vision. Their career paths in the new organization need to be clearly understood.

Technophile Start-Ups

Propellerheads often start businesses. The technie metamorphosizes into a businessperson. It can be an uneasy transition. Jim Clark, one of the founders of Netscape, comments, "Spiritually at least, Netscape is a place where the inmates run the asylum."[11] Netscape's founders come from the Dungeons and Dragons culture, where dominating the Internet is like a game in virtual reality. It is full of intensely absorbed young programmers who can work 100-hour weeks and have a chance to become fabulously wealthy.

The technophile businessperson is always prone to fall in love again with another brilliant technological idea, but love is blind. Many technophile start-ups fail. Some have wild rides on Wall Street, their share price rising meteorically and plunging even faster when the magic becomes suspect.

Margaret Hamilton was a Mozart of programming who masterminded the creation of the software for Project Apollo's Lunar Landing Module. She watched the first moon landing from the NASA control room, knowing that one bug in her very complex software would wreck the landing, leave two men to die, and give her a unique place in history. The first landing, in fact, skated very close to disaster.

Margaret Hamilton and her inseparable companion, Zaydeen Zeldin, became obsessed with a technique for building ultrareliable software from mathematically described constructs. They built an impressive tool and created a company called HOS. The black-stockinged pair, wearing clothes that should have been given to the Salvation Army, assembled a high-octane board with prestigious representatives of two venture capital firms, Venrock and Frontenac.

The board urged them to spend more money on marketing and adapting the product to customer needs. To the customer the tool needed to be easier to use; to Hamilton and Zeldin the mathematics and philosophy of software design were all-important. The culturally alien groups said honeyed words across the board table, but when board meetings ended the technophiles did what *they* believed in. It was the era when Frank Sinatra was singing, "I did it my way," and Hamilton and Zeldin believed that their ownership must never go below 51 percent. The company desperately needed cash to build its sales capability but could not dilute.

Then Ross Perot's powerhouse EDS (before he sold it to General Motors) offered $36 million in cash to buy HOS. To the disbelief of the board, Hamilton and Zeldin refused. The situation turned into a venture capitalist's nightmare. Hamilton and Zeldin insisted that their technology could change the software world; HOS could be a billion-dollar corporation one day. The board meetings turned into grand theater, with one Venrock executive literally banging his head on the boardroom table. A year later, HOS was bankrupt.

Cyberpunk

If the world of IT professionals seems weird to businesspeople, it pales by comparison with the world of cyberspace hackers.

Cyberspace is full of loners who are happier in virtual worlds than in real ones. The world behind the screen holds an uncanny fascination for some teenagers. They tell each other to regard real life as "the other thing you do." They apply themselves with a fierce intensity and often become astonishingly skilled. J. C. Herz, lovingly describing the cyberpunk world, says, "I stand in awe at the netter's capacity to obsess."[12] Prime time, she wrote, is between midnight and 3 A.M., and if you're sleeping you'll miss it. There are three things in life: sleep, social life, and life on the Net. You can have any two, but not all three. Herz comments that the union of man and machine is one of the defining characteristics of our age but that it will ultimately make the human race look goofy! As if technical alphabet soup wasn't bad enough, net-heads now entertain themselves with acronym phrases like IANAL (I Am Not A Lawyer) and IRL (In Real Life!). "Newbies" are detected by their failure to understand such jargon.

To the cyberpunk generation, worldwide interaction with computers is as natural as riding a bicycle, but they radiate extreme contempt for an earlier generation of computer users. Herz says: "Creaky technophobes are infinitely preferable to the dreaded boomer cyberpunk wannabes who crash through the Net making idiots of themselves." She describes a meeting with a corporate vice president who was reading his e-mail when the phone rang:

> Reaching over his executive desk pad and copy of *Wired* magazine, he picked up the receiver, grinned, and told the corporate president, "Hey,

you'll never guess what I'm doing right now. I'm *surfing* on the Internet."
He looked at me. "This is really *cyberpunk,* isn't it?" I blinked, struggling
desperately to keep a straight face, then shifted to Plan B, the all-purpose
coughing fit. "Sorry to break this to you, Sir, but there aren't too many
cyberpunks in America Online."

Asset Sales

There will be many stories of cybercorp success depending on brilliant hackers. An extreme example of what has happened to the financial community
with the design of derivatives. Ph.D.-level geniuses have used exotic computing techniques to design investments of a level of complexity unheard of ten
years ago.

The top management of one large bank decided to enter the asset sales
business with an all-out assault that they compared to the Allied invasion of
Normandy. This involved selling corporate loans and packages of investments to regional banks, subsidiaries of foreign banks, and large institutional
investors. The activity needed complex computer applications. Medium-term
asset sales require different computing from short-term asset sales; they include leveraged buyout financing and recapitalizations, loan syndications,
and restructurings. The legal requirements are complicated and constantly
changing. Each deal is unique and requires a dedicated computer application
written to support it, often with as little as ten days' advance notice.

A brilliant hacker was employed who could generate code quickly with
his own family of reusable designs.[13] He created nearly a million lines of code
with over 500 menu choices. With the traditional software development life
cycle this would have taken hundreds of person-years. In one year the bank
sold $400 billion worth of corporate loan assets, earning $100 million with a
staff of about 50—a remarkable profit per person.

The Silicon Ceiling

In 1995 *Computerworld* conducted a survey of 200 senior executives, asking
them, "To what future position would you consider appointing your senior
information technology manager?" Forty-eight percent said that they would
not appoint their head of IT to *any* senior business position.[14]

In today's corporation, if the senior IT executive cannot be considered
for the ranks of business management he is the wrong choice. He is not only
in charge of what is probably the company's largest capital budget, he is the
backbone of the company's ability to operate. If the CEO does not have
confidence that that person could occupy a business position, then the CEO

has made a serious hiring mistake. In reality, most IT executives are very bright and are as able to listen, budget, plan, and execute as their peers. They manage complex and difficult activities. The *Computerworld* survey is an illustration of the culture gap. When businesspeople do not understand technology, they become frustrated, angry, and fearful of IT. This translates into prejudice, so IT executives are repeatedly left out of critical management decisions, which often results in wrong decisions. There are lost opportunities or a lowered ability to compete well. The culture gap reduces the profitability of many corporations. Anthony Fedanzo, vice president of IT at Harding Associates, called this "the silicon ceiling": "Most managers of IT are unknowingly involved in a sick relationship with their organizations. We buy the idea of improving our business skills and other techniques to enter the ranks of senior management. But such thinking is like that of an abused wife who believes that learning to cook better or wearing nicer clothes will end the beatings."[15]

As corporations inexorably move toward the cybercorp world this culture gap becomes much more dangerous.

Bridging the Culture Gap

> An essential part of cybercorp management is the bridging of the culture gap and eliminating any harmful effects of separate cultures. The traditional way that IT is managed does not do that adequately.

To fuse together the alien cultures, IT organizations should be divided into two layers, like an onion, with an outer layer and an inner layer. The inner layer contains the technical professionals who build systems, make networks operate, provide security, and know their way around cyberspace. The outer layer consists of cybercorp professionals who communicate well with and are totally credible to the businesspeople. The outer layer speaks two languages, the language of the businesspeople and the language of the technical professionals (Exhibit 19-1).

The professionals in the outer layer might be referred to as cybercorp engineers or enterprise engineers. Enterprise engineering is a complex body of knowledge concerned with identifying the most appropriate enterprise architectures and establishing the most effective change methods for reengineering.[16] It identifies and uses the best change methods, including TQM, procedure modeling and redesign, radical reinvention of value streams, and enterprise redesign. It bases the necessary changes on the strategic vision and culture of the enterprise. It is concerned with integrating these change methods so that the whole is greater than the sum of the parts. It teaches manage-

Exhibit 19-1. A two-layer IT organization

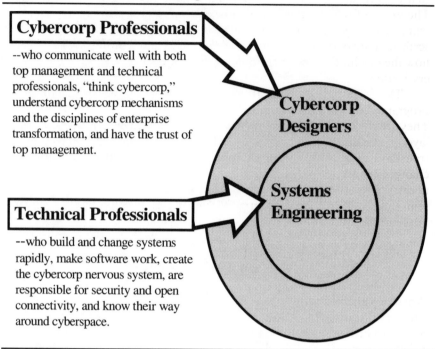

Cybercorp Professionals

--who communicate well with both top management and technical professionals, "think cybercorp," understand cybercorp mechanisms and the disciplines of enterprise transformation, and have the trust of top management.

Technical Professionals

--who build and change systems rapidly, make software work, create the cybercorp nervous system, are responsible for security and open connectivity, and know their way around cyberspace.

Cybercorp Designers

Systems Engineering

ment, in practical terms, what are the best mechanisms for their unique situations, how best to make the necessary transition. The goal is a cybercorp designed for fast evolution, which continually learns at all levels, in which all employees contribute the maximum value.

Enterprise engineering is concerned with cybercorp thinking, its pragmatic implementation, and how you get there from here. The two-layer structure helps to deal with the language problem. No one is in the outer layer unless they communicate well with the businesspeople and are respected by the businesspeople (and by top management, in particular). The outer-layer professionals are translators. They speak the language of the technical professionals and the businesspeople and are comfortable in both worlds. The jargon-filled language of IT disempowers IT. Businesspeople do not want to be embarrassed by talk that they do not understand. One purpose of the two-layer IT organization is to hide the IT language from the businesspeople.

However, the layered structure is concerned with much more than language; it is concerned with concepts and their realization. It is concerned with how the professionals view their world. The world of the inner layer is that of software design, programming, system details, and implementation. The world of the outer layer is that of cybercorp design along with the spectrum of change methods that are used for transforming corporations (described in my book *The Great Transition*).[17] The inner layer is concerned with how the machinery works; the outer layer is concerned with how the machinery is used.

This is entirely different from the old distinction between analysts and programmers. Now the analysts and programmers are on the same team. They are the system implementers, and both are in the inner layer. The outer-layer professionals are concerned with corporate design, architecture, and transition. They can conduct detailed dialogs with businesspeople about changes in business policies, rules, and procedures. They can do the modeling necessary to redesign complex procedures. They can ensure that systems for reinvented value streams are correctly specified and prototyped and that their implementation will not bring nasty surprises.

A New Profession?

When two alien cultures have to communicate intimately there must be translators who translate, not just language, but cultural mindsets. There must be people to bridge the cultures. The outer layer of Exhibit 19-1 are the bridge people.

Executives in some corporations debate whether the skills in the outer layer of Exhibit 19-1 should be in the IT organization or not. Should the bridging people be in the business units, not in the IT organization? A reason for putting them in the IT organization is that they must be completely cross-functional; they must relate to multiple business units. Should the outer layer of Exhibit 19-1 be populated with businesspeople, not IT people? Or a mixture of both? Or should all management be trained in the cybercorp-engineering skills?

Many corporations have implemented a restructuring of their IT organization something like Exhibit 19-1, and different names are used for it in different organizations. The two-layer structuring of IT focuses IT on the business needs and cross-functional cybercorp reengineering. It fundamentally changes the hiring policies in the IT organization.[18] If the outer layer is not part of IT, IT tends to be too inwardly focused on tuning the technology rather than on the return on investment from using the technology. (Too many IT activities have a net negative return on investment.) The head of the outer layer of Exhibit 19-1 *must* report to the CEO. The outer-layer professionals need to be involved with the strategic vision and overall design of the cybercorp.

> However it is organized, the outer layer of Exhibit 19-1 is essential to the future of the cybercorp. The cybercorp bridge people, whatever they are called, are a new profession, essential for this vital new evolution of business.

The Once and Future King?

Nicholas Negroponte, the founder and director of MIT's prestigious Media Lab, wrote in his 1995 book: "The MIS czar is an emperor with no clothes, almost extinct. Those who survive are usually doing so because they outrank anybody able to fire them, and the company's board of directors is out of touch or asleep."[19] A sad joke around the world says that "CIO" stands for "career is over." Many CIOs lost their power because of the trend to downsizing.

With the typical irony of human affairs this happened at a time when an urgent new need was arising for the IT management. The cybercorp needs an architect. You cannot build a cybercorp out of incompatible fragments. The architect needs to be able to weld together the new business and IT paradigms. The IT organization needs sophisticated new skills because it has a new role to play with major financial consequences.

The CIO lost control because of the revolt of the masses. Everybody got a PC. This revolt of the masses was caused by the same technology that made the cybercorp possible. The cybercorp needs user computers everywhere, linked to networks. But the cybercorp needs an architecture that enables all the pieces to work together. If the same corporate data is represented differently in different systems because each department has designed its own data, that is chaos. If computers cannot work together because they are incompatible, there may be islands of automation but not a cybercorp. Worse, the cybercorp needs a fundamentally different structure from traditional enterprises. Most of today's departments should not exist in their present form. Cybercorp design replaces many traditional departments with creaturelike value-stream units.

In most enterprises the old departments are busy automating the old procedures. Not only is this a waste of effort and money, it makes the task of building the new structure more difficult. In many corporations different departmental systems represent the same data in incompatible ways and so make the building of value-stream mechanisms very difficult.

Some corporations, as commented earlier, have *combined the jobs of head of computing and head of the most critical value stream*. This helps bring the best use of technology into play in making the predator value stream world-class, and it makes the head of computing focus very directly on adding business value.

The name "chief information officer" sounds old-fashioned. Cybercorp architecture is concerned with much more than information; it is concerned with the entire organizational ecosystem that enables the corporation to compete. In various Ford Motor companies around the world the head of IT has the title "vice president of process leadership." This title emphasizes the importance of the role of IT in fundamentally reinventing Ford's cross-functional operations, including those with computerized links to suppliers and dealers. It seems an excellent model for the top IT executive.

> **The modern corporation needs a "chief cybercorp architect" rather than a "chief information officer."**

References

1. C. P. Snow, *The Two Cultures* (Cambridge: Cambridge University Press, 1959).
2. Leo J. Heile, "Primer on Managing Information Technology from the Top," *Forbes ASAP,* December 1994.
3. Charles Wang (CEO of Computer Associates), *Techno Vision* (New York: McGraw-Hill, 1995).
4. Bank of England Report on the Collapse of Barings Bank, July 18, 1995.
5. "Catastrophic Culture Clash," *Newsweek,* March 13, 1995.
6. "The Final Chapter," Insight report on the collapse of Barings Bank, *Sunday Times,* July 9, 1995, Business section.
7. Interview with Louis Gerstner, *Business Week,* May 1, 1995.
8. James Martin, *Rapid Application Development* (Englewood Cliffs, NJ: Prentice-Hall, 1991).
9. James Martin, *Rebuilding the IT Profession* (Carnforth, England: Savant, 1995), chap. 16.
10. Martin, *Rebuilding the IT Profession.*
11. *Fast Company* 1, no. 1 (1995): 86ff.
12. J. C. Herz, *Surfing on the Internet* (New York: Little, Brown, 1995).
13. Quoted from a press release about Security Pacific's Asset Sales Group, from Cortex Inc. (Waltham, MA, August 23, 1989).
14. *Computerworld* CEO/CFO survey of 200 senior executives (1995).
15. Anthony Fedanzo, "The Silicon Ceiling," *Computerworld,* July 17, 1995.
16. James Martin, *The Great Transition* (New York: AMACOM, 1995).
17. Ibid.
18. Martin, *Rebuilding the IT Profession.*
19. Nicholas Negroponte, *Being Digital* (London: Hodder & Stoughton, 1995).

Index